MW01257727

SURVIVOR

THE CULTURAL HISTORY OF TELEVISION

Breaking Bad: *A Cultural History*, by Lara Stache

Cheers: *A Cultural History*, by Joseph J. Darowski and Kate Darowski

Doctor Who: *A Cultural History*, by Graham Gibson

Fierce Females on Television: A Cultural History, by Nicole Evelina

Frasier: *A Cultural History*, by Joseph J. Darowski and Kate Darowski

Friends: *A Cultural History*, by Jennifer C. Dunn

Gilmore Girls: *A Cultural History*, by Lara Stache and Rachel Davidson

The Golden Girls: *A Cultural History*, by Bernadette Giacomazzo

In Living Color: *A Cultural History*, by Bernadette Giacomazzo

Law & Order: *A Cultural History*, by Bernadette Giacomazzo

Mad Men: *A Cultural History*, by M. Keith Booker and Bob Batchelor

Mystery Science Theater 3000: *A Cultural History*, by Matt Foy and Christopher J. Olson

Northern Exposure: *A Cultural History*, by Michael Samuel

Seinfeld: *A Cultural History*, by Paul Arras

Sex and the City: *A Cultural History*, by Nicole Evelina

The Simpsons: *A Cultural History*, by Moritz Fink

Star Trek: *A Cultural History*, by M. Keith Booker

Survivor: *A Cultural History*, by Joseph J. Darowski and Kate Darowski

The Wire: *A Cultural History*, by Ben Lamb

SURVIVOR

A Cultural History

JOSEPH J. DAROWSKI
KATE DAROWSKI

ROWMAN & LITTLEFIELD
Lanham • Boulder • New York • London

Rowman & Littlefield
Bloomsbury Publishing Inc, 1385 Broadway, New York, NY 10018, USA.
Bloomsbury Publishing Plc, 50 Bedford Square, London, WC1B 3DP, UK
Bloomsbury Publishing Ireland, 29 Earlsfort Terrace, Dublin 2, D02 AY28, Ireland
www.rowman.com

86-90 Paul Street, London EC2A 4NE, United Kingdom

British Library Cataloguing in Publication Information Available

Library of Congress Cataloging-in-Publication Data Available

ISBN 978-1-5381-9655-7 (cloth) | ISBN 978-1-5381-9656-4 (electronic)

For product safety related questions contact productsafety@bloomsbury.com.

♾™ The paper used in this publication meets the minimum requirements of American National Standard for Information Sciences—Permanence of Paper for Printed Library Materials, ANSI/NISO Z39.48-1992.

To Kate's survivor, Summer.

CONTENTS

INTRODUCTION

"**F**rom this tiny Malaysian fishing village, these sixteen Americans are beginning the adventure of a lifetime."

On May 31, 2000, Jeff Probst's opening monologue played over shots of contestants walking down a thin dock to board a fishing boat and introduced American audiences to a show that would revolutionize the television industry. *Survivor* is, without hyperbole, one of the most significant productions in entertainment history. Its impact was shockingly instantaneous and surprisingly enduring. For over twenty years, *Survivor* has been a steady presence on CBS, and in its wake has come a tidal wave of reality TV on mainstream television. At the time of this writing, forty-six seasons have aired and CBS has already begun to tease the fiftieth season which is scheduled to air in 2026.[1]

Survivor is a pop culture constant. It has endured long enough that familiarity with references to the show are necessary for cultural literacy. As television critic Alison Herman wrote, "You can't talk about America without talking about television; you can't talk about television without talking about reality TV; and you can't talk about reality TV without talking about 'Survivor,' the one reality show that's ascended to a permanent state of monoculture."[2] Even if you prefer sitcoms over reality TV, you will catch references to *Survivor* on *The Simpsons* (1989–present), *How I Met Your Mother* (2005–2014), *30 Rock* (2006–2013), or *The Office* (2005–2013) (the last of which used camera operators who had worked on *Survivor* to capture a documentary feel), while if you prefer dramas, you'll still encounter allusions to *Survivor* on shows like *Lost* (2004–2010) or *Supernatural* (2005–2020).

The shape of *Survivor* has remained largely the same since the beginning, but the contents of every season vary incredibly. There is an astonishing breadth of tone, material, and content that happens on *Survivor*. As

Survivor commentator Shannon Guss explains, the core of the series is "a group of people from different walk of life, who have to work together and vote each other out, and then the jury votes for a winner."[3] Each season viewers can expect anywhere from sixteen to twenty players to face off in challenges that range from obstacle courses to puzzles to endurance contests. If they win, they are safe and cannot be voted out. Each episode one player is eliminated by a tribal vote, until the last players standing try to win a million-dollar prize and the title of Sole Survivor. Along the way, the blend of teamwork and camaraderie with self-interested backstabbing allows for infinite variation of result.

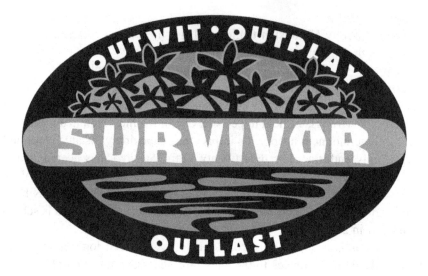

Survivor: Borneo *(Season 1, 2000) Logo.* CBS / Photofest © CBS

    Survivor is one of the most successful franchises in the history of television. For the 2023–2024 television season— almost two-and-a-half decades after its premiere—*Survivor* was the "most watched entertainment series" among adults eighteen to forty-nine on American television.[4] That is the most coveted demographic for advertisers, meaning the show is especially valuable to its network. While live sports, like NFL football games, do boast higher ratings, for entertainment programs *Survivor* has had enduring popularity.[5] This is not only true of ratings when it airs on Wednesday nights on CBS, but *Survivor* has also proven very popular as a show to binge on streaming services. Paramount+ is the home of all the seasons of *Survivor*, and it is "the No. 1 reality program and the No. 3 overall series on the platform." Amy Reisenbach, the president of CBS entertainment, has also revealed that *Survivor* is CBS's most co-viewed series with children, meaning entire families are watching the show together and creating a fandom that is "a huge community, it's a multi-generational community."[6]

While there are versions of the show that have been produced in dozens of countries—including Argentina, Australia, Denmark, France, Greece, New Zealand, Russia, Spain, South Africa, Ukraine, and others—this book is focused on the American version of *Survivor*. There is ample material to cover for a book-length study in just this version, but there would be similarly fruitful avenues of research in the international versions of the show.

At the time of this writing, 46 seasons of *Survivor* have aired, and the inevitable 50th season can be seen on the horizon, an astonishingly long run for a television program. Already, 697 people have played *Survivor*, and there are 36 new players filming the two new seasons right now. We have done our best to stay up to date and draw on content from all eras of production, but there is simply too much material to cover everything, even in a book-length study. This is not the final statement on any aspect of the show, and undoubtedly there will be more commentary, analysis, and interpretation of *Survivor* for years to come. *Survivor* is still in active production, and there will be much more to say as new content is produced.

A thriving community of *Survivor* commentary already exists, and we are entering a very long-lasting and still-going conversation. We are indebted to the reporters, podcasters, and fans who have offered in-depth coverage of the series and its players through the years. A glance at our bibliography shows how frequently we consulted the work of people like Dalton Ross, Mike Bloom, Andy Dehnart, Martin Holmes, Mario Lanza, Rob Cesternino, Tyson Apostol, Riley McAtee, Steve Helling, and many others. There is also significant academic discourse around *Survivor* and reality TV from scholars like Misha Kavka, James Friedman, Sallie Tisdale, Christopher J. Wright, Matthew J. Smith, Andrew F. Wood, and others who informed our discussion.

Within this book, when a *Survivor* player is referenced for the first time in a chapter it will be by their full name. Any reference after will refer to them by the name or nickname that they are most commonly known by (i.e., Cirie Fields is Cirie; Oscar Lusth is Ozzy; John Cochran is Cochran; Benjamin Wade is Coach), followed by the name of the season or seasons they played. Each season will be referenced by the full title of each season, followed by the season number and year the season aired in parentheses, for example, *Borneo* (Season 1, 2000); *41* (Season 41, 2021). For ease of reference, a chart below includes details for each season, including the season number, title, location, air dates, and winner.

There are many different aspects of *Survivor* that warrant close analysis. This book approaches three main areas: "The Production," "The Game," and "The Social Experiment." In the Production we provide a thorough history of reality TV and *Survivor* and discuss how the show is made. This section is more historical in nature, providing information about the origins of the show and also its impact on the entertainment industry. In "The Game," we explore game theory and strategy and break down the changes that have been introduced on the show. This is an aspect of analysis that drives many podcasts and fan discussions as the seasons air. What are the factors determining player choices and what are the optimal moves that could be made? In "The Social Experiment," we analyze how controversial subjects have been addressed and how the evolution of various aspects of society have been reflected in *Survivor*. Pop culture entertainment is reflective of the times when it is produced, and with the length of time *Survivor* has been on the air there are identifiable shifts in our culture that are reflected in the show. We are also including an appendix where we address many of the favorite topics of fan discussions—best players, ranking the seasons, and dividing the show into eras.

There have been many great television shows, but there are far fewer that have changed the entertainment industry forever. *Survivor* is a hinge point for the entertainment industry. The content of American television and the nature of celebrity swung after *Survivor* aired on CBS in the year 2000. As one of the most transformative shows ever produced, *Survivor* needs to be analyzed; not just by fans who love the series, but also by anyone who is invested in the history of popular culture. Survivor: *A Cultural History* is the contribution of two long-time fans to the fascinating conversation around this important piece of American entertainment history.

Season	Title	Location	Airing Dates	Winner
I	*Survivor: Borneo*	Malaysia	May 31–August 23, 2000	Richard Hatch
2	*Survivor: The Australian Outback*	Australia	January 28–May 3, 2001	Tina Wesson
3	*Survivor: Africa*	Kenya	October 11, 2001–January 10, 2002	Ethan Zohn
4	*Survivor: Marquesas*	French Polynesia	February 28–May 19, 2002	Vecepia Towery
5	*Survivor: Thailand*	Thailand	September 19–December 19, 2002	Brian Heidik

(Continued)

Season	Title	Location	Airing Dates	Winner
6	Survivor: The Amazon	Brazil	February 13–May 11, 2003	Jenna Morasca
7	Survivor: Pearl Islands	Panama	September 18–December 14, 2003	Sandra Diaz-Twine
8	Survivor: All-Stars	Panama	February 1–May 9, 2004	Amber Brkich
9	Survivor: Vanuatu	Vanuatu	September 16–December 12, 2004	Chris Daugherty
10	Survivor: Palau	Palau	February 17–May 15, 2005	Tom Westman
11	Survivor: Guatemala	Guatemala	September 15–December 11, 2005	Danni Boatwright
12	Survivor: Panama	Panama	February 2–May 14, 2006	Aras Baskausas
13	Survivor: Cook Islands	Cook Islands	September 14–December 17, 2006	Yul Kwon
14	Survivor: Fiji	Fiji	February 8–May 13, 2007	Earl Cole
15	Survivor: China	China	September 20–December 16, 2007	Todd Herzog
16	Survivor: Micronesia	Palau	February 7–May 11, 2008	Parvati Shallow
17	Survivor: Gabon	Gabon	September 25–December 14, 2008	Bob Crowley
18	Survivor: Tocantins	Brazil	February 12–May 17, 2009	J. T. Thomas
19	Survivor: Samoa	Samoa	September 17–December 20, 2009	Natalie White
20	Survivor: Heroes vs. Villains	Samoa	February 11–May 16, 2010	Sandra Diaz-Twine
21	Survivor: Nicaragua	Nicaragua	September 15–December 19, 2010	Jun "Fabio" Birza
22	Survivor: Redemption Island	Nicaragua	February 16–May 15, 2011	Rob Mariano
23	Survivor: South Pacific	Samoa	September 14–December 18, 2011	Sophie Clarke
24	Survivor: One World	Samoa	February 15–May 13, 2012	Kim Spradlin
25	Survivor: Philippines	Philippines	September 19–December 16, 2012	Denise Stapley
26	Survivor: Caramoan	Philippines	February 13–May 12, 2013	John Cochran
27	Survivor: Blood vs. Water	Philippines	September 18–December 15, 2013	Tyson Apostol
28	Survivor: Cagayan	Philippines	February 26–May 21, 2014	Tony Vlachos
29	Survivor: San Juan del Sur	Nicaragua	September 24–December 17, 2014	Natalie Anderson
30	Survivor: Worlds Apart	Nicaragua	February 25–May 20, 2015	Mike Holloway

(Continued)

Season	Title	Location	Airing Dates	Winner
31	*Survivor: Cambodia*	Cambodia	September 23–December 16, 2015	Jeremy Collins
32	*Survivor: Kaôh Rōng*	Cambodia	February 17–May 18, 2016	Michelle Fitzgerald
33	*Survivor: Millennials vs. Gen X*	Fiji	September 21–December 14, 2016	Adam Klein
34	*Survivor: Game Changers*	Fiji	March 8–May 24, 2017	Sarah Lacina
35	*Survivor: Heroes vs. Healers vs. Hustlers*	Fiji	September 27–December 20, 2017	Ben Driebergen
36	*Survivor: Ghost Island*	Fiji	February 28–May 23, 2018	Wendell Holland
37	*Survivor: David vs. Goliath*	Fiji	September 26–December 19, 2018	Nick Wilson
38	*Survivor: Edge of Extinction*	Fiji	February 20–May 15, 2019	Chris Underwood
39	*Survivor: Island of the Idols*	Fiji	September 25–December 18, 2019	Tommy Sheehan
40	*Survivor: Winners at War*	Fiji	February 12–May 13, 2020	Tony Vlachos
41	*Survivor: 41*	Fiji	September 22–December 15, 2021	Erika Casupan
42	*Survivor: 42*	Fiji	March 9–May 25, 2022	Maryanne Oketch
43	*Survivor: 43*	Fiji	September 21–December 14, 2022	Mike Gabler
44	*Survivor: 44*	Fiji	March 1–May 24, 2023	Yamil "Yam Yam" Arocho
45	*Survivor: 45*	Fiji	September 27–December 20, 2023	Dee Valladares
46	*Survivor: 46*	Fiji	February 28, 2024–May 22, 2024	Kenzie Petty

Part I

THE PRODUCTION

CHAPTER 1

REALITY TV AND FANS

There are many ways to define a successful show. Ratings, the devotion of a fanbase, or a positive critical response are all elements of success. *Survivor* is a ratings hit, has a very active fanbase, and is praised by critics. In addition, *Survivor* can make a claim that very few programs in the history of television can make: *Survivor* forever changed the American entertainment industry. In pop culture history, there are landmark shows that result in clearly identifiable transformations to the entertainment industry. *Survivor* is one of those shows.

Fascination with *Survivor* and the players on the show exploded during the summer it first aired. Decades on, when there are hundreds of new reality television participants every year, the fame from appearing on a reality TV show is considerably more muted. In contrast, the players from *Borneo* (season 1, 2000) became instant celebrities, appearing on late-night[1] and day-time talk shows,[2] being featured on popular magazine covers,[3] playing on game shows,[4] and acting in soap operas, sitcoms, and motion pictures.[5] Players who were only in two or three episodes appeared in national Reebok television commercials.[6] One example that serves as a cultural time capsule of the year 2000 is that Sue Hawk, deliverer of the infamous "Snakes and Rats" monologue in the first season finale, co-hosted the network morning show *Live! With Regis* on September 21, 2000, when George W. Bush was a guest as part of his presidential campaign.[7]

Survivor: Borneo (Season 1, 2000) Cast: Shown from left: standing, Ramona Gray, Dirk Been, Gretchen Cordy, Richard Hatch, Sonja Christopher, Susan Hawk, Kelly Wiglesworth, Sean Kenniff, B. B. Anderson, Rudy Boesch, seated, Gervase Peterson, Jenna Lewis, Joel Klug, Stacey Stillman, Greg Buis, Colleen Haskell. CBS / Photofest © CBS.

In terms of *Survivor*'s long-term impact, it first must be noted that *Survivor* is still being produced at the time of writing this book. While viewership has waned since the staggering heights of its earliest seasons, a sizable audience remains engaged with the series even after hundreds of players, dozens of seasons, and more than two decades of time on the air. An additional impact is the omnipresence of reality TV on networks, cable channels, and streaming services. Since the summer of 2000, *Survivor* has aired on CBS continuously—its production only interrupted by the global COVID pandemic in 2020. Its impact goes far beyond becoming a network tentpole program; it made the genre of "reality TV" an acceptable and familiar genre in broadcast television, moving it from a few niche shows on cable to mainstream audiences. That influence, for good and bad, has shaped the media landscape of the twenty-first century.

REALITY TELEVISION

In the summer of 2000, *Survivor* was so new and so different, people did not even know what genre to call it. Now the term reality TV is ubiquitous (as are shows that fit into that broad and elastic genre). But what exactly is reality TV? On the one hand, viewers know reality TV when they see it. On the other, when you sit down to write out a definition, it is difficult to set parameters that do not unintentionally exclude some shows that are part of the genre.

Reality TV is clearly not scripted programming like a traditional sitcom or hour-long drama. But do game shows like *Jeopardy!* (1964–present) constitute reality TV? Talent shows like *Star Search* (1983–1995), *American Idol* (2002–2016, 2018–present), or *America's Got Talent* (2006–present) also cause some debate. *The Bachelor* (2002–present) is definitely reality TV, but so is *Duck Dynasty* (2012–2017), and those shows are not very much alike. The very broadness of the term leads to it being used as "a catch-all category" for television shows featuring real people rather than actors.[8] Cultural theorists have landed on different definitions: Anita Biressi and Heather Nunn explain that the many different shows that are grouped as reality TV share "an emphasis on the representation of ordinary people and allegedly unscripted or spontaneous moments that supposedly reveal unmediated reality."[9] Sam Brenton and Reuben Cohen argue that the term "reality TV" is an oxymoron, stating, "The genre never sought to portray real life" and "is about 'reality' only inasmuch it features neither actors nor scripts."[10] Annete Hill has concluded that "There is no one definition of reality programming, but many, competing definitions . . . because the reality genre is made of a number of distinctive" types of programs.[11] In the year 2000 it was revolutionary for a traditional broadcast network to put an unscripted show starring ordinary people on primetime television. MTV began airing *The Real World* (1992–2017) in the 1990s, but was considered an experiment on a niche cable channel for young kids. By contrast, CBS was "the Tiffany network," home of only the highest quality programming.

That lack of familiarity made it difficult for producers to get a network to agree to broadcast *Survivor*. Charlie Parsons, who originated the idea for *Survivor*, explains, "They had never seen a show like this—it didn't fall into any normal category. It wasn't an entertainment show set in a studio, it wasn't a documentary, it wasn't a drama."[12] The show he was pitching was unlike anything on TV, which can be a good thing. Networks don't want to air content that is too obviously derivative of the competition. But if it's too different, networks may not want to air it at all. The idea of a show following Americans competing on an island for $1 million "broke the mold—but too much for the buyers."[13] Networks weren't clear on what this show was or if their audiences would watch it. In attempting to codify entertainment, labels oftentimes prove problematic—particularly with new media when tropes have not yet been established. When groundbreaking media emerges, it doesn't conform to a set of established generic expectations. Retroactively, those genre tropes can be identified. The producers of these shows often aren't concerned about what people call their product, only that the shows find an audience. But these labels do help audiences know what they're about to watch, and networks develop brand identities around the types of shows they air. Leslie Moonves, the president at CBS at the time, recalls that upon hearing the pitch for *Survivor*, his first reaction was, "That's the stupidest thing I've ever heard. This is not a cable network. This doesn't belong on CBS."[14] Eventually, when CBS did agree to air *Survivor*, it was as a trial run in a non-traditional time of the year.

Mainstream television broadcast schedules were very different in the year 2000. During the summer months, the main American broadcast networks (NBC, CBS, ABC, and FOX) would primarily air reruns of their scripted sitcoms and dramas in primetime, with new episodes of their news magazine shows (*60 Minutes*, *20/20*, and the like). In a time before DVD box sets or streaming options, and when TiVo was just entering the market as the first DVR, summer months were a chance to let audiences catch up on shows they had missed when they first aired. Occasionally networks would air original entertainment programming to see if it could find an audience. For example, in the summer of 1997, FOX tried unsuccessfully to launch *Roar*, a show with a teenage Heath Ledger in the lead as a Celtic warrior trying to fight off Romans in 400 AD. Like most summer trial shows in that era, it failed to find an audience. *Roar* only aired eight of thirteen produced episodes before being canceled.[15]

Survivor was one of these infrequent instances where a network aired an original program in the summer months. This was, in part, because CBS did not have faith that the show was worth a slot in the more valuable fall schedule. The program was relatively cheap to produce—a *New York Times* article from 2000 notes that "CBS executives did not disclose the cost, but when ABC was in the running to buy the show, it was priced at $700,000 an episode"[16]—and if it did manage to find an audience the network would be able to turn a profit with little risk. The profit was actually massive, with CBS able to charge $600,000 per thirty-second spot during the two-hour finale.[17] The first episode of *Survivor* attracted over 15.1 million viewers in its initial airing in May (CBS would air it again as buzz grew),[18] and the audience grew to over 51 million watching the final episode on August 23, 2000.[19] *Survivor* was an instant phenomenon, but it definitely had its detractors. Television critic Tom Shales opined that the show "is a piece of crap. What's scary is that it's going to start a really big new crap trend."[20] While many can disagree with the subjective analysis

Shale offered of *Survivor*'s artistic merit, it is objectively true that *Survivor* did, in fact, start a trend.

Viewers and reviewers saw this trend, but it took some time to settle on what to call it. A *New York Times* article from 2000 about CBS's summer shows *Survivor* and *Big Brother* (2000-present) uses the term "televoyeurism" rather than reality TV.[21] When networks began to air shows like *Temptation Island* or *The Mole* in 2001, *Survivor* producer Mark Burnett would push back when his show and those were all called reality TV. Burnett would insist he made "nonscripted drama—dramality," not reality TV.[22] Shales, that early critic of the show, balked at calling *Survivor* a "reality show" "since it's really a heavily edited game show."[23]

Disagreements about what to call TV shows featuring people who are not playing a role go back much earlier. In 1972, *An American Family* aired an edited presentation of footage that had been shot following one family's life for seven months. At the time, debates ensued whether it was a documentary or something else entirely. An anthropologist quoted in *TV Guide* mused, "I do not think that *American Family* should be called a documentary. I think we need a new name for it, a name that would contrast it not only with fiction, but with what we have been exposed to up until now on TV."[24] Annette Hill, a noted British scholar who studies reality TV, acknowledges that "the type of hybrid programming we have come to associate with reality TV is difficult to categorise."[25] A 2002 academic essay on *Big Brother* posits that "One of the first questions that arises concerns the question of genre: what exactly is *Big Brother*? A documentary, a game show, or a psychological experiment?"[26]

For a show to be considered reality TV must it be unscripted with real people in everyday situations? That would include attempts to document the experiences of people living their lives (like MTV's *The Real World* [1992–2019], or the longform documentary *7Up*), but what about contrived scenarios like *Joe Millionaire* (2003)? As scholar Misha Kavka argues, there is a "generic haziness" around reality TV even as its impact is seen on television sets around the world.[27] If a show is billed as reality TV, it is expected to include real people in unscripted situations, but edited and packaged for narrative clarity and easy audience consumption. That broad umbrella definition of reality TV absolutely includes *Survivor*, as well as very different shows like *Keeping Up with the Kardashians* (2001–2021), *Hell's Kitchen* (2005–present), *The Great British Baking Show* (2010–present), *The Amazing Race* (2001–present), and literally hundreds of other productions.

Whether *Survivor* is considered a reality-based program, a second-generation reality show, a reality gameshow, a game-doc, a game of group governance, a constructed documentary, popular factual television, or any number of terms[28] that have come and gone in the decades since it premiered, it is one of the most impactful pieces of entertainment in American television this century. While many of those labels have fallen out of usage, there are some useful sub-divisions underneath the larger generic umbrella term of reality TV.

Survivor stands out first as a competition, not a pseudo-documentary. But there are many reality competition shows that are not very much like *Survivor*. A cooking competition like *Chopped* (2009–present), a dating show like *The Bachelor* (2002–present), and a weapon-making competition like *Forged in Fire* (2015–present) are all reality competitions, but *Survivor* feels essentially different. A clarifying label of "adventure competition" differentiates it from the cooking competitions, dating competitions, or knife-making competitions that have been produced. There is undeniably a reputation for cheapness that many associate with the reality TV genre, but *Survivor* defies that association. So, the genre label that best fits *Survivor* is "Prestige Reality Adventure Competition." This sets expectations for its production values and content. While this specificity increases accuracy in defining what *Survivor* is, there is also no denying that in common usage, all sub-labels have been swallowed up for the pervasive shorthand of "reality TV."

One of the immediate and long-term impacts of *Survivor*'s popularity was the acceptance of reality TV as a viable product for network television. In the capitalistic entertainment industry, imitation is the inevitable result of a ratings phenomenon. When *Survivor* shattered ratings records and television executives' expectations, it was only a matter of time before reality shows began to populate the networks. In 2022, a *Time* article explained that "Once dismissed as a noxious fad, reality TV has hardened into an institution."[29] The increase in reality TV on the airwaves was so dramatic, that from 2005–2010, Fox Reality was an American cable channel devoted solely to reruns of reality TV shows. Several cable channels have become closely associated with their reality TV offerings, even if the channels originally had completely different identities. MTV, long mocked for no longer airing music videos, has become more well-known for *The Real World* (1992–2019), *Road Rules* (1995–2007), *The Challenge* (1998–present), *Jersey Shore* (2009–2012), and many other reality shows. Bravo began as a cable channel focusing on fine arts and cinema, and is now well-known for its reality shows like *Queer Eye for the Straight Guy* (2003–2007), *Project Runway* (2004–present, though not on Bravo for every season), *Top Chef*

(2006–present), and the *Real Housewives* (2006–present) franchise. Reality TV has been fully embraced by producers, networks, and streaming outlets.

The immediacy of *Survivor*'s shockwaves through the media landscape can be seen in news articles from the week the show premiered. In reporting on its high ratings for the first episode, Bill Carter wrote in the *New York Times* that "networks were said to be lining up yesterday to acquire the rights to other such televoyeur shows" that "record real people doing real-life things."[30] In 2006, Richard M. Huff published a book, *Reality Television*, that noted that reality television had created a "revolution" in television broadcasting and the "newfangled genre has infiltrated virtually every corner of the television world and quickly become a staple of every television programmer's arsenal of program choices."[31] In 2009, television critic Scott D. Pierce wrote "it's impossible to count how many other series [*Survivor*] launched on umpteen different networks."[32] In an effort to do just that in 2015, a *Washington Post* article about *Survivor*'s influence identified more than 300 reality shows that had moved into production since its premiere.[33] In a 2021 book about *Survivor*, Sallie Tisdale reported that there were "More than 700 reality shows being produced now around the world."[34] *Survivor* wasn't the first reality show, but it definitely popularized the genre and also introduced it to mainstream network television. This is why an article in *Variety* in 2022 argued that Parsons is one of "Only a handful of people who [can be] credited with changing the face of television"[35] and an article in 2023 called *Survivor* the "original reality competition show that caused a stir not only in the United States but worldwide."[36] Or, as B. J. Sigesmund poetically declared in 2001, "'Survivor' didn't just change the face of television. It got all the way into its blood."[37]

Almost as quickly as reality TV became a recognized genre, a backlash began. In October 2000, critic Scott Donaton wrote a piece condemning the "exploitative tube trend" of reality TV and sounded an alarm that the reality TV craze may get out of hand.[38] A *Newsweek* article notes that there were concerns being raised even prior to *Survivor*'s premiere,

> Before "Survivor" debuted 13 weeks ago, the pundits whined that "reality" shows were the beginning of the end of television—or worse. They'd kill the sitcom, because they don't require writers and are cheaper to produce. They'd obliterate what's left of Americans' sense of privacy and dignity, too.[39]

While these concerns were raised frequently at the time, as with many things in life, TV production is all about the money. Writing in 2009, Jason Mittell notes,

The success of *Survivor* triggered a rush to reality programming across all networks and channels, as they saw the genre offering the potential for solid overall ratings, strong performance among younger demographics, lower production costs, and opportunities for co-production arrangements to maintain ownership in hit programs.[40]

Mittell also notes that the profits don't always come from the established streams: "Even though back-end revenues from reruns and DVD releases of reality television have not been typically as strong as scripted programs, a hit show can export its format around the globe, creating a huge revenue stream for the original producers."[41] The imitative logic of the entertainment industry rushed to capitalize on the reality trend as soon as it was identified. While many programs like *The Apprentice* (2004–2017) and *The Traitors* (2023–present) mimic the gamedoc structure of *Survivor*, the unscripted format proved amenable to a wide range of scenarios and genre mixtures: reality romances (*Love Is Blind*, 2020–present), talent shows (*America's Next Top Model*, 2003–2018), lifestyle makeovers (*Queer Eye for the Straight Guy*, 2003–2007), sports (*The Contender*, 2005–2009, 2018), competition shows (*The Challenge*, 1998–present), and even parodies (*The Joe Schmo Show*, 2003–2004, 2013).

FROM BIG IDEA TO SMALL SCREEN

Survivor's presence on a major American television network was never inevitable. Several key figures are involved in the journey from a seemingly unfilmable concept to one of pop culture's most recognizable franchises. The exact history is sometimes hard to parse. When "fairly ugly"[42] negotiations and lawsuits[43] have occurred in intervening years, determining who thought of what or who deserves credit for which decision can become difficult. Using articles, interviews, and retrospectives, it appears that among the most important figures leading to *Survivor* airing on CBS in 2000 are Charlie Parsons, Mark Burnett, Ghen Maynard, and Leslie Moonves.

Parsons is a British television producer who conceived of the basic premise of *Survivor* in the 1980s and spent more than a decade trying to get his idea produced. The seeds of the idea for *Survivor* began when Parsons was working on a television magazine show and they created a segment where four people from different walks of life were sent to an island for a couple weeks. Later, when Parsons founded a production company called Planet24, they laid out a series bible for a game show on an island that he called *Survive*.[44] "It took 12 years, during which it was rejected by every network in Britain and two in the United States, before it finally emerged into the relative obscurity of Swedish television."[45] This first version of Parsons's show was called *Expedition Robinson*, an homage to the castaway tales of *Robinson Crusoe* and *Swiss Family Robinson*. But Parsons had been actively pursuing development of this project in many markets.

Moonves, the president of CBS at the time, says that Maynard—an executive who would eventually also bring the European reality show *Big Brother* to CBS[46]—tried to pitch a show idea called *Survivor* to him, based on the Parsons idea. Moonves rejected it because it was completely off-brand for the network. Maynard, who worked in drama development at the time, continued to push the new type of show even though Moonves was "clearly not responding to" the pitch.[47] Maynard eventually convinced Moonves to meet with a producer named Mark Burnett.

Burnett and Parsons had met at a party by chance. They were both British and living in America trying to work in the entertainment industry. Parsons told Burnett about his idea, and Burnett wanted to help produce it. After Parsons had spent "horrible years" in the United States trying to get his show made—what he describes as "truly the most awful experience of my life"[48]—he decided to license the North American rights to his show to Burnett and let him deal with it.[49] While Burnett tried to get the show greenlit on American television, Parsons was able to produce *Expedition Robinson* in Sweden.

Burnett had an interesting history before becoming involved in American television. He served in the British military at the age of eighteen and after his discharge moved to Los Angeles to pursue his dream of making a lot of money. Early jobs Burnett had included working as an au pair, in telemarketing, insurance sales and credit card sales, and working at a modeling agency.[50] After attending a Tony Robbins motivational seminar, Burnett signed up for several extreme adventure races as a participant. After this, Burnett produced his own adventure race in the United States and filmed it as a TV show that initially aired on MTV Sports as *Eco-Challenge Expedition Race*. Seasons of *Eco-Challenge* aired from 1995–2001 on multiple networks, including Discovery and ESPN. Burnett felt that with his experience filming extreme races, he could produce a show set on a desert island.[51]

When Burnett pitched *Survivor* to Moonves, he explained that with product placement, they could produce the show cheaply. Moonves, who called Burnett "incredibly charming," was convinced to give the show a try for a summer season if Burnett could get the show paid for with product placement and advertising commitments.[52] Burnett worked with CBS to redefine the terms by which the show would be financed. Instead of CBS paying a standard licensing fee to help fund the show's production, Burnett negotiated to self-fund the production, but split the program's advertising revenue with CBS, pre-selling some sponsorships before the series aired. For the first season in 2000, eight sponsors paid roughly $4 million each to run ads during the series and have their products featured in the program.[53]

This unique sponsorship system led to some natural product placement during *Borneo* (season 1, 2000)—host Jeff Probst sharing a cold Bud Light with Kelly Wiglesworth during a reward—and some incredibly awkward product placement—Probst unenthusiastically offering a barefoot Wiglesworth Dr. Scholl's shoe inserts after a balance beam challenge. One of the major sponsors to buy in on the first season was Reebok. Reebok's deal included space for two ads that would air each week during the show, and also exclusive representation on the show. During *Borneo* castaways are either wearing Reebok branded clothing and shoes, or generic clothing with no labels. There is no evidence of Nike or Adidas on the desert island world of *Borneo*.[54] With *Survivor*'s ratings success, Reebok ads were rushed into production featuring B. B. Anderson[55] and Stacey Stillman[56] (the second and third players booted from the show) interacting with the regular "Reebok Guys" ad spokesmen. "The Reebok Guys" were also given camera time and had a lower-third chyron identifying them as they sat in the audience of the reunion show, but now their appearance mostly confuses viewers who are binge-watching old seasons.

In the end, it took Charlie Parson's idea, Mark Burnett's salesmanship, Ghen Maynard's persistence, and Leslie Moonves's eventual willingness to greenlight the show for *Survivor* to premiere in the summer of 2000. Audiences quickly became familiar with something that was initially new and strange and shocking.

VIEWERS AND FAN ENGAGEMENT

Somewhat surprisingly, since the first season of *Survivor* was aired during the summer months, the show has never matched the ratings heights it achieved. In fact, in terms of ratings, the long-running series demonstrates a general downward trend since the first season. The most-watched episode of the first season was the finale, with an estimated 51.7 million viewers.[57] The chart in figure 1.2 shows the viewership number in millions of the highest viewed episode of each season (typically either the premiere or the finale).

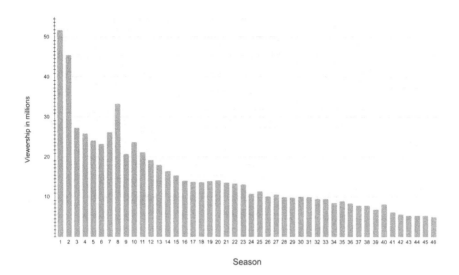

Survivor *ratings by season*. Created by the authors. Source: *"Survivor* (US)." *Survivor* Wiki.
Accessed July 30, 2024. *https://survivor.fandom.com/wiki/Survivor_(U.S.). Data from Nielsen ratings.*

While the downward trend might be alarming, it is also worth noting that from the year 2000–2024 ratings across the board for network television have declined. Time-shifted viewing due to DVRs, increased competition from streaming services, and a general increase in fractured viewing habits has disrupted the traditional viewing patterns of television watchers. *Survivor*'s lower ratings are still considered very successful. At the conclusion of the 2023–2024 television season, *Variety* reported that among the coveted eighteen to forty-nine demographic of viewers, *Survivor* was "this year's top-rated entertainment series. Not bad for a show that just ended its 46th edition."[58] Also, with the increase in streaming has come an increase in new viewership and rewatching past seasons from fans. There was a steep drop in ratings between season 2 and season 3, and that is when the country's attitude toward entertainment shifted dramatically as 9/11 happened weeks before season 3 premiered. In terms of the real-world impacts of 9/11, television viewer's loss of interest in reality TV is inconsequential, but it is part of the reason why *Survivor* lost its previous popularity.[59]

Once the finale of a season of *Survivor* airs, spoilers about who won the season are not only available; they are also prominent in headlines, podcast discussions, and social media posts. Despite this, *Survivor* has found new life with old seasons available on streaming sites. Seasons that aired years ago have become hits on Netflix and the series as a whole features prominently in advertising for the Paramount+ streaming service. Many fans who

watched seasons when they originally aired have found the show surprisingly rewatchable. There is so much strategy between the marooning and
the final Tribal Council, even if you remember the final outcome the journey
there can still surprise on a rewatch. In fact, some fans who are particularly
interested in the strategy side of the game find a rewatch more illuminating
than the initial viewing. Mike Bloom, a prominent *Survivor* commentator,
has said that "I tend to only judge a season of *Survivor* after I've watched it
at least twice."[60]

Rewatching can also yield different experiences if viewers have learned
facts about the players. Theorist Linda Hutcheon writes about the idea of a
"knowing audience" who will have a different experience with a text than
an unknowing audience.[61] This can be true of adaptations—if you know the
plot of *Pride and Prejudice* you may be fascinated by the changes between
one adaptation and the next, for example—but can also be true of reality TV. Fans who know more about the real people who played in a season have different reactions than fans who only see the edited content on
screen.

Perhaps the most notable example of this is, unfortunately, Michael Skupin. In *The Australian Outback* (season 2, 2001), Skupin was something of a
breakout character. His hunger led him to some bizarre but memorable decisions, but when he fell into a fire and was the first contestant "medevacked"
(meaning medically evacuated via helicopter or airplane) in the show's history, his place in fan lore was secured. He was popular enough that producers
brought him back for a second appearance eleven years later in *Philippines*
(season 25, 2012). A new fan who discovers *Survivor* and binges those seasons on a streaming service may find themselves rooting for Skupin. But
a knowing fan who is aware of news headlines of his high-profile arrest in
2016 may have difficulty watching the season at all. After computers were
seized because Skupin was being investigated for running a Ponzi scheme,
images of child pornography were discovered on the computers. Skupin was
subsequently sentenced to one to four years in jail.[62] Fans familiar with the
abhorrent accusations leading to Skupin's arrest and jail time cannot watch
episodes with him in the same light they did before. Unfortunately for the
other castaways in his season, Skupin's reputation casts a pall over their
Survivor experience as well.

Even specific moments in the season take on odd, completely different
connotations depending on how knowing the viewer is. In *Philippines*, the
player Abi-Maria Gomes has something of a villain edit. At one point, she is
trying to open coconuts with a machete, and one coconut goes flying and hits
Skupin in the head. An unknowing viewer may read the scene as indicative

of Abi Maria's selfish clumsiness, but a knowing viewer may find themselves rooting for the coconut.

The Australian Outback has another moment that hits longtime *Survivor* fans in a very different emotional way. Tina Wesson participates in a family online chat at one challenge. As the contestants type their instant messages on a large iMac from circa 2001, viewers see footage of their families back home typing their responses. Tina's two children, Taylor and Katie, are shown on screen. Katie, who was thirteen years old at that time, will later join Tina as a *Survivor* contestant on *Blood vs. Water* (season 27, 2013). During that season finale, Tina and Katie tearfully share the news with *Survivor* fans that their son and brother, Taylor, died in a drunk driving accident while the season was airing.[63] They make a tearful plea for people to buckle up and be safe. It's an undeniably moving moment, and having seen Taylor on screen as a child in 2001 makes Tina's pleading all the more resonant for viewers.

Similarly different emotional reactions are felt when rewatching a season with castaways who have passed away since their seasons aired. In some instances, this isn't as shocking due to the player's age. Rudy Boesch from the first season was seventy-two years old when he first appeared on the show, so his passing in 2019 at age ninety-one was saddening but not as tragic as others. When Keith Nale (*San Juan del Sur*; *Cambodia*) passed at age sixty-two after battling cancer in 2023,[64] there was an outpouring of sadness from the fanbase, but it was not as shocking as when thirty-seven-year-old Jenn Lyon (*Palau*) lost her battle with cancer only five years after her season aired. One of the most unexpected and tragic deaths occurred when twenty-six-year-old Caleb Bankston (*Blood Versus Water*) died in a railway accident in 2014, not even a year after appearing on the show.[65]

Rewatching can also lead to reassessing a player's reputation, especially when players have appeared multiple times. In *Tocantins* (season 18, 2009), J. T. Thomas and Stephen Fishbach had a strategic alliance that allowed them both to reach the final two, but J. T. swept all of the jury votes in one of the most dominant wins in the show's history. J. T. was considered one of the best strategic and social players ever. But when he was asked back on *Heroes vs. Villains* (season 20, 2010), he made one of the stupidest moves in the show's history when he assumed an all-women's alliance was running the Villain's tribe and he passed an immunity idol he had found over to the lone man remaining on that tribe, Russell Hantz. Russell was, in fact, leading the alliance on the Villain's tribe. In a third appearance on *Game Changers* (season 34, 2017), J. T. made another strategic blunder by not playing his idol that led to him being voted out fifth. In a rewatch of *Tocantins*, knowing how poorly J. T. does without Fishbach helping to strategize, some holes in J. T.'s game appear and the importance of Fishbach in their strategic alliance becomes more apparent. The opposite occurs with a player like Kelley Wentworth, who was voted out pre-jury in her first appearance (*San Juan Del Sur*) but became a dominant force in her next outing on the show (*Cambodia*).

The relationship between a fan and a reality TV contestant is different from the relationship between a fan and a character in a fictional tv show. In part, this is due to the parasocial relationship viewers develop with the real people appearing on their television screens. First introduced by anthropologist Donald Horton and sociologist R. Richard Wohl in 1956, the concept of a parasocial interaction is a type of relationship between users and mass media performers. Horton and Wohl identified this most prominently with television, where the viewer "would feel like being in an interaction with a television performer, despite of the nonreciprocal exposure situation."[66] Researcher Dong-Hee Shin has published research about parasocial relationships and television viewers, noting, "Often called pseudo-interaction, imaginary social relation-ship, and pseudo-friendship, [para-social interaction] creates users who are not mere passive viewers, but involved, active parts of the process."[67] Parasocial relationships are unidirectional but can feel validating to the participant. Listeners who feel like they've gotten to know a podcast host, viewers who feel a connection to a reality TV contestant, or readers who follow an author on social media are examples of parasocial relationships. With the advent of social media, which did not exist when *Survivor* instigated the first wave of reality TV superstars, the opportunities for viewers to develop a parasocial relationship with a contestant on *Survivor* are far more plentiful than ever before.

The relationship of current contestants and social media has been mediated and controlled in various ways through the years. Obviously, CBS is wary of spoilers appearing on Twitter,[68] Instagram, or other social media platforms. And with fans of the show desperate to interpret and read the tea leaves, what may seem innocent to a player on the show can be inferred as a spoiler. Even the level and amount of time players spend posting is seen as a signal to fans about how well a player has done. A rule of thumb for a time was that the more active a player was in the lead up to a season the more likely they are to be an early boot. They're enjoying the experience and building up a social media following before their time on television comes to an unfortunately early close. Of course, this rule of thumb does not always hold true.

After the cast was announced but before *Cagayan* (season 28, 2014) began airing, players Spencer Bledsoe, Kass McQuillen, and Tony Vlachos got into a public feud on Twitter. Following some of the patterns fans had seen before, many assumed this meant they all would be leaving the show early and likely had some feuding during the pre-jury trip for players. Instead, they all made remarkably deep runs. Tony's erratic gameplay made him a surprise winner for everyone who watched the show, but especially for those who thought they'd discovered evidence of an early exit.

Some posts on social media just outright aren't allowed. Alec Merlino from *David vs. Goliath* (season 37, 2018) broke his Non-Disclosure Agreement by posting a photo on Instagram with fellow player, Kara Kay, shortly after filming ended. The caption read "F*** it," implying Alec knew the post went against the confidentiality agreement each contestant signs.[69] Alec was disinvited from that season's reunion show, and his appearance fee was withheld.[70]

When *Survivor* first aired, it was the early days of the internet, but fans were there. In online posts, fans dissected and analyzed information about *Survivor*, and made predictions about who would be voted out each week. Some of the earliest online fan sites actively engaged in trying to spoil the boot order of *Survivor*. Almost immediately, survivorsucks.com came into existence and had posts analyzing individual frames of the show. As a *Newsweek* article from 2000 explained,

a crafty Web site calling itself survivorsucks.com predicted who would be booted off next. It based its forecasts on clues gleaned from the show itself. During the third episode, one eagle-eyed fan noticed that the opening sequence featured a new tribal-council scene—with only nine people, as opposed to the 14 people who still remained on the island at that point. Using that apparent slip, the survivorsucks.com folks deduced—correctly—who the next five victims would be. CBS didn't make that mistake again. In fact, it went on the offensive. The next time the show changed the opening council shot, in week eight, it featured only four people: Gervase, Rudy, Sean and Colleen. Was this another slip? Would they be the final four? For a while survivorsucks.com thought so. "It was a Trojan horse," says Paul Sims, who maintains the site. "Some people believe that video footage was digitally doctored." CBS won't confirm or deny that, though it admits waging a disinformation campaign.[71]

One of the famous parts of CBS's disinformation campaign was on its own website. The cast of *Borneo* had their headshots on the site, and each week a red X appeared over the headshot of the contestant who had been voted off. James Poniewozik confessed in *TIME* magazine that he believed he had been spoiled to the fact that Gervase was the winner because "A few weeks ago, a hacker announced that he had cracked the area of the official 'Survivor' web site that contained the photos a head shot marked with a red 'X' that identify contestants voted off the island. The site had an 'X' for everyone except Gervase." Fans deduced that CBS was playing games with fans' heads on purpose. This story, of fans discovering the absent red X for Gervase, had been picked up by national media outlets like ABC News,[72] even though—like the eagle-eyed analysis of a Tribal Council—it had first appeared on the survivorsucks.com.[73]

The very nature of *Survivor* invites speculation about who will be the next player voted out. Media scholar Henry Jenkins argues that the part of what makes *Survivor* so compelling for fans is the "giant cat and mouse game that is played between the producers and the audience." The coincidental rise of online fan communities at the same time *Survivor* first aired was serendipitous, but *Survivor* is a perfect series for engaged fan content. As Jenkins declares, "*Survivor* is television for the Internet age—designed to be discussed, dissected, debated, and critiqued."[74]

Fan engagement with a franchise can take many forms, and *Survivor* fans are as devoted as any other fanbase. Sports fans expect to find analysis of game results, strategy, and decisions to fill up hours of airtime on radio and podcasts. While the coverage of *Survivor* is nowhere near as pervasive as popular sports analysis, there is ample content generated for fans to consume after any episode of *Survivor* airs, or even in *Survivor*'s off-season. While the total viewership of *Survivor* has decreased since its record-breaking first season, the depth of fan engagement has increased.

In 2016, an international team of researchers including Thiago Oliveira Santos, Abel Correia, Rui Biscaia, and Ann Pegoraro analyzed fan engagement through social media sites.[75] They identified three constructs of fan engagement: fan-to-fan relationships, team-to-fan relationships, and fan co-creation. The emergence of social media and online communities has transformed fandom and facilitated the emergence of unique performative aspects to fandom. While the work of Santos et al. was specifically geared toward understanding sports fandom, there is significant overlap in how *Survivor* fandom has emerged. Identifying some of those affinities will allow a theoretical framework for understanding *Survivor* fandom, even if the specificity of their original research does not always correlate perfectly between sports teams and reality TV.

The fan-to-fan interactions are relationships where viewers would interact with other viewers. These online interactions initially came about through forums, most notably survivorsucks.com, but are carried on in different social media platforms. Whether it is Twitter polls about the best seasons, Redditors debating strategy, or discussions about favorite players on the Survivor Facebook Fanpage, opportunities for fan-to-fan interactions are commonplace.

Team-to-fan relationships are "an interactive relationship created by the team aimed at building a long-term relationship with fans." For *Survivor*, one clear example of this would include the fan voting, most famously done in "America's Tribal Council" after *All-Stars* (season 8, 2004). Fans could text in the name of their favorite contestant from *All-Stars*, and the one who received the most votes would receive a million dollar prize. In *Panama* (season 12, 2006) and *Cook Islands* (season 13, 2006), fans could vote on a player to receive a truck or a car. From season 15 through season 26 the winner of a Fan Favorite or Sprint Player of the Season award as voted on by fans would win $100,000. While the winner of these fan votes definitely sees an immediate, monetary prize, for the producers allowing fans to have a role in the voting increases a sense of ownership and connection between the fans, the players, and the series.

Probst's official Twitter feed, and the official *Survivor* social media accounts are also examples of team-to-fan relationships. The social media presence of past contestants can also be a part of team-to-fan interactions. There is also the possibility that fans can one day be on the show. While some reality shows focus on the seemingly unattainable lifestyles of the upper-class or an exclusive high-profile family, in the case of *Survivor*, fans can easily fantasize about becoming part of the show and many desire to do so. Academics Beverley Skeggs and Helen Wood explain that "The speed with which television executives seize on the easy replicability of formats is matched by the eagerness of audiences to present themselves as television participants for others to watch and criticize."[76] The proliferation of competition reality shows required an equivalent increase in participants. Fans of these shows could become participants. Fan engagement is, for some, driven by the idea that understanding the game will make them better players if (when?) they get onto the show.

Aside from participating in the game itself, there are other means by which fans can engage with the show. Fan co-created content increases engagement with the original product, while allowing fans to be content creators. An entire industry geared around *Survivor* commentary has arisen during the show's decades on the air. There are prominent figures from traditional media, go-to fan websites, popular podcasts, and former players who have become commentators. There are academic journal articles analyzing various facets of the game and entire books written about the show. Multiple

YouTubers regularly post videos of *Survivor* highlights, analysis, or retrospectives that can garner hundreds of thousands to millions of views.

The world of *Survivor* commentary is somewhat akin to the thriving ecosystem of sports commentary. Sports reporters debate what will happen in future games, break down what happened in previous games, and have long conversations about the quality of various players and teams. In sports media, there are fan comment boards; podcasts from fans, media, and players; and traditional media in print and video. This is also true of *Survivor*. During a season there is speculation about what will happen in the next episode, intense scrutiny of what happened in the previous episode, and debate over who is playing the best game. Choices by producers and editors are debated, with people second-guessing about what the optimal strategy could have been, and what the losing player did wrong is analyzed.

Survivor fandom has proven extremely invested in discussion of the show. For many years *Survivor* has aired one season in the fall and one in late winter/early spring. But even during the summer months, content is still produced. Articles ranking seasons, podcasts highlighting obscure parts of *Survivor* lore, and YouTube videos breaking down twenty-year-old seasons are still released.

Survivor's wealth of analysis and discussion range from online coverage on websites like *EW*, *The Ringer*, *Parade*, *Vulture*, and *Newsweek* to academic books that analyze the series from various angles. Books about *Survivor* include Sallie Tisdale's *The Lie About the Truck: Survivor, Reality TV, and the Endless Gaze* and academic essay collections like *The Psychology of Survivor*, *Survivor Lessons: Essays on Communication and Reality Television*, and *Tribal Warfare: Survivor and the Political Unconscious of Reality Television*. There are also websites like Martin Holmes's Inside Survivor,[77] Andy Dehnart's Reality Blurred,[78] or Jeff Pittman's True Dork Times[79] which provide news, analysis, and recaps.

There are many websites where fans discuss the show. Perhaps the most famous is SurvivorSucks, but Reddit has a large, active *Survivor* subreddit. The website FanFiction.net, a repository of unlicensed fiction writing by fans of existing properties, has thousands of stories written using aspects of *Survivor*'s aesthetic, rules, storytelling style, and players.[80] Other sites also house numerous fanfiction tales of contestants battling it out to win the million-dollar prize. The stories can range from writing a season made up of previous contestants on the show[81] to imagining Pokémon characters participating in a season and writing about how that would play out.[82]

Several YouTube channels present commentary about *Survivor* and receive hundreds of thousands of views, or even more. The YouTube videos with the most views come from the official SurvivorOnCBS channel,[83] with several videos with more than 13 million views. But there are several channels with names like Land of Survivor,[84] Idoled Out,[85] Peridiam,[86] Survivor Geek,[87] or Once Upon an Island[88] that also have videos about *Survivor* with millions of views. Peridiam has a video titled "5 Times Survivor Players Hacked Challenges" with 3.5 million views which includes footage from *Survivor*, but also fifteen minutes of original voice-over analysis.[89] Other videos, like "Survivors Falling Over for 17 Minutes"[90] on the channel Eager Tortoise, are just montages of footage from the episodes with no commentary added.

When a new season of *Survivor* is airing, there are dozens of podcasts that provide analysis and commentary. These range from the *On Fire with Jeff Probst*, the official CBS podcast, to podcasts with former players, or media members who cover *Survivor*, to fans who have become commentators. Just as many pro athletes retire and move into sports commentary providing a unique point of view, these former contestants provide a deeper understanding in analyzing the strategy seen on the show as well as behind-the-scenes information.

Rob Cesternino (*The Amazon*; *All-Stars*) has founded an entire podcast network that discusses pop culture. The most prominent part of the network is its *Survivor* analysis, which features multiple shows released each week, even during the breaks in *Survivor*'s airing of new episodes. Stephen Fishbach (*Tocantins*; *Cambodia*) appears on Rob Cesternino's *Survivor Know-It-Alls* podcast, analyzing the strategy of every new episode that airs. David Bloomberg and Jessica Lewis (*Millennials vs. Gen X*) co-host *Why ____ Lost* after every episode, breaking down what the eliminated player did wrong. Tyson Apostol (*Tocantins*; *Heroes vs. Villains*; *Blood vs. Water*; *Winners at War*) hosts a podcast on *The Ringer*, titled *The Pod Has Spoken,* in which he recaps the episodes each week typically with a former player as a guest. And in early 2023, Probst himself got into the podcast scene with *On Fire with Jeff Probst: The Official Survivor Podcast* which releases a weekly episode during *Survivor* seasons. Other popular *Survivor* podcasts include *Snuffing Torches*, *The Purple Rock Podcast*, and *Survivor Historians*. This is far from an exhaustive list, as there have been hundreds of *Survivor* podcasts made throughout the years.

One of the most amusing expressions of fandom was the "Wandoff," a piece of absurdist postmodern theater that is almost impossible to describe with any concision. *The Wiggle Room* was a podcast with Rob Cesternino and Josh Wigler. Occasionally during an episode of *The Wiggle Room*, Wigler would sing a parody song in a falsetto voice, which he said was an imitation of Wanda Shirk, a contestant with an amazingly brief stay on the show who was notable for singing songs in her one-episode appearance during the premiere of *Palau* (season 10, 2005). Out of that silly bit on the podcast, The Wandoff was born. It is a contest in which fans of *Survivor* submit song parodies based on some event that occurred in the previous week's episode of the TV show. However, the fan engagement doesn't end with recording a song to be played on a podcast. The songs have to be curated, because there are too many submissions each week to be played on a single podcast episode. The top five songs of the week are then voted on by listeners, and a winner is declared. The winner receives a prize from Cesternino and Wigler, but will also be entered into the season finale of the Wandoff, where past winners can submit a song that captures the season as a whole. There are dozens of YouTube videos which splice together relevant footage from the episode to align with the parody lyrics.

Some examples of winning song parodies include transforming "Since U Been Gone" into "Since Yul's Been Gone" for the episode in which Yul Kwon was voted off of *Winners at War*. And lest you think the absurdity is over, Rob Cesternino introduces the parodies in the voice of Casey Kasem, and creates a pun name for the performer of the song, usually based on the original artist and a past contestant on the show. In this example, "Since Yul's Been Gone" was credited to Reed Kelly Clarkson. Reed Kelly was a contestant on *San Juan del Sur*, and Kelly Clarkson is the singer of "Since U Been Gone."

What is so fascinating about The Wandoff is not only how immensely insular it is as a form of fan expression, but also how devoted the artists and listeners are to it. The Wandoff requires familiarity with Casey Kasem's career as a radio DJ, the most recent episode of *Survivor*, the original songs that are being parodied, Wanda Shirk's one-episode stay on *Survivor*, Rob Cesternino's impressions on his podcasts, numerous in-jokes between the podcasters and their listeners, and very often obscure bits of *Survivor* episodes. To add to the strangeness of it all, Wanda Shirk's singing has been edited out of her episode on Paramount+ without any explanation, though we can assume it has to do with music rights. It took several paragraphs to explain what The Wandoff even is, but even with that foundation attempting a simple summary becomes absurd: former *Survivor* contestant Rob Cesternino pretends to be possessed by the ghost of Casey Kasem to present song parodies to *Survivor* journalist Wigler. The songs are written and recorded by fans reacting to the most recent episode of *Survivor* and released on the podcast only days after the episode airs.

The *Survivor* fandom is both broad—the casual fans who watch all the episodes but don't listen to podcasts or post online about it—and very deep—those who write fan fiction or song parodies about the show. Because *Survivor* is an ongoing media property, fan response can literally change the content. Mike White—a Hollywood writer and producer and eventual *Survivor* contestant (*David vs. Goliath*)—reacted negatively when Probst told him a twist would be reused in *San Juan del Sur* in 2014. Probst described that interaction in an interview, stating:

> He was over at our house for dinner just a couple of weeks before we started shooting. I confided in him about the basic creative for the *Blood vs. Water* season and when I mentioned Redemption Island coming back he had a very lackluster response—"Oh, you're doing Redemption again?"[91]

Because of White's response, the production shifted away from using Redemption Island that season. White also swayed Probst away from developing an entire, elaborate island economy based on the Fire Token twist from *Winners at War*.[92] Probst explained the plan to White, and White said "Well . . . it sounds . . . in-ter-est-ing. But is it fun?" and with that Probst threw the entire plan away.[93] Similarly, Probst told a story at the *Cagayan* reunion about how actor and filmmaker Tyler Perry suggested a more powerful immunity idol be introduced, and it has since been dubbed "The Tyler Perry Idol" by fans.

Aside from creating The Wandoff, Wigler campaigned on social media to end the Edge of Extinction twist which allowed players who had been voted out a chance to return to the game. After #EndEdgeofExtinction trended on social media, Probst acknowledged that this pressure would lead to them not returning to that aspect of the game for the foreseeable future.[94] In an opposite situation, there was an interaction between Probst and *Entertainment Weekly* writer Dalton Ross in which Probst said they're likely to phase out memory-based challenges. Ross said he likes to play along with those at home. Probst decided to use social media to ask fans if they liked to play at home too. "I went to Twitter tonight to ask the fans what they thought. Are memory challenges fun because you can play along or boring to watch? The overwhelming majority was 'fun to play along!' So never mind what I said about taking a break from them! They're back in the rotation!"[95] Knowing that their reaction and interaction has led to changes in the format of the show is likely to deepen engagement from fans.

More seriously, several former players formed organizations with the effort of changing how CBS cast its shows and how characters of color were portrayed on their reality shows. The Black Survivor Alliance (BSA) was founded by Jolanda Jones (*Palau*), who was very upset with her edit on the show, stating:

> My edit, and that of so many other Black people, caused me to organize the BSA and move to end systematic racism on *Survivor*. Mark Burnett foreshadowed portraying me as a "b*tch," his word not mine, and I didn't figure out that that was what he was actually going to do because I hadn't watched previous *Survivor*. I actually thought *Survivor* honestly portrayed players. I was wrong.[96]

Crystal Cox from *Gabon* also addressed how players of color are edited:

> Because there's limited representation in the editing room, many minority female castaways are edited as angry, loud, intimidating, and outspoken. But if there is representation in the editing room, maybe our other strengths can shine through and we are given a fair shot and reap the rewards of being on reality television, like many of our white female counterparts.[97]

In November 2020, CBS announced that they would cast 50 percent Black, Indigenous, People of Color (BIPOC) across all of their reality television shows and also committed to adding more diversity behind the camera.

FAN JARGON

Any dedicated fandom is likely to develop a jargon of terms associated with the thing they love. Sometimes these terms will come from the text themselves or sometimes they develop organically from fan discourse. Fans of *Star Trek: The Original Series* (1966–1969) have popularized the term Red Shirt—referring to a disposable member of the crew who is much less likely to survive a battle than the core cast of Kirk, Spoke, or McCoy (who wear gold and blue)—so much that there is even an award-winning parody novel by John Scalzi that borrows the term for its title.[98] Many other devoted fandoms develop jargon that can be based on in-universe terms or self-aware commentary about aspects of the production. As *Survivor*'s online fandom has migrated through various forums, message boards, and social media sites, in-community terminology has arisen as fans commiserate about their problems with the show and celebrate the aspects they love. Terms like "pagonging"—when the tribe with more members at the merge is in a tight alliance and consecutively votes off all the members of the other tribe (named after the Pagong tribe that had five members voted out in a row on

Borneo)—"advantage-geddon,"—when there were too many advantages in a season, and at Tribal Council every player but one was able to play an advantage that kept them safe—"gamebot,"—a player who only focuses on game strategy—or "mactor"—a model/actor who was recruited to appear on the show without applying—have become shorthand within the fandom to describe certain moments or types of players. Some terms have come directly from things said in the show. In *Blood vs. Water*, Kat Edorsson lamented that her boyfriend would be disappointed when she was voted out before the merge, saying, "Nobody wants to date someone who didn't make the merge."[99] This has led to some later players declaring that they are now dateable after they make it to the merge. In *46* (season 26, 2004), the first player booted out, David Jelinsky, argued that "several means seven."[100] Subsequently, the *Survivor* fandom started swapping "several" in for the word "seven," and production even gave the seventh episode of the season the title "Episode Several."

Some jargon stems strictly from how fans choose to engage with the series. "Edgic" is a term for a reading into the editing of a season in order to determine who the winner will be in the season finale. Martin Holmes, writing on the Inside Survivor website, explains, "Edgic is a portmanteau that combines the words Editing and Logic. It is a concept that was originally devised by the good folks on the Survivor Sucks forums to try and determine the winner of each Survivor season based on the edit."[101] In analyzing an episode, Edgic analysis considers a complex scale of rating how invisible or over-the-top a contestant's personality is in an episode, how positive or negative a castaway's portrayal is, and how visible a character is in terms of confessionals, conversations, and performance in challenges. After an episode airs, the content of the episode is coded into the preestablished Edgic scales, and each contestant receives ratings. Based on the trends recognized in previous seasons, Edgic readers would attempt to determine who is receiving a "winner's edit" that would result in a satisfying conclusion to the season. This may sound extreme, but when contrasted with how many hours of statistical analysis and sabermetric math is done on every major sporting event in America, it stops feeling like an outlier of fan engagement.

Some jargon is instantly discernible to anyone, even if it's not commonly used outside of *Survivor* fan discussions. Saying that a particular castaway received a "dodo edit" is easily comprehended. The moments chosen to be highlighted, the music that was used, and the way the events were edited made the castaway look foolish. Similarly, a "Winner's Edit" is where fans feel like a particular contestant's positive attributes have been highlighted, thus leading to a more emotionally satisfying conclusion to the season. The producers of the series are aware of these interpretations and analyses. Mike Bloom conducted an interview with the editing team behind the series. Brian Barefoot, an editor on *Survivor* since 2000, said, "Some viewers will read a lot into 'the edit,' and I love that they're passionate about it. It's a fun game between us and the audience, but they often read more into it than what is actually there." In the end, for the editors, the goal is to tell a clear and entertaining story in each episode. Some contestants are more entertaining or provide a clearer summation of strategy, and so they may get used more. As a result, fans may assume it's a Winner's Edit, when in reality choices were made for clarity. Plowden Schumacher, an editor with *Survivor* since 2009, points out that naturally the winner will become more familiar to the audience and have more screen time. "The people who last longer get more screen time and appear to be 'highlighted' but that's not something we consciously do. They appear 'highlighted' because they are the story. They survived." Matt Van Wagenen, a producer of the show since 2007 says the goal is to give every contestant a Winner's Edit,[102] though that clearly does not happen in some instances. The opposite of the Winner's Edit is not a Loser's Edit, but rather what has come to be known as a "Purple Edit."

To say a contestant got a "Purple Edit," means they basically were not present in an episode (or season). No confessionals to camera, no storylines to follow, no impact on votes or strategy. It comes from the twenty-first season of the show, *Nicaragua* (season 21, 2010). There were two castaways named Kelly on the same tribe. This is not the first time this has happened on the show, and a way to distinguish the two castaways is always developed. For example, in *Pearl Islands* (season 7, 2003), when there were two Ryans on the same tribe, Ryan Shoulders was referred to as "Skinny Ryan" and Ryan Opray was known as Ryan O. or Ryno. For the two Kellys, Kelly Bruno was Kelly B. and Kelly Shinn became known as Purple Kelly because she had purple highlights in her hair.

Through the first ten episodes, Purple Kelly only had one confessional to camera that aired. In the eleventh episode, when she quit the game she had four confessionals. Five confessionals across eleven episodes is remarkably low. Additionally, she was never shown as engaged in strategic conversations and her performance in challenges or around camp was never highlighted. Despite making it deep into the season, she was in eleven of fifteen episodes, Purple Kelly is presented as a complete nonfactor. The editors and producers had obviously minimized her role in the season. So now if a castaway has an episode they are not prominent in (even if they are a popular character), people will say they had a purple edit for that episode.

It could be assumed that because Purple Kelly quit late in the game, producers chose not to make her a prominent figure in the season so as to discourage quitting by future contestants. But another contestant from the same season, NaOnka Mixon, quit in the very same episode. NaOnka was the most prominent player in the edit, having fifty confessionals, the most of any castaway in the season.

It is worth noting the heavy speculation that Purple Kelly quit her season due to being extremely cold most of the days and being unable to handle it any longer. Nicaragua was rainy and wet most of the season. At the time of this season, production still limited clothes contestants could wear more strictly and Purple Kelly only had her yellow sundress and pink bikini. In an interview with Dalton Ross, Purple Kelly noted that her biggest regret from her *Survivor* experience was her dress, stating,

> Many of you probably know, *Survivor* asks you to send them an "interview outfit." Thinking this was an outfit I would be interviewed in, I sent them one of my favorite dresses that also fit within the required color scheme they had given me. This was that dang yellow dress that I lived in for my time on *Survivor.* I definitely regret not doing more research into this. Who knew I'd be tricked like that! I froze!

Despite this, Purple Kelly can be seen throughout the season wearing fellow contestant (and the season winner) Jud "Fabio" Birza's jacket. Fabio only won the final jury vote 5–4, so that kindness may have won him the game, as Purple Kelly also noted in the same interview, "I also wore Fabio's jacket for the majority of my time on *Survivor*—that's one reason he earned my million-dollar vote."[103]

SURVIVOR'S IMPACT

In 2009, *Variety* declared, "'Survivor' is the most influential program of the soon-to-be-concluded decade," claiming "from a business and a cultural standpoint, nothing was as game-changing as 'Survivor.'"[104] The television landscape was wildly different when *Survivor* premiered in May 2000 than the world we know today and *Survivor* has thrived as the industry shifted around it. The longevity *Survivor* has enjoyed is surprising. It was a ratings monster when it premiered, but many reality TV shows that attracted huge audiences were comets for the networks, burning bright then trailing off and disappearing. There were hit shows like *Who Wants to Be a Millionaire* (1999–2002) or *American Idol* (2002–2016, 2018–present), and others that seemed like unstoppable juggernauts that were canceled, even if they were later revived. According to John Koblin in a *New York Times* article, the enduring appeal of *Survivor* is "surprising enough that CBS executives have taken to calling it the 'miracle show' and the 'marathon show.'" Koblin notes, because "Reality shows are generally less expensive to produce than scripted shows," *Survivor* "provides CBS with a ratings magnet at a relatively low cost."[105] And, with some exceptions for controversies, the show requires little care and maintenance from the network. While salary demands nearly derailed hit series like *Seinfeld* (1989–1998) and *Friends* (1994–2004), the $1 million prize in *Survivor* was unchanged for twenty years—until it was doubled for the show's fortieth, all-winners season. But when the series returned for season 41 in 2001, the prize was back down to $1 million.

For a generation of TV viewers, *Survivor* has simply always been there. It has become as indelible a part of the television landscape as *Jeopardy* (1964–present) or *The Simpsons* (1989–present). Having been on the air since the year 2000, the franchise is so embedded into American pop culture that it is a steady presence even for people who don't watch it. It's part of the wallpaper of the entertainment world, a franchise that's constantly there. Jairus Robinson played *Survivor*'s forty-first season and was the first player who was younger than the show itself.[106]

While hundreds of reality shows have come and gone since *Survivor* first became a phenomenon, the show endures. Its concept captivates audiences and lures in new viewers. Though producers have introduced gimmicks— some that have become staples of the games; others that are loathed by fans—the show doesn't have to rely on twists to be compelling. Its very format forces the players into tough decisions, compelling strategy, and choices that fans love to debate. Writing for the *New York Times* in 2021 before the show's forty-first season premiered, Brenna Carley argued, "Most shows aren't having fun this many seasons in, but 'Survivor' isn't most shows. It has, remarkably, run for 21 years now, reinventing just often enough to keep devoted viewers guessing, with game wrinkles (some popular, some decidedly not) that make for consistently electrifying television."[107] Perhaps the most important thing to note about *Survivor* is that it is good, entertaining television. Production may like to highlight the social experiment, fans may have favorite players, the challenges can create drama, but none of that would matter if the show was boring. Yes, *Survivor* changed television, but if it wasn't a good show, it would have been canceled decades ago.

CHAPTER 2

MAKING *SURVIVOR*

THE HOST

Just as it takes a lot of individuals and effort to get a show like *Survivor* on the air, it takes a lot for it to keep going—from the pre-production to the cast and crew to the post-production. While thousands of people have been a part of making *Survivor*, the most recognizable, public face of the franchise is the host, Jeff Probst.

It is impossible to imagine what *Survivor* would be without Probst as the familiar, constant presence. The players change for each season. At the time of this writing, there have been almost 700 players in *Survivor* history, and only ten have ever appeared in back-to-back seasons. (Rupert Boneham [seasons 7 and 8]; Bobby John Drinkard, Stephenie LaGrossa [seasons 10 and 11]; Amanda Kimmel, James Clement [seasons 15 and 16]; Russell Hantz [seasons 19 and 20]; Malcolm Freberg [seasons 25 and 26]; Joe Anglim [seasons 30 and 31]; Michaela Bradshaw, Zeke Smith [seasons 33 and 34].) This makes the familiar face and voice of Probst extremely impactful. He is the singular persistent face each season for both players and viewers.

Probst has become synonymous with the franchise. This is, in part, because he was fairly unknown before *Survivor* began so he was not bringing existing fan familiarity into his role. He had worked as a freelance host in the entertainment industry, but was not a well-known name. This could have held him back, but he explains it motivated him to pursue *Survivor* specifically, admitting that he really wanted a project he could "sink his teeth into."[1] And in the case of *Survivor*, show creator Mark Burnett said, his "relative anonymity allowed them to build the show from the ground up."[2]

Probst reached out to Burnett directly when he heard about the show. As part of his application, Probst included a tape of an interview with actress Sandra Bullock for *Access Hollywood* that caught Burnett's eye. Burnett stated, Probst was "hilarious" and "had a great human quality." But it was something else that really sold him to Burnett. Sharing similar ways of thinking, Probst pitched himself by sending a "mockup of press stories about him and *Survivor* once it was a huge success." Amazingly, this was something Burnett himself had done when he was pitching the show to CBS, creating *Newsweek* and *Time* covers showing *Survivor* as the number one show on TV. Probst didn't know that Burnett had done a similar thing, but they had similar instincts and methods, which signaled to Burnett that Probst was the right man for the job. Burnett then brought in Probst for an interview, initially spending forty-five minutes telling him why he could not do the job. He explained that the nature of the production would include being out in the field, "living in a tent," not having "much water or food," and "getting bitten by bugs, chased by snakes," which wasn't something for a casual host. Burnett wanted to be sure Probst was up for everything the job entailed. Probst simply responded saying, "I really want to do this." The role came down to two people—Jeff Probst and Phil Keoghan (the eventual host of *The Amazing Race*). Both have become established reality television hosts, but in that moment, Burnett told Leslie Moonves, president of CBS, his instincts told him to go with Jeff Probst.[3] And so they did.

Survivor: Vanuatu *(Season 9, 2004) Shown: Jeff Probst.* CBS / Photofest © CBS, Photographer: Monty Brinton.

Over the years, Probst has been not only the host of *Survivor*, but also promoted to executive producer and showrunner. Burnett admits, "It was the second greatest decision I have made with Jeff Probst and 'Survivor.' First was choosing Jeff as host and second was having him become the showrunner."[4] The journey to showrunner was not a smooth one. At one point in 2009, Probst quit the show. While *Survivor* had made him famous, he was feeling pigeonholed, as he explained in a *New York Times* article:

> My Achilles' heel for a lot of my life was that nobody saw me as a storyteller, that they saw me as a white guy with dark hair who was just a game show host. . . . And that in terms of my own self-image was the thing that could gut me. It was like a kidney punch.

Probst explains in the same article that Moonves told him to take a break rather than leave the show, and after "a few months off" he returned to the show "re-energized," determined to focus on the formula that works: "serving the loyal audience and not worrying about doing more than that."[5] It is difficult to find the exact timing of Probst's quit, return, and promotion, but it appears Probst left the show sometime after season 17, *Gabon,* aired at the end of 2008 (and season 18, *Tocantins,* had already filmed). Probst is credited as an executive producer starting in *Nicaragua* (season 21, 2010). In an interview in early 2024, Probst noted that "maybe 12 years ago or so, I took over as a showrunner. That's ultimately when I saw where I wanted to be. I had to learn how to be good enough to have a shot at it."[6] Although he had frustrations after nearly a decade working on *Survivor*, it seems evident that these promotions helped reinvigorate Probst for his next chapter with the show.

Along with the position of executive producer and showrunner, Probst has to take on many roles as host toward the players. He has to be the guide, walking the players through the overall game, rewards, and challenges. He is the therapist at Tribal Council, asking questions and navigating answers. He is the comforting friend during medical evacuations and heightened situations. He has to hype up emotion when it's flat, deescalate emotion when it's too high, has to be a storyteller for the audience, and an interrogator of the contestants. Four-time player Cirie Fields (*Panama*; *Micronesia*; *Heroes vs. Villains*; *Game Changers*) explained her view of all his different roles in an interview with the *New York Times*, stating, "Jeff sees all and he's saying it, whether you see it or not. And he does it so authentically that you attach yourself to him. He's like your brother, your cousin, your friend, your fiancé."[7] And some players have noted that Probst is a tool to be used in your own game. Multiple-time player, and *Micronesia* (season 16, 2008) winner,

Parvarti Shallow says, "Think of him as an ally that you can use to unnerve people. He's not an omniscient Wizard of Oz character. He's a key player."[8]

Despite his presence today as the guardian of the *Survivor* brand, it took a while for Probst to find his role. He acknowledged at the beginning of the initial season, "We were making it up as we went along out there,"[9] so some transformation of role, tone, and style is expected. In the first season, *Borneo* (2000) Probst is very calm, placating, and comforting with the players. The Tribal Councils are fairly informal, with people talking over each other and Probst seemingly having little control. In episode 3, he even institutes a *Lord of the Flies*-style conch shell to try and ensure only the player holding it will speak. That gimmick passes quickly. Eventually, Tribal Council becomes Probst's domain. He guides the conversation, ensures questions are responded to, and probes into tribe dynamics. Regarding how he leads Tribal Council, Probst states,

> I used to approach Tribal as though anytime there was a really great answer, I would try to put a button on it, so that we could have a little moment. Then I realized maybe I would be more effective if I talked just a whole lot less. Now, though you don't see it in the cut, I'm very likely to ask a question and if I don't get the answer I'm looking for, I'll just wait. . . . The key to my job is to keep turning the story, without being seen as the one holding the key.[10]

In *Borneo*, Probst is concerned with the quality of everyone's experience. His first direct question to players is "How was the journey over here?" and the next is "How are you holding up, physically?"[11] But as Probst settles into his role, he mostly becomes more distanced from the players. Initially, Probst would often join reward excursions with players and be seen more frequently throughout each episode. However, after a few years Probst stopped joining rewards and after about a decade of the show occasionally did not even run challenges, but rather left do-it-yourself challenges for the players to run on their own.

At present, Probst is involved with all aspects of the show—from casting, producing, and at times testing out the challenges. As Probst admitted in an interview, "Anyone that works on the show will tell you I'm intimately involved in every single part of the show," explaining that over the years as host he has evolved:

> I was learning a lot and mostly I was learning by making mistakes. I was learning how to trust my instincts. The one thing I've always noticed about good hosts is they're able to see when a moment is unfolding and they know what to do, whether to create space for the moment to happen or whether to get in and grab the moment and make sure it has a spotlight on it.[12]

Gervase Peterson, who played in *Borneo* and thirteen years later in *Blood vs. Water* (season 27, 2013), describes the evolution of Probst between the two seasons: "Jeff is totally in control now. The first season he was just along for the ride with us. But now he has this authoritative aura. He knows all he has to do is ask the right question and push the right button and people will go at each other."[13] It is quite the change from barely being able to control the first few Tribal Councils to how he is presented as asking pointed to questions to guide each Tribal Council in the following seasons.

There have been multiple phases of Probst as the host that are clear to identify with a consecutive rewatch of the show. In the earlier seasons, Probst was learning and figuring out his role, toward the time he quit and after as he grew in his executive producer role, he was arguably more checked out and definitely less involved in rewards and challenges. Seasons after he was more stern with players, refusing to put up with much from them. And in the most recent seasons post-COVID in 2020, he has been kinder and more of a friend toward the players. In an interview regarding this change, Probst states, "My personality was shifting into much more uplifting, positive, encouraging . . . You can have a change of heart personally in how you see the world, but you still have to run this show in a way that holds players accountable."[14] Probst admits he is still learning: "I'm not always perfect on the show . . . I said things that I regret now, I've had points of view that I would change now. That was also me in the moment, being vulnerable and learning."[15] Evolution and growth are two things seen throughout the twenty-plus years of the show and of its host.

What carries on the show so well is Probst's clear passion and love of the game. Speaking on his experience as host for over twenty years, comparing the first season to now, he noted,

> I just had this unbridled enthusiasm and I thought it would be the greatest summer of my life and then I would do something else but I was going to enjoy those 39 days. Here's the kicker to that, I've enjoyed every single season since. I still have that same enthusiasm today that I had 20 years ago.[16]

Probst also stated in an interview with *Entertainment Weekly*,

> It's impossible to describe what Survivor represents to me. Impossible. It goes beyond creative expression or professional recognition. It's much deeper. It's right in line with the ideas I try to impress on our players. It's about pushing myself further than I think I can go, about trying to stay in the moment and adapt to my surroundings, about being a good "tribe member," about being open to new ideas and new people. The same opportunities *Survivor* offers the players, it offers me. I love *Survivor* and I still need *Survivor*.[17]

Survivor and Jeff Probst are inextricably linked to one another. Probst is as much a part of the show as the island location, and whenever the time comes for a new host to step in it will be one of the most jarring changes to date.

THE CASTING

With a strong host as the consistent presence, a season of *Survivor* is defined by its players and the success is dependent on each cast. No matter the theme or twists and advantages put together by the producers—what matters most are the players reacting and adapting to each scenario. Iconic players, such as Russell Hantz (*Samoa*; *Heroes vs. Villains*; *Redemption Island*) or Tony Vlachos (*Cagayan*; *Game Changers*; *Winners at War*), can instantly take hold of a season and whether as a hero or a villain, make for compelling television.

The ability to be cast on the show *Survivor* is, in theory, available for all. Anyone can apply by sending in an application, or attend an open casting call offered in various cities throughout the year. But there are specific qualities and traits that the casting directors are looking for in each player. At the end of the day, it is a television show for entertainment. Interesting characters who can narrate the story comfortably on camera are essential. It is difficult to estimate the exact number of applicants; however, in recent seasons there have been approximately 25,000 applications for each season.[18] Whittle that down to just eighteen (or sometimes sixteen or twenty) individuals who get on a season, and the odds of getting on the show are very low.

There needs to be something about an applicant that will set them apart from the thousands of others. In an interview with *Entertainment Weekly* regarding what he looks for in casting, Probst says, "First of all, there has to be drive," and second, "Do you know who you are? . . . you need to know how you see yourself. And it really helps if you have an idea of how the world sees you because they're not always the same."[19] Lynne Spillman, who worked as the casting director for *Survivor* for the first eighteen years of the show, noted a similar desire in that she looked for individuals who "have really strong opinions, they know who they are, they have a foundation, they've worked, they're in college or a fraternity. They've had a lot of social interaction."[20] Evidently, a strong sense of self is a must for being on *Survivor*.

What else are producers going for when building a cast of players for a season of *Survivor*? Burnett stated,

If a bunch of people were marooned and a ship went down, there'd probably be a lawyer, there'd be a doctor, there'd be a homemaker, there'd be a student, there might be someone from the military. A wide range of people from different ages, different races, different geographies, different incomes, who never would meet unless thrown together in this new society.[21]

The first season of the show showcased a wide variety of demographics between the players who would most likely never come into contact otherwise. Players included Rudy Boesch, a seventy-two-year-old former Navy Seal from Virginia; Sue Hawk, a thirty-eight-year-old truck driver from Wisconsin; Kelly Wiglesworth, a twenty-two-year-old river rafting guide from California; Richard Hatch, a thirty-eight-year-old corporate trainer from Rhode Island; and Sean Kenniff, a thirty-year-old neurosurgeon from New York in the top five alone. In what other scenario would these individuals end up spending over thirty-five days together?

Sean Foley, an editor on the show from 2000–2006, and director of photography from 2011–2015 stated in an interview, "The iconic characters of season one became the benchmark of the series. Originally cast from key demographics across the country, each character was chosen to appeal to a given group of viewers. Ideally, there would be someone for everyone to root for."[22] This goal of demographic diversity is reflected in various themes used through seasons to give a cross section of different types of individuals—such as *Worlds Apart* (season 30, 2015) which divided the players by their profession of white collar vs. blue collar vs. no collar and *Heroes vs. Healers vs. Hustlers* (season 35, 2017) similarly divided the players by their professions. This was also the goal in the controversial thirteenth season, *Cook Islands* (2006), in which they divided the cast into four tribes by race: African American, Asian America, Hispanic American, and Caucasian.

This desire for such specific types of players is perhaps what led to individuals being recruited for the show, which is not an uncommon practice for reality TV shows. Despite having thousands of applicants, recruited players have appeared in most seasons. There have been recruited players who won, such as Brian Heidik in *Thailand* (season 5, 2002), Yul Kwon in *Cook Islands*, and Natalie Anderson in *San Juan del Sur* (season 29, 2014).[23] *Gabon* (season 17, 2008) winner, Bob Cowley, was recruited for the show, and played "to have a good time," having only seen the show "a couple of times."[24] Some of the most memorable players were recruits and have played multiple times, including Rudy Boesch, Jonny Fairplay, Phillip Sheppard, and Jessica "Sugar" Kiper.[25] Of course many recruits were voted out early on in their season, confirming that the wide range of outcomes for recruits is the same as the wide range for those who actively apply on their own. Notably, even if you were recruited you still had to formally apply for the show. Spillman explains, "They still have to make a video, they still have to go through the process, they still have to come to finals, they still have to go to the network and get approved. It's just a shorter process."[26]

For those who are not recruited, there are endless articles, videos, and former players who can help guide and advise one through the application process. While some individuals claim to have winning techniques that help you get on the show, casting directors adamantly deny that anything like a coach could help an applicant get cast.[27] What we do know for sure, though, is that the process to be cast currently is different from how it was in early seasons. There are two distinct changes. The first is that production is no longer recruiting and now only casting applicants who know the show well. Jodi Wincheski, former casting producer for *Survivor*, explained why only fans are now cast: "They really just want people who really know the show and are going to be good strategists. . . . That's the way they'd rather go, [rather] than finding somebody and then having them cram and become a fan."[28] This change seems to have come from a transition in who leads the casting. As noted, Lynne Spillman led the casting for *Survivor* for the first eighteen years of the show. In 2018 she was reportedly let go from *Survivor* as her contract was up and didn't get renewed[29] and casting is now led by Jesse Tannenbaum, with Jeff Probst much more involved as well.[30]

The second big change occurred in 2020 when CBS introduced a new policy that "50% of its casts for its unscripted shows must be Black, Indigenous or People of Color (BIPOC)."[31] *41* was the first season filmed under this change. Regarding the policy, Probst stated, "It's one of the most exciting things that's happened to 'Survivor' in my 21 years. It opened the door to something we hadn't seen, one of our own blind spots."[32] It is a change that many cast members have pushed for over the years. Probst also noted the improvement this diversity target would lead to with each cast for a season, stating, "We quickly realized we are not what we could be. By diving into our casting in a completely different way, we have found so many people that we never would've discovered before. The people we're finding are so interesting and layered and they love *Survivor*."[33]

It is worth noting, that along with these other changes, Probst has declared they will no longer be casting villains on the show. "In the hands of somebody else, I can tell you, for sure, there would be more 'villains,' more negativity, more yelling at each other. . . . It's just not going to happen when I'm part of the show. I'm just not interested in it. There's too many other things we could do and still have fun."[34] While there is an argument for the entertainment and drama villains can bring to the show, it is admirable the effort the show is now making to present a positive environment with no need to have players tear each other down. However, with the nature of the show, backstabbing remains an inevitability. Also, while Probst may say he does not want to cast villains, he cannot control how audiences perceive the players. After the finale of *46* (season 26, 2024), the online backlash against Maria Shrime Gonzalez's choice to vote for Kenzie Petty rather than her longtime ally Charlie Davis in the final vote was so intense that a rare admonishment was published on the *Survivor* Instagram account:

> One of the best things about the Survivor community is the passion, engagement and excitement around the show, gameplay and those brave enough to compete. So, a reminder as we watch and discuss the entertaining competition, epic blind-sides and emotional journeys these players go on, remember that who you see on screen are real people navigating this experience. Please consider embracing kindness, respect and compassion before commenting.[35]

Though Maria's actions hardly reached the level of villainy seen previously on the show, some fans were rooting for Charlie so much they interpreted her vote as the act of a true villain.

Even with focusing on casting fans and those who love *Survivor*, there will still be players who love to watch the game, but turns out, don't love to play the game. There have been quitters throughout *Survivor*, the first being Osten Taylor from *Pearl Islands* (season 7, 2003). Throughout the years, individuals have quit for various reasons, whether it be physical health, mental health, or assuming they're about to be voted out so they leave on their own terms. Some inform Probst and then leave the game while others ask their tribe to vote them out. In *45* (season 45, 2023), two of the first four eliminations were quits rather than vote outs. Despite both the individuals being super fans, it's impossible to know for certain how an individual will react when having to actually live the game. The casting process is very thorough to try and prevent casting individuals who are likely to quit. Probst has explained, "During casting it gets very personal, and we learn a lot about everybody, and they go through a deep psychological process with us so that we know that they're ready for this adventure and that they can handle this adventure once the game starts."[36] Despite this, the elements, the gameplay, or the stress of being constantly filmed can all wear down a player.

"Watching someone quit is very frustrating for fans of the show, but less than one percent have quit."[37] Even so, in November 2023, Probst said, "I want to declare right here on your show that from this point forward if you are a Survivor player and you quit, your torch will not be snuffed. That's over. To get your torch snuffed, you got to play the game."[38] It may be a minor consequence, but *Survivor* is built on symbolic actions, and preventing a fan from participating in one could possibly serve as a deterrent, but more likely just gives fans some minor satisfaction.

Survivor: Panama *(Season 12, 2006) Shown: Courtney Marit, Jeff Probst.* CBS / Photofest © CBS, Photographer: Bill Inoshita.

Survivor is a game and a reality television show, but just like in real life, things are out of the players' control. Injuries happen. Illnesses occur. And even events back home take over and pull them from the game. These are very different circumstances than quitters of the game. There are times when a player will beg to stay in the game, but their injury is so critical that they are given no choice and leave the game to receive medical care. As a returning player and "favorite" in *Micronesia*, Jonathan Penner suffered a knee injury during a reward challenge. Days later, as the injury worsened, the infection was determined to be potentially life threatening, doctors ordered that he be removed from the game for treatment during the sixth episode. When pulled from the game for any medical reason, players are not allowed to return. Sometimes players leave the game due to family situations. In *All-Stars*, Jenna Morasca left the show during the third episode on day eight after beginning to feel the need to go be with her sick mother. *Survivor* noted at the end of the episode Jenna's mother passed away only eight days after Jenna returned to her. And in *Cambodia*'s sixth episode, returning player

Terry Deitz immediately left the show on day thirteen to return home after Probst arrived in the middle of the night to inform him his son was in the hospital with an emergency heart condition. Ultimately, *Survivor* is a game, most players are playing for their family back home, and family emergencies seem to be more important than what is happening on the island.

THE LOCATIONS

For eighteen seasons *Survivor* traveled around the world filming in new locations. The only early back-to-back seasons in the same location were seasons 7 and 8 filmed in Panama. Seasons initially were filmed months apart in order to get set up in the new location. Then beginning with seasons 19 and 20 the show began filming two seasons in a location back-to-back. The countries used as locations were Samoa, Nicaragua, Philippines, and Cambodia. Staying in the same location allows for significant cost-cutting. Since *Millennials vs. Gen X* (season 33, 2016) the show has filmed solely on the Mamanuca Islands of Fiji. The show also used to film at all different times of the year (most likely depending on the location, weather, and permits) and now films back-to-back during the early summer months in Fiji.

While it is exciting as viewers to see new locations around the world for players to "survive" in, there are many more logistics, costs, and issues that come with each new location, such as climate, governments, permits, moving crew, and sets. Traveling to a new location each season requires hours of research and setup, all of which come with a higher price. Considering this through the production side of things, rather than a viewer, it is easy to comprehend why the show would begin to film back-to-back in a location, and eventually settle in Fiji permanently.

Everything with TV production comes down to cost. In a podcast interview with film producer Todd Garner in 2018, Probst discusses the benefits of filming in Fiji, disclosing much of the show's costs are aided by Fiji offering a 45 percent rebate. That is significant cost savings that would allow the budget to be put toward other things, such as large sets for challenges (or perhaps the $2 million prize for season 40). Probst continues in the podcast to note that staying in one location with good relationships eases a lot of logistical burden: "It just takes the stress of having to break down, put stuff in containers, ship it across the ocean, pull it out of the containers, set it up again, make new deals with island owners which are not easy to do."[39] All of this adds up to make it a logical situation to stay and film there rather than anywhere else.

Importantly, Fiji offers everything needed in a filming location on an island. Visually it is stunning—beautiful water with endless shades of blue, white sandy beaches, and diverse jungles. The climate is not as extreme as many other locations *Survivor* has filmed in. A big storm here or there certainly adds drama to a season, but it's fun to watch people fish and scavenge for food to survive against the elements in creative ways. It is not fun to watch people starve and have the elements be so intense to the point that each player is so depleted they can barely function, much less strategize.

There are a lot of reasons as to why the show has chosen to film only in Fiji for the past decade, but Probst summed it up best when he stated, "The real truth of the world is, when we started *Survivor* 18 years ago, there were lots of places we could go. It's been two decades. It's a different world. There are not as many places we can go for lots of reasons—the economy, population, political unrest, weather patterns."[40] At least for the foreseeable future, fans and players should expect the show to film on the same beaches. This is why David Wright (*Millennials vs. Gen X*) flew to Fiji on his own, hired a boat to take him to the island where *Survivor* films, and buried a fake idol where he could find it if he was ever asked back. David did return in *Edge of Extinction*, but chose not to dig it up, and it is still buried at a campsite that is regularly used.[41] No one from production seemed to know he had done this as it was only revealed by David in a Q&A in 2021.

Despite any negatives that come with filming in one location, there doesn't seem to be any chance that it will change while Probst is host and showrunner. "It would be great to say, no we're going to go all over the world. No, there is nowhere to go. This is our home. I hope we end our show here."[42] In recent years, the only consideration for filming in a different location than Fiji has been during the COVID pandemic, such as Hawaii and Georgia, merely as a means to get back into production while the world was in shutdown, although neither location worked out.[43] Once back in Fiji, production has been there ever since, with no plans to go anywhere else as Probst has declared, "I hope we stay here forever."[44]

THE CHALLENGES

Every episode of *Survivor* features a challenge for immunity—either tribal immunity or individual immunity after the merge. Frequently, there is also a challenge for just reward, in which the tribe or individuals compete for food or an experience. Sometimes the reward and immunity challenges are combined into one. Over the years there have been more than 800 challenges played on *Survivor*.[45] That is a staggering number, even with challenges having been repeated, or elements of former challenges incorporated into new challenges. The types of challenges can be categorized into general themes, including: physical, obstacle course, hit a target, endurance, balance, and puzzle. There are other more specific types, such as: *Survivor* Auction, "Gross" Food Eating, Q&A, Blindfold, and Loved Ones Visit. Commonly now, challenges combine a few of the general categories, such as beginning with a physical water section or obstacle course, leading into a balance section, and ending on a puzzle or hitting a target.

Survivor: Heroes vs Villains *(Season 20, 2010) Shown: Tyson Apostol, J. T. Thomas Jr.* CBS / Photofest © CBS.

The show occasionally incorporates other means to make the challenges more difficult, such as tying up one arm of the players, so they can only use one hand or only allowing players to use their feet. In some extreme instances, both arms and feet are tied up and players have to slither through the sand to get from point A to point B. Occasionally players are offered food if they will step out of a challenge, revealing how secure they feel in the game, or simply showing their lack of confidence in winning the challenge. Rewards for the tribe can also be offered, such as when the tribe is in need of rice and can receive it only if a specific number of individuals opt out of competing in the challenge.

Challenges are a very significant part of *Survivor*, yet there are times when a challenge doesn't go the way production may have expected. The most iconic example of this is from the finale of *Palau*. The last challenge comes down to Tom Westman and Ian Rosenberger in which they stood on a buoy in the water for just under twelve hours in an endurance contest. On his podcast, *On Fire*, Probst describes this challenge noting, "We did it with the Dream Team, and it lasted about an hour, because it was painful."[46] Clearly, production was not prepared for the challenge to go well into the night, forcing a scramble to figure out how to get lighting for the end of the challenge. A crew member was unable to compete with the same level of drive and desire as a player who had a million dollars on the line.

Puzzles are another type of challenge that have had unforeseen dedication by players. Recent seasons have featured players who have either bought, created, or printed versions of previous *Survivor* puzzles that are then solved extremely quickly. In the eighth episode of *41* (season 41, 2021), Evvie Jagoda solved the pyramid puzzle almost instantly after seeing it in a previous season and realizing she could replicate it and practice it at home. And Carson Garrett in *44* (season 44, 2023) used a 3D printer to create common puzzles from earlier seasons and was able to complete some puzzles very quickly.[47] Due to some players practicing before the season begins, some fans have argued *Survivor* needs new puzzles and challenges to be created. However, there are also fans practicing at home in the hope that they will get on the show and happen to have a puzzle they can solve quickly. While there have been new puzzles created for recent seasons, it seems unlikely that all puzzles will be retired. As Probst said on his podcast, "Sometimes you get lucky in the season you're on has a puzzle that you made a 3D model of and you kill it. I love that because it rewards preparation."[48]

Sometimes players excel at certain challenges so much that fans claim that specific challenges must have been used in seasons to cater to them. Probst has declared this cannot be true. "People say, I bet you put challenges in to help your favorite players. That's impossible, we don't even know who the players are when we're making these challenges."[49] And there have been players who looked like they would do well at a certain type of challenge who completely failed.

A lot goes into creating and building the challenges and each challenge is tested by the Dream Team, a group of individuals who run through every challenge onsite to be sure it works correctly before filming. They also help to be sure the right shots can be captured on camera. Former dream teamer, Heimata Hall, who worked on the show in 2009 in Samoa, said in an interview of his experience,

Throughout the day, our primary job was to test all the challenges. . . . We'd shoot a complete run-through every few days with all the cameras, crew, and producers watching. It was fun because everyone would make side bets on which "Dream Team" players would win. Our job was to play as hard as if we were actual contestants.[50]

The challenges are also monitored by a standards of practice individual, to ensure fairness and that nothing would favor one player or tribe. Every knot is tied by the same individual and everything is measured to be equal, either directly or proportionally to each player's size.[51]

Regarding the creation of challenges, John Kirhoffer, challenge producer since the first season, said, "One of our mantras that Jeff established years ago is, 'Simple in concept, difficult in execution.'"[52] Many challenges may seem simple, and seem like something as a viewer you could do. But many players point out they are much harder than you realize when playing on *Survivor*.

THE PRODUCTION

One of the miracles of *Survivor* is that it successfully presents the illusion of island castaways that are separated from anyone else. While it's obvious to anyone who thinks about it, a production crew must be around to get the footage they're watching. The same production crew does an amazing job of encouraging the viewer to forget that. Very rarely does the existence of the crew members—whether through the stray leg of a camera operator appearing in a shot or shadows from a boom mic passing over a castaway—break through the carefully cultivated "reality" that the contestants are alone on the island. The consistent illusion that is presented to viewers is that the castaways are alone on the island, except when Probst guides them through challenges and Tribal Council. The reality, of course, is that the number of production crew involved in making the show while filming on the island is much higher than most viewers would likely guess. In 2019, Dalton Ross wrote an in-depth piece about the opening scenes of *Edge of Extinction* (season 38, 2019) for *Entertainment Weekly*. In the impressive piece of journalism, Ross notes that the production crew consists of "approximately 275 international crew members and 370 local Fijian workers"[53] After having visited on-site, Reporter Mike Bloom expertly described the production set up, stating,

Survivor production is an iceberg. Everything we see in front of the camera, including the castaways and Jeff Probst is just a small portion of everyone who is there. Between the camera and sound guys and producers and challenge coordinators, even the people behind those people, the ones who are scouting locations, the ones who are cooking the food for the staff, there are so many people integral to every single day of production who very rarely get talked about.[54]

Rarely, but at times, the show allows viewers a peek behind the curtain. The first time viewers saw the illusion of isolation fully pulled back was in the second season, *The Australian Outback* (season 2, 2001). In the sixth episode, Michael Skupin was badly injured when he fell into the fire and burned his hands. He had to be medevacked via helicopter and transported to a hospital for trauma treatment. Sean Foley, an editor and director of photography on the series for many years, recalled in an interview, "The imaginary world of 'Survivor' was shattered when Michael had to be medevacked after falling into the fire. In the edit suite, editor Ivan Ladizinsky faced a difficult challenge because the injury itself happened early in the morning when there was no camera on Michael."[55] Because there was no footage of the actual moment of the accident, the audience sees B-roll footage of nature and hears the audio of Skupin screaming and then the visual footage cuts to Skupin in the river cooling his burned skin.

Another notable example of seeing behind the curtain is when several players began to suffer from heatstroke in *Kaôh Rōng* (season 32, 2016). Due to the severity of the situation, Probst called for all hands on deck during the medical emergency, and footage aired that revealed the dozens of crew members and medical personnel that were present during the challenge. Probst recalls in an interview with Ross, "Having three people down within one challenge was unprecedented and it quickly became clear that this was a very serious situation." He would conclude, "This was the most frightened I've been in all my time on *Survivor*. Three people down at once and one of them in very serious condition." Probst continues in the interview, stating,

Later in the day as we were doing our debriefing, our safety and security team reminded me that despite being in the middle of a jungle in the middle of an ocean, that Caleb was in the air on a chopper with a doctor at his side within twenty-two minutes of collapsing. And, he was being tended to in a hospital not long after that. My point in sharing this is that it would be very hard to get that same kind of fast response in most cities in the United States. We go to great lengths and expense to be prepared for a situation like this and it's rewarding to see it pay off.[56]

Although *Survivor* strives to give the illusion of being stranded in a location with just your tribe, the players are never abandoned. However, editing such a scene is critical to the tone of the show. Challenge editor, Dave Armstrong, explains, "The tricky part of this sort of thing is showing the viewer what is happening without editing it in a sensationalized way. So, I let many of the shots play out in a raw documentary style, even if it meant revealing our crew, medical staff and our entire 300-crew set up."[57] The intensity of the scene is translated for viewers, as the panic in Probst and the crew is palpable as players are struggling.

In contrast to any other season opening, in *44*, a producer's voice is the very first sound heard, as he says to a contestant, "Alright Carolyn, you ready?" To which Carolyn Wiger replies, "So I'm just like talking?" And the producer confirms, "Yeah, to me."[58] It is a charming opening that becomes even more charming as the viewers get to know Carolyn over the course of the season. The show does a callback to this exact moment in the finale episode as Carolyn has made the final three. In her last confessional she says to the camera, but clearly talking to her producer, "Remember day one when you interviewed me?" The producer replies off camera, "Yeah, I do. We're here on day 26, this is full success."[59] It's a choice never before made by the editors to show a conversation between contestant and producer like that. But after forty-plus seasons, it's natural that new ideas and formats would be explored. Similarly, in *41*, as a tonal experiment, more of the crew was shown to viewers. The season's opening montage included crackling voices over walkie-talkies, shots of entire boats full of crew were shown to the audience, and camera operators were spotted in some early scenes. This experiment did not last through season 41, and hasn't been used again in subsequent seasons.

THE EDITING

It's a massive undertaking to edit a season of *Survivor*. Mike Bloom, after interviewing multiple *Survivor* editors, said,

> Fourteen hundred and forty minutes. That's how much raw footage the "Survivor" production team captures of the brutal challenges, bonding, and backstabbing that occur within every three-day cycle that usually makes up an episode of the hit reality franchise. Millions of people have seen countless tales of betrayal and survival play out on their screens. But before the footage gets to the fans, the "Survivor" editing team takes all that coverage and trims it down to forty minutes per episode, spinning the stories that have kept viewers tuned in for two decades and 600 episodes.[60]

Survivor: Panama *(Season 12, 2006) Shown: Aras Baskauskas, Danielle DiLorenzo, Shane Powers, Cirie Fields.* CBS / Photofest © CBS, Photographer: Bill Inoshita.

How do you take all the footage and form it into a cohesive narrative for an approximately forty-minute television show? (However, some episodes within seasons have been given ninety minutes or even two hours. And in seasons 45 and 46 all the episodes were ninety minutes.) The first step is to stick to the format. Part of the comfort of watching *Survivor* is the familiarity of what to expect. There will be a challenge for immunity. There will be a Tribal Council. Someone will go home. And Probst will say at some point:

"Wanna know what you're playing for?"
"Fire represents your life."
"It's time to vote."
"I'll go tally the votes."
"The Tribe has spoken."

The show is so aware of the repeat phrases that Probst has adopted over the years that they sometimes become part of the puzzle in a challenge. In a particular challenge during *Worlds Apart* the players could not solve a word puzzle which was supposed to read "A reward with all the fixin's." Probst tried to give them clues by stating, "Start thinking *Survivor*. It's been on for thirty seasons. I say the same 200 words over and over and over and over and over. I'm in therapy I say the words so often."[61] The repetitive nature of these phrases and formulaic format allows viewers to connect deeper with the show. Some things are unpredictable, like the actions of the players, but to have enough of the show be familiar is comforting. An article from the *Washington Post* interviewing Burnett, noted, "Burnett credits this combination—a viewer's need for familiar, comfortable programming while still injecting twists—for keeping 'Survivor' a fan favorite for so long. The format rarely changes—host Jeff Probst is always there—but producers can throw in a gimmick each season. For some, it's a soothing routine."[62] Routine and comfort are part of why viewers make a habit of watching a series.

There are plenty of variables in a season of *Survivor* to make each episode unique, but viewers also want something familiar when they tune in. They hear the familiar musical cues scoring scenes, there are shots of wildlife used as transitions, the players compete in a challenge, and someone is voted off at Tribal Council. These beats provide audiences with the familiar trappings that they already know they enjoy, but they want to be surprised as well. Finding that balance between the comforting familiar and the surprising new is key for the long-term success of any show.

Bloom published an informative article about the behind-the-scenes work that goes into *Survivor* titled "Outwit, Outplay, Out-cut: How the Editing Team Has Kept the 'Survivor' Tribe Together Through 40 Seasons." Much of *Survivor*'s familiar style was established in its first season in the year 2000 by Burnett and his production team and has remained consistent across all its seasons. Because of this, the editors can build an episode around that known format. Brian Barefoot, who has been an editor on the show since the beginning, describes the initial part of this process: "At the start of each episode, we'll have a story meeting with our producer who was out on location, so they know what happened in detail. They give us an outline of the important beats for that episode." He continues, noting what the editors look for, "Then we screen hours and hours of footage. Sometimes that's the hardest part of the whole process. While screening, we search for important story points and any fun or revealing moments with the contestants."[63]

However, even with the goal of keeping a consistent format, there is a natural evolution to the editing of the show. Watching the first season after having become used to current season styles, there are several striking elements that have changed. The season featured lots of montages around camp, no commentary during challenge, Probst monologuing to explain everything, Tribal Council is essentially a mess as Probst asks random questions and people talk over each other, and some of the key story beats are told through confessionals rather than actual footage of events (likely due to smaller crew and fewer cameras). Production-wise, the absence of any play-by-play commentary from Probst during challenges feels like a glaring omission. There are other familiar aspects missing too. No tribe swap to mix things up before the merge. No hidden individual immunity idol. Simple terms that have become commonplace aren't there yet. In *Borneo*, Probst and the show refer to "the merge," as "the merger," an individual can win the "Immunity Talisman" instead of the "Immunity Necklace," and in the fifth episode a player calls "Tribal Council" "Immunity Council."

Bloom's article includes insights from other members of the *Survivor* production team. Executive Producer Matt Van Wagenen states, "A big difference in storytelling over the years is the speed of the show. That's probably the most obvious change." Initially, the strategy was almost nonexistent and the idea of alliances was alien to many castaways. Whereas now, the strategy starts even before the game begins. And the emphasis of this strategy is highlighted in the edit. Bill Bowden, a *Survivor* editor since 2008, explained what this change has allowed them to create with the show:

> The more complex the strategy and game gets, the more interesting it gets. So we strive to show as much of the complexities as possible. That quickened pace also allows us to slow down for powerful moments with the players that are not strategy as well. These moments give our audience a chance to really get to know the players.

It is easy to take for granted the style of the show, when in reality, *Survivor* set the stage for other shows to follow. The editors had to figure it out as they went, as Foley explained,

> Season 1 was a challenge because there was no blueprint. There were no other shows like "Survivor" and reality TV was in its infancy. In terms of style and tone, we started with a blank canvas. Since every episode had a dramatic reveal at the end, we began to emulate traditional drama, crafting scene work from scraps of moments to create a sense of cause and effect that viewers could track. Today, the techniques we experimented with back then have become commonplace in good non-fiction. But at the time, we were struggling to figure it all out.

It is so easy to forget that techniques that are commonplace today once had to be invented by someone. Bob Matthews, another *Survivor* editor since 2001, explained a specific example from *The Australian Outback*, which featured in the first episode a blowout vote in the Tribal Council. A vote of this nature could have zero suspense if all the votes are shown. Matthews describes how they solved the issues, "In an effort to create suspense, I introduced the classic 'Survivor' over the shoulder shot, showing the contestants holding up the vote without revealing who they were voting for. It was the start of something we would continue to do for seasons to come."[64] This type of shot has become so common within seasons of *Survivor* a viewer may not even note when it happens, as we expect not to have the vote revealed before Probst reads them off. Naturally, over forty seasons later, the production is a well-seasoned crew who know more of what to expect, and what works well for the show, integrating the new styles seamlessly.

Interestingly, the show has had to adapt to societal changes, just as all other media must to stay current. Armstrong stated, "American attention spans have never been shorter. Our viewing choices now consist of YouTube or Instagram clips lasting all of one minute. Inevitably 'Survivor' will feel some of the effects of that: Challenges have been ranked up, season opens are cut shorter, and the season recap blazes through." With this the editors aren't afraid to try new techniques. Barefoot noted, "One of the great things about being an editor on 'Survivor' is that we've always been free to try new things and mix it up. We have a distinct editing style on the show, but we're also free to break those rules whenever it feels right. Lately, we've been doing more flashbacks and out-of-chronological order storytelling. Anything to keep it feeling fresh." Some may not always be a fan of the new editing tricks *Survivor* tries, but it's clear the show is treading the line of keeping the show familiar while allowing it to also evolve.

THE SHOW

In analyzing *Survivor*, it is important to always center on the idea that this is a television show first and foremost. The events from the thirty-nine days on the island are being edited and presented to the audience with the goal of providing entertainment. There is no writer's room creating a plot or director calling for reshoots after filming has completed to capture a moment. Producers only have the footage shot on the island to reshape into a cohesive narrative for the viewers, but there are hours and hours of footage from different cameras that can be shaped into a forty-minute story for an episode or a season-long story. What is chosen to be revealed or hidden from an audience can create fan-favorite characters, lead to suspenseful vote-offs, or leave former contestants complaining that they had a bad edit. When looking closely at how the show chooses to condense so much material into an easily consumed episode of television, interesting patterns emerge.

   The visual aesthetic of the show is meant to denote a sense of a pre-industrial natural environment rather than civilization. The visual language of *Survivor* deliberately connotes an experience that is separate from what audiences associate with civilized everyday life. Even the large builds for challenges, though built with the aid of power tools, are meant to look rough and lashed together with rope. There is no technology, few creature comforts, and very little in the way of "topical references" that date many other shows.

   As part of this aesthetic, the production attempts to present a timelessness to the island life that is completely separate from a fast-paced corporate world. But there are visual markers that create a temporal rhythm for viewers. While there are dozens of counter-examples that could be identified in the show's twenty-year history—episodes with medical evacuations or double eliminations, for example—there is an overall pattern to a *Survivor* episode that has been standardized. Open an episode with shots of dawn and conversations around camp. Proceed to a midday challenge (or two if there are both a Reward and an Immunity Challenge), then feature some late-afternoon scrambling at camp. A shot of the moon alerts the viewer that it's time for the nighttime Tribal Council where a contestant is eliminated. This morning/afternoon/night pattern gives a clean sense of continuity, and makes each episode feel as though it has followed a day in the life of the contestants. However, in actuality, an episode covers multiple days of the players at camp.

   One of the most common variants to this is the insertion of a nighttime scene to open the episode. This scene is often included if the previous episode's Tribal Council was contentious. It is now used in almost every episode, whereas in earlier seasons it was less frequent. The brief opener will see the immediate fallout as the tribemates return to camp. Then the episode will begin the rhythm of portraying a linear day anew.

   For the majority of its seasons, *Survivor* used a thirty-nine-day shoot schedule and the standard break between Tribal Councils was three days, so each episode has three mornings, afternoons, nights to cull material from. Even if events are presented nonlinearly for views (a conversation from day fourteen may be shown before a conversation from day thirteen, for example), the illusion of a single day between vote-outs makes the story simple to follow. Scholars Misha Kavka and Amy West note that, with the show's castaway aesthetic omitting clocks and watches, "the production conveys the time of day to the viewer through the use of suggesting shots of dawn, high noon or sunset. These images help structure the narrative of each episode and provide a visual shorthand for such cultural cliches as 'a new day' and 'a new beginning.'"[65] Production doesn't hide that multiple days are occurring in a single episode, both on screen cues and contestants often refer to the day number. There is no attempt to trick viewers, but rather, encapsulating an episode with the sense of the familiar daily cycle of time presents an easily consumed pattern. With cameras rolling essentially nonstop and following so many contestants, it would be very easy for the story to become disjointed without the visual time markers to orient viewers.

There are two aspects of the show that can completely break the facade of a "world out of time" that is often presented to viewers. On rewatches of old seasons, these become particularly notable. These are (1) the use of technology and (2) the intrusive presence of product placements that are undeniably from an earlier era.

A show with the pretense of being set on a deserted island shouldn't have much in the way of technology, but there are some moments that completely center on technology. For example, in the eighth episode of *Borneo* a major emotional beat revolves around a VHS tape. As a tease for a reward, Probst brings out an old, boxy television and VCR out onto the beach and plays clips from videos that players' families mailed to the production crew after they left. Jenna Lewis' family did not get a video to producers in time, and she is upset about not seeing her daughters on video. The footage viewers do see from other players' videos is vintage VHS quality, far below the quality of video most readers of this book have available in their pocket at all times.

There are other examples that litter the early seasons. In the thirteenth episode of *The Australian Outback*, a reward includes an instant messenger chat with loved ones, but with the technology available at the time, the chat is far from instant. Players sat at a large computer and one player, Keith Famie, even typed out a proposal to his girlfriend and is shown eagerly awaited her typed response. When Sprint became a sponsor of the show, the most up-to-date phone was often used as part of a reward challenge, but with the passage of time those phones have become relics of old tech. And before it was discontinued due to the "car curse," contestants had a chance to win a new car, many of which are becoming outdated vehicles (Pontiac Aztek, Chevrolet Avalanche, Saturn VUE, Saturn ION, GMC Envoy XUV, Pontiac G6) to viewers who watch those old episodes on streaming services.

For reward challenges, occasionally there are advertising tie-ins. In *Nicaragua*, the team that won a reward challenge watched the Jack Black film *Gulliver's Travels*. In *South Pacific* it was a new Adam Sandler film, *Jack and Jill*. In both instances, strained efforts were made to thematically tie the films into the experiences of the players on the island. For all of Jack

Black's boundless charisma and Adam Sandler's box office success, neither film remains in the cultural zeitgeist at the present day, and the films feel like odd time capsules of earlier years that Probst is shilling for as part of an episode. Similarly, in *Borneo*, there is one challenge that features Probst performing a *Blair Witch Project* spoof. This was in no way a marketing ploy from the movie's production company, it was just *Survivor* embracing a very relevant pop culture reference from the year 2000. But as that reference is not part of the current cultural zeitgeist it has become more of a curiosity in the subsequent decades.

Unexpectedly, some companies involved in sponsorships have gone bankrupt or have merged with other companies and no longer exist. Sears sponsored several seasons of the show, but declared Chapter 11 bankruptcy in 2018.[66] The company has emerged from that bankruptcy but with a fraction of the store presence it had before and is not as well-known a brand as when it was featured in *Survivor* challenges. Sprint became synonymous with both loved one rewards and also a "Sprint Fan-Favorite" award where viewers could text in their pick for favorite player of the season and the castaway with the most votes would win $100,000 at the reunion show. In 2020, Sprint merged with T-Mobile.[67] However, despite these odd instances, as intended the overall experience while watching *Survivor* transports the viewer to a faraway location removed from real life.

There are beats to the storytelling in *Survivor* that all fans have come to recognize, and they happen fairly frequently. We see a majority alliance identify their target for the next Tribal Council and the only thing that will disrupt their plans is that person winning individual immunity. Sure enough, that person does. There are many examples of this happening and it's always satisfying. It's natural to root for the underdog. But how much of this narrative is shaped through the editing? Obviously, the producers don't alter who wins a challenge, but do they select material from their hours and hours of footage to set up and present that storyline? The answer is seemingly yes, as Foley explains:

> Tribal Council is the destination of the story arc, so we typically work backward from there. Who got voted off and why? Who else was in jeopardy? Who were the shot-callers pulling the strings? We start by creating a simple outline of the A, B and C stories for each tribe and then watch virtually every bit of footage we can to find enough moments to craft compelling scenes.[68]

Jeff also confirms this:

Let's start with how we approach our episodes from an editing standpoint as it will give some context to how we end up with an episode that features one player so prominently. We always start at the end and work backwards. We start with who is voted out, then we identify the players responsible for the vote out, then we look at the impact the immunity challenge may have had, etc. We continue this process all the way back to the tribes returning to camp from the previous Tribal and how the fallout of that vote may impact the next vote. That's our process.[69]

Contestants are constantly scheming and talking through scenarios and debating strategy. It's entirely possible that footage exists of the majority alliance debating whom to vote out or exploring multiple potential outcomes. But it's more satisfying storytelling to present a singular plan that is thwarted by the outcome of the immunity challenge. So, through omission, that's the story that is told to viewers.

Every episode of *Survivor* is built around the tension of someone's game ending, someone's dreams being smashed. There is a balance to be struck in making this culmination of an hour of storytelling feel satisfying. Viewers should be surprised, but it should make sense. It needs to feel logical, but not inevitable. Often, producers try to give reasons why multiple players may be voted out, so the drama is about which player of multiple options goes home. Sometimes, in order to maintain that tension, it feels like the vote out comes without reason, and that frustrates viewers.

In the end, on reality TV (as with all television shows) a story must be told. The editors craft the narrative. While they may try to be fair to each contestant, what is shown must be compelling. Producers and editors change and influence the viewers' perspective. There's an interesting layered effect—you have regular people out playing a game being filmed and then edited by a team of producers and editors to provide entertainment for a television show. Arguably, this scenario has nothing to do with "reality." But that doesn't matter. What matters is that we as viewers are watching raw, unscripted people interact in various situations and navigate among each other to eventually win the vote for one million dollars.

Despite any story the editors can try and tell, they can't put words into a player's mouth or change actions that they performed. Yet players may complain about the edit they receive as they might not like what they see. *Survivor* is an environment of extremes—hunger, stress, exhaustion, coupled with zero privacy between other players and the crew and cameras—it is a setting that can break even the strongest of humans. Three-time player Andrea Boehlke (*Redemption Island, Caramoan, Game Changers*) said regarding playing the game, "When you're playing 'Survivor,' it shows the best and the worst of humans. And sometimes you do things that you wouldn't normally do or say because you're hungry and miserable, and that's on national television."[70]

A player may not recall what they did or said. Whether you thought you were a villain or not, the editors only have the footage they are given to work with. Three-time player Colby Donaldson (*The Australian Outback, All-Stars, Heroes vs. Villains*) said of players' edits, "You can't go after the show and say 'That's not me!' Because clearly it is. They're not putting words in your mouth. If you said it and they show it, that doesn't mean you didn't say it. You still said it."[71]

Although *Survivor* is a reality TV show without reshoots and retakes like on a scripted show, some shots have been revealed to be set up and reenacted to get it just right. Karishma Patel (*Island of the Idols*), said in an interview on her season they would reshoot the walk to Tribal Council on the beach, stating, "[When] they get that shot of us walking down the beach holding our torches . . . they do that shot about three times. We have to rewind and do it again from different angles."[72] Back in 2001, Burnett admitted this as well, exclaiming some shots are staged purely for aesthetic reasons. In an interview he stated, "Nothing that we do changes the dramatic outcome, or the sporting outcome or the emotional outcome of anything."[73]

While having players redo something for cinematic effect is a rather inconsequential reshoot, it has been revealed by players that they were asked to redo more impactful scenes. In April 2024, chaos Kass herself (Kass McQuillen from *Cagayan*; *Cambodia*) took to Twitter to reveal that a famous moment from the finale of *Cagayan* was reshot due to a mic issue. Initially, @SurvivorquotesX posted this iconic quote from the final Tribal Council, with Trish Hegarty grilling Tony:

> "I'm saying to you, heart to heart, friend to friend, human being to human being. ANSWER THE QUESTION! Is it worth it to you to be here, to play a game for a million dollars on your father's soul and memory? Yes or no! It's a million-dollar question."

> "Yes."[74]

Kass (@KassMcQ) replied:

This had to be redone because Trish's mic wasn't working the first time. I always laugh about how authentic everyone thinks it was. Trish should have won an Emmy for it.[75]

This led to other players responding to reveal scenes in which they had to reshoot a moment. Davie Rickenbacker (@WheresDavie) from *David vs. Goliath* responded on Twitter with his own reshoot story, which is a significant moment to not have been captured by the cameras.

Lol since we talking about reshoots when I found the 1st idol on screen that was all acting, I found it without the producers and they were PISSED. Oops ur bad for not thinking u was a serious contender until then [emoji][76]

These are all moments that carry significance to the game, and production wants to capture, but reshooting them does not impact the game. Notably, Probst has stated on his podcast that in regard to challenges, *Survivor* does not do reshoots. When asked by his co-host, Jay Wolff if they miss a shot during a challenge, would they make a player redo that scene? Probst answered, "We just don't do it. We never have, we would never ask a player to go back and run the balance beam again. We either get it or we don't."[77] The "reality" of reality TV is always packaged, edited, and scored in ways far removed from what it's like when filming takes place. On some occasions, it is also reshot, but never in a way to misrepresent what happened on the island.

There are many pieces to *Survivor* that bring the show together as a whole. One without the other and the puzzle couldn't connect in the integral way it does for each season. *Survivor* needs to be led by a great host, filled with a strong cast, filmed in an interesting location with dynamic challenges, backed by a phenomenal crew, and curated by a powerful team of editors in order to continually entertain audiences for forty-plus seasons. The best product is the result of each team performing its best, and the whole becoming greater than the sum of its parts. A great cast is more interesting when they're competing in a well-designed challenge and a well-designed challenge becomes riveting television when the editing increases tension. When it all comes together, the result is one of the most important television shows of this century.

Part II

THE GAME

CHAPTER 3

GAME STRUCTURE AND PLAYER STRATEGY

THE RULES

A televised game with a million-dollar prize. With that amount of money on the line, it is inevitable that complex plans, strategies, and plots will be hatched. And while players are fond of reminding each other "It's just a game," the stakes in *Survivor* are more significant than a family round of Monopoly or a little league T-ball game. In *Vanuatu* (season 9, 2004), as the game was nearing an end and backstabbing had left the jury embittered, Twila Tanner declared, "People kill for less than what we're playing for right now."[1] While it's never gone anywhere near that far—physical violence is strictly forbidden in *Survivor* and that rule is definitely enforced—lying, manipulating, scrambling, and stretching the loose framework of rules are rampant. It's all been done to try and reach the cash prize. As player Sue Hawk explained all the way back in the first season, "The idea of money—money makes the world go round. Money is greed, money is what everybody strives for. . . . Big fights . . . divorces happen over shortages of money, so [there's] a lot to be said about money."[2] And a lot has been done for money on *Survivor*.

The basic framework of *Survivor* is that there are regularly held Tribal Councils where one player is voted out of the game until the final survivors remain. Then, at the final Tribal Council the group of players who have most recently been voted out make up a jury who votes for a winner from the small pool of players who have never been voted out. This is the setup for each season, but through the decades there have been many twists and advantages that alter the gameplay within that general structure.

In 2010, news made its way through *Survivor*'s internet fandom that journalist Andy Dehnart's website Reality Blurred had posted what appeared to be a leaked but official player's contract.[3] The coverage of this contract and the accompanying rules that players agree to abide by even reached more mainstream news outlets like *Time* magazine.[4] The thirty-two-page document is full of legalese, but is easily understood. Besides confirming what the varied payouts were depending on when players were eliminated— beginning at $2,500 for the first player eliminated and rising to $100,000 for the runner-up—for the first time it clearly laid out several rules that were implicit to any viewer, but had never been explicitly said on camera. The contract also codifies substantial flexibility for the producers to change aspects of the game. For example, it notes that the "number of teams" will be determined by the producer and Tribal Councils will occur "at intervals determined by" the producer.[5] Heading into a season, players don't know whether there will be two, three, or four tribes at the start or even how frequently Tribal Councils will occur. Occasionally, producers have forced multiple tribes to go to Tribal Council the same night, or every tribe to vote someone out no matter who won the challenge that day. Players may not expect it based on past precedent, but producers are allowed to make those changes.

In the version of the rules that was leaked in 2010, the first sections detail the prize, supplies that can be used by players (producers can prohibit contestants from using certain protected foliage in the filming location), and participation at challenges and Tribal Council. But it is stipulated that "Enforcement of the Rules will be at Producer's sole discretion."[6] This flexibility may lead to inconsistencies on how certain events are handled. For example, when a medevac occurs, in some instances, that takes the place of a vote at Tribal Council and viewers do not see a player voted out that episode. But there have also been episodes with medevacs where a Tribal Council still takes place and a player is voted out. The same happens with players quitting; sometimes that means there is no vote off of a player who is still in the game, other times Tribal Council is still held. In *Kaôh Rōng* (season 32, 2016), Caleb Reynolds was medevacked from the game in an episode that still saw Alecia Holden voted out at tribal council. In the same season, Neal Gottlieb was medevacked at the merge and Joe del Campo was medevacked at the final five, and in both instances there was no Tribal Council in the episode they were pulled from the game. The choice about whether a player who was pulled from the game or who quit means that there is no Tribal

Council varies. It is tempting to look for a pattern of when it happens during the season, but players have been evacuated in the first episode and they are the only player to leave the game. Conversely, players have been evacuated in the first episode and Tribal Council still happens. The same is true of post-merge evacuations and quits. There isn't consistency.

The next section of the contract about challenges establishes that all decisions about who wins a challenge are at the discretion of the producer and are not subject to review. Winning challenges can make or break a player's game, particularly when immunity is the prize. A player who wins immunity cannot be eliminated from the game at the next Tribal Council, and many players have prolonged their time on the island with a clutch immunity win. With the aid of video footage giving angles Probst didn't see at the time, viewers have identified some instances in challenges where a player broke a rule that should have disqualified them. Of course, with the game happening months previously, nothing changes and Probst's call on the island stands. For example, in the twelfth episode of *The Australian Outback* (season 2, 2001) there is an individual immunity challenge where players must always have a carabiner clipped onto a rope and Colby Donaldson clearly (though apparently inadvertently) is completely unclipped at one point. He goes on to win the challenge and it's never mentioned by production.

There are also instances where the ruling by Probst is just wrong. In *All-Stars* (Season 8, 2004) there is a challenge where players face off on a narrow beam above a pool of water and Probst explains, "First person to hit the water returns to the start."[7] The other player can continue on in the challenge. "Boston" Rob Mariano tackles Colby but Boston Rob's foot hits the water first. This is clear in television footage at an angle Probst did not have from where he was judging the competition. From Probst's vantage point, it appeared Colby hit the water first, and Boston Rob was allowed to continue the challenge while Colby returned to the start. After the episode aired, fans voiced discontent with the ruling. Probst responded to the controversy, explaining, "Part of the rules and the contract [the contestants] sign is that during the challenges I'm the sole arbiter and final call. They're often judgment calls. . . . This is one I just blew."[8] Similar to sports fans complaining about a referee's blown call, it may make fans feel better to complain but doesn't change the outcome of the game.

This doesn't mean that there are no rules at all. As a game show, a member of CBS's standards and practices is present at every challenge, to "make sure one tribe doesn't have an advantage over another."[9] Rules before a challenge are clearly laid out, but sometimes contestants try things that were not anticipated. In *South Pacific* (season 23, 2011) the majority alliance was desperate to prevent Ozzy Lusth from winning an immunity challenge. During a challenge in the finale, Sophie Clarke called out for Albert Destrade to stop what he was doing and come help her, but Probst announces that this is an individual challenge, and they can't help one another. Likely, producers hadn't considered players helping one another and Probst made a call about how to handle it that was applicable to all the players. However, in the *46* (season 46, 2024) finale, a similar situation arose as Maria Shrime Gonzalez was considered the biggest threat. When Kenzie Petty, who was ahead in the challenge, couldn't figure out part of a puzzle, Liz Wilcox left her station and interpreted the puzzle clue. Realizing that Kenzie needed to count the number of holes on a board that had been used earlier in the challenge, Liz went and retrieved the board for Kenzie. Kenzie won the challenge and Maria was voted out. After the season, Kenzie explained that "Liz just started helping me out of nowhere" and "I think it caught everyone off guard, including me, including Jeff [Probst]."[10] Perhaps because he had not explicitly said anything about not helping one another, or because Liz voluntarily helped on her own without Kenzie asking her, Probst allowed Liz to help Kenzie. However, Kenzie also explained that in the next challenge, "Jeff was like, 'Y'all are playing your own game. Don't help each other,'"[11] so the option to team up was removed. Dehnart, in writing about the fan backlash to Liz's aid in the challenge, noted that it was "allowed, or the producers would have stopped the challenge and restarted, as the rules allow them to do."[12]

While Probst's word is final, there is a challenge in the second episode of *Cook Islands* (season 13, 2006) that goes to video review. While viewers don't see Probst or other staff watch a replay, the episode shows Probst announce that the Puka Puka tribe won and the Rarotonga tribe got second place. After the other teams complete the challenge, Probst explains that they went and double checked the footage and confirmed that Puka and Raro had in fact tied and both would win the first-place reward. This instance is contrasted with a challenge in the twelfth episode of *Ghost Island* (season 36, 2018), where Wendell Holland clearly finishes a puzzle before Laurel Johnson but does not call for Probst to check his puzzle. Probst declares Laurel the winner after she calls him over. Probst sees Wendell's completed puzzle and says that a puzzle is not finished until you call Probst to check it—despite there being many examples from previous seasons of Probst announcing puzzles completed without being called over—and explains that his call of Laurel winning the challenge will stand.

There is one significant mistake that was not caught during filming, but came to light after the finale aired. As a result of this incident, CBS awarded the third- and fourth-place finishers $100,000, the amount typically only awarded to the second place finisher.[13] In *Africa* (season 3, 2001), there was a challenge with four players left that involved answering questions about their eliminated contestants from that season. One question was "Which female survivor does not have anything pierced, including her ears?" Kim Johnson wrote down Kelly Goldsmith, and was awarded a point. Lex van den Berghe wrote down Lindsey Richter, but was not given a point.[14] After the finale aired, producers were informed that Lindsey had no piercings. Ethan Zohn, Tom Buchanan, and Lex were in an alliance that would have voted out Kim had she not won immunity at that challenge. After Kim won immunity, she eventually sat next to Ethan at the final two, where Ethan won the $1 million prize. Because Lex and Tom's games were upended by production's mistake in this immunity challenge, they were both awarded the second-place prize amount of $100,000. A spokesman for *Survivor* said, "This was a screw up, not a scandal" and production took steps to rectify things with Lex and Tom as soon as they learned about it.[15]

If these examples feel like inconsistencies to viewers and players, that is because they are. These types of inconsistencies are allowed in the contract players sign and are part of a reality competition show with unexpected choices by players. Many of these inconsistencies come about because an unforeseen event occurs and a call has to be made in the moment about how to address it. Probst makes that final call. While there are some instances where Probst's initial call of a winner has been overturned, considering the hundreds of challenges that he has judged, it appears that Probst's track record in judging competitions overall is very good.

GAME STRUCTURE

Just as the official contract offers a fair amount of leeway to the producers in terms of how aspects of a season will play out, there is considerable free room for contestants to decide how they will play the game. The contract gives some specific rules and some general guidelines, but the shape of players' strategy is astoundingly elastic. Player's gameplay is limited more by lack of individual creativity than the game's rules. There are many options. Play with loyalty or lies, rely on challenge dominance or strong social ties, avoid drama or actively strategize. Many different styles of play have won the game, from Bob Crowley (*Gabon*) who seemed to avoid drama as he enjoyed the adventure, to Tony Vlachos (*Cagayan, Winners at War*) who brought an overabundance of chaotic energy to the island. Even more styles of play have failed.

One thing to keep in mind is that, while producers love to tout *Survivor* as a social experiment, it is a game. Many of the strategies that feel transgressive or immoral in real society are integral to the game portion of *Survivor*. As Mary Catherine Bateson wrote in the *New York Times* after the first season had become a pop culture event:

> The directors of "Survivor" designed their game to require the players to eject other members of their own group and to betray their allies. They surrounded the game with an elaborate and corny setting and a set of rules and rituals that seemed to be inspired by memories of some ill-understood Introduction to Anthropology course. The trappings of a popular image of the primitive were used not only for cosmetic purposes, but also to legitimize behavior that many people would find unacceptable in other contexts.[16]

Bateson was writing this before the game became riddled with twists and advantages that encourage the "unacceptable behavior" she referenced in the year 2000.

When it comes to strategy, one of the most fascinating parts of the game is that what is safe in one stage of the game is dangerous in another. Attempting to play with an inflexible strategy is likely to result in failure. Attempting to play with no strategy is all but guaranteed to end in failure. Players must be willing to adapt, respond, and alter course. There are different aspects of the game where players may excel or struggle, including camp life, challenges, social awareness, or strategic planning. Of course, the game also requires luck. No player can win without some luck going their way, no matter how much they may think otherwise. When Tom Westman, who won *Palau* (season 10, 2005), was asked about Sandra Diaz-Twine winning *Heroes vs. Villains* (season 20, 2010) during the season reunion despite never winning an individual challenge, offered this analysis: "I've always said the game is a third physical, it's a third strategic and social, and it's a third luck. A lot of luck comes into it. One thing I've always maintained is whoever won that season deserves to win that season."[17] Not every player may agree with that assessment. As Tom said this, in a wide shot of the jury you can see Amanda Kimmel, who made the finals twice but lost both times is making a questioning smirk. Danielle DiLorenzo, who made it to the finals but lost to Aras Baskauskas, is staring at the ground. Russell Hantz, who had just lost his second consecutive season, is turning confrontationally to Tom. Parvati Shallow, who just lost this season minutes ago, is leaning back in apparent frustrated disagreement. J. T. Thomas is staring off in the distance, and it's tempting to speculate that he's wondering if he actually deserved to win *Tocantins* (season 18, 2009) after his disastrous performance in *Heroes vs. Villains*.

The stages of the game that have largely remained consistent across more than forty seasons are the marooning leading to the tribal immunity stage, the merge leading to the individual immunity stage, and the final Tribal Council where the power shifts to the jury. As players master the best way to play a stretch of the game, producers may introduce a wrinkle that disrupts the established methods. When producers think something is working out, players may find a loophole that alters the expected style of play. This keeps the game fresh for viewers and prevents a player from being able to dominate the entire game—with an exception or two.

THE MAROONING

Every season begins with the marooning. The marooning is the moment when all the contestants meet each other, see the location where they'll be filming, learn about the tribe divisions, and—most importantly for the TV show—viewers form first impressions of the players. How it is done has varied significantly. If a season is to be played on a beach there may be a literal marooning where players are ordered to scramble off a boat with a few meager supplies to be left on an island. But, if it was a landlocked season, the players may ride in on a truck before having a long hike to their tribe's camp.

Survivor: Thailand *(Season 5, 2002) Shown from left: Penny Ramsey, Ken Stafford, Shii Ann Huang, Shephanie Dill, Jed Hildebrand, Robb Zbacnik, Jake Billingsley, Erin Collins.* CBS / Photofest © CBS.

Because it was used in *Borneo* (season 1, 2000), the most iconic version of the marooning involves players grabbing supplies, jumping in the water, and making their way to shore. That first season was invested in the idea of sixteen Americans being left on a desert island to form their own society, and the opening is inspired by that idea. The chaos of more than a dozen people experiencing an adrenaline surge as their dreams are coming true provides a fantastic burst of energy to begin a season. The audience begins to make assessments of the players, as this instant action shows who is assertive, who stumbles, and who connives their way into extra supplies.

As the series has settled into using Fiji as the shooting location since season 33 in 2016, a literal marooning is frequently possible. But in the earlier globe-trotting era, there were several locations that were used where an ocean marooning was not an option, so other ways have been employed. In *The Australian Outback*, the players were flown in and then had to hike to their camps from the airstrip. In *Africa* they were driven in on a truck with gun-toting men. Players have arrived by boat, plane, trucks, and even trains in *China* (season 15, 2007).

Palau had one of the strangest openings, as all of the castaways were left alone on a beach with no instructions for a full day. Players talked with each other, started forming alliances, and began to build a shelter. The next day, Probst arrived and announced that they would be selecting their own tribes. A woman and a man were selected as captains for the tribes, and each had to select one member of the opposite sex to become the second member of the tribe. Then that new member chose the next tribe member, and so on. In a twist, one man and one woman would be left unchosen for the tribes and they would not participate in *Survivor* at all, other than their time on the beach for that one day before the schoolyard pick of tribes.

While this particular marooning highlights the need for instant bonding and strategizing—likely one of the reasons producers introduced the twist— it also comes across as harsh and emotionally manipulative in an unnecessary way. Everyone who signs up for *Survivor* knows that the vast majority of players in that season will be voted out, that is the nature of the game. But this is the only time, outside of medevacs or an extremely rare producer removal of a contestant, that players were eliminated without a chance to compete, strategize, plead their case at a Tribal Council, or even cast a vote in an effort to sway the results.

Longtime fans who have the chance to play may think they know what's coming when the game starts but producers do try to keep players off balance. Some seasons have featured wild scrambles for individual immunity necklaces (or the laughably named Medallion of Power), schoolyard picks to determine the tribes, or immediate challenges for a reward. *Winners at War* (season 40, 2020) began with champagne and a toast to the players' past triumphs. In a truly unfortunate result in *44* (season 44, 2023), an immediate challenge before the teams went to their camps resulted in Bruce Perreault hitting his head hard on a wooden part of an obstacle course. Though he was bleeding from a head wound, he completed the challenge. But a concussion Bruce sustained forced him to be pulled from the game before the first official Tribal Council.

Guatemala (season 11, 2005) began with a grueling eleven-mile hike through the rainforest before the tribes found their camps. Neither tribe reached their destination before nightfall, and both tribes camped for the night in the middle of the forest. The trek clearly was too much, and wiped out several members of both tribes who suffered from dehydration and other injuries that occurred during their nighttime hike. Bobby John Drinkard collapsed and his eyes rolled back into his head, Blake Towsley had a branch covered with barbs fall onto his shoulder, Jim Lynch tore his bicep, and Judd Sergeant was shown vomiting after the harsh hike.

Most often, producers decide the tribe divisions before the season begins. There generally seems to be an intent to balance the tribes in terms of likely challenge performance, gender dispersal, age range, and overall strength. Seasons have started with two tribes of eight, two tribes of nine, two tribes of ten, three tribes of six, four tribes of four, and four tribes of five. In *Fiji* (season 14, 2007), one player dropped out very close to the start of filming due to a panic attack. There was no time to bring in an alternate player, so production had another player, Sylvia Kwan, divide the other castaways into two tribes of nine and then joined the tribe that lost the first immunity challenge and eliminated one player. Production does have alternates prepared in case players are unable to participate. Former player RC Saint-Amour and her father Craig were cast in a season that featured returning players and their loved ones, *Blood vs. Water* (season 27, 2013), but due to a health condition he was deemed unable to play at the last minute and alternates Candice Woodcock Cody and John Cody were flown in.[18] But in the case of *Fiji*, the panic attack came the day before filming began and there was not enough time to bring in another player. There have been other seasons with late changes to the cast due to medevacs, but production was able to bring in an alternate player or make adjustments that retained an even number of players in those instances. Recently, in *45* (season 45, 2023) Austin Li Coon played as a last-minute alternate and came in second place, losing to Dee Valladares in a 5–3–0 vote.[19]

Whether it includes alternates or not, once a cast of players is starting the game they will be divided into tribes. There are a variety of ways tribes divisions have been made. In a few seasons, players have selected their own tribes which can create drama, but it has also tended to produce some of the most lopsided results. Production has divided tribes based on age, gender, and (controversially) race. Other times, divisions align with a season theme such as brawn vs. brains vs. beauty or David vs. Goliath. Three times, the series has featured one tribe of returning players against a tribe of new contestants. In all three instances, a member of the returning players' tribes won the game, indicating that there is a learning curve and experience can go a long way in improving one's game. In terms of gameplay, the instant assessment that players make of one another can be the most important thing to happen at the marooning. Decisions are made rapidly in *Survivor*, often based on too little information.

TRIBAL IMMUNITY

The first goal of the game is surviving the tribal immunity phase. In this portion, the players are divided into tribes and must work together to build a shelter and compete in challenges. Often, there are two types of challenges during this phase of the game: reward and immunity. Sometimes those are combined, sometimes there is only an immunity challenge. Winning a reward challenge could result in something mundane, like a supply of spices, or something essential like flint or a tarp, or something extravagant, like a crew building a super shelter to live in. Winning the immunity challenge means that the tribe does not have to go to Tribal Council where a member of the tribe is voted out of the game.

As players are eliminated tribes become uneven in numbers. Most often each tribe is required to use the same number of players in a challenge, so a tribe that has not yet voted anyone off will have to sit someone out of a challenge. Generally, the same player cannot sit out of consecutive challenges.[20] So, teams have to choose who they want to sit out when, and significant thought and strategy can be put into those choices. Sometimes, a player is desperately hungry and has a tribe sit out people who are perceived to be their weakest players during a reward challenge in the hopes of winning food, even though that means the "weaker" players will have to play in the immunity challenge.

Among all the tribal variations, one consistency remains through every single season—the tribe that loses the immunity challenge must go to Tribal

Council and vote off one member. Except, of course, for the exceptions. *One World* (season 24, 2012) has a truly unexpected exception, unlikely to ever happen again. After the men's tribe win the immunity challenge, they bizarrely unanimously agree to go to Tribal Council to vote out a member of their tribe, sparing the women's tribe from having to vote someone out. In fact, the men had been on a streak of wins that had been demoralizing the women's tribe. Dalton Ross, in recapping this episode for *Entertainment Weekly*, titled his article, "Dumbest. Tribe. Ever." The decision was truly bizarre, and most notably it was absurd because it required a unanimous vote by the tribe to go to Tribal Council in the first place. As Ross explained in his article,

> It's dumber than a single individual giving up immunity because it is easy for one person to be a moron, but very, very difficult for there to be such a high level of collective idiocy. All it took was one single person among the eight Manono tribe members to say, "Nope. I don't agree with it. Worst case scenario I get voted out. Best case scenario we lose our numbers advantage going into the merge. No thanks." And yet no one did.[21]

This was a season where, at times, Probst seemed frustrated with the gameplay when grilling contestants at the Tribal Council. This remains one of the most unexpected strategic choices in the history of the show.

Instances where groups won immunity and believed they were safe but still had to go to Tribal Council also arose in *41* (season 41, 2021) and *42* (season 42, 2022), but this time from a production twist not a player vote. The twist was called "Change History," but fans have taken to calling it "The Hourglass Twist." In this twist, at the merge the players are divided into two teams, but there is one player left out. After the challenge has been won the winning team is told they're safe, the losing team is told they'll be going to tribal. But the one player who was left out can smash an hourglass to signal they're "changing history" and the team that won now has to go to Tribal Council. This twist was retired after what Probst calls "amazing" feedback from the fans.[22] Online discourse was overwhelmingly negative about the twist.[23] In 2024, Probst stated in an interview regarding this twist, "The idea was 'dangerous fun' . . . and I went too far. I loved the title. I had it on my whiteboard for 10 years and I knew it'd never work. But I just got a little drunk on the idea of dangerous fun, and boy did I hear about it!"[24]

There are also a few instances when both tribes must go to Tribal Council and vote someone out after a challenge, but the winning tribe receives a food reward and gets to watch the other tribe's Tribal Council. Generally speaking, Tribal Council has become the finale of each episode of *Survivor*, the moment where all the tension that has built is finally released. Writing for *The Ringer*, Mara Reinstein has argued, "Tribal Council remains *Survivor*'s greatest invention—and one of the few elements of the show that hasn't changed. Twenty years and 40 seasons later, the ritual of sending a player home at Tribal Council has become the bedrock of the entire series." Mark Burnett noted, "Tribal Council has largely remained unchanged over 20 years because it works perfectly."[25] Tribal Council is not only the place where one player's hopes go to die; it is also where players can see what alliances have formed, who likely targets are, and what information is revealed by Probst's probing questions.

Outside of dealing with twists, the logical strategy to employ in the tribal stage of the game is to avoid going to Tribal Council. After all, that is the only place where you might be voted out of the game. This often leads to a mentality of "Keep the tribe strong" early on in the game. The stronger the tribe, the less likely anyone has to be voted out. Of course, what strength means can vary in terms of individual player perception. When so many challenges in the tribal immunity stage can come down to a puzzle, physical strength should not be the only consideration—though it often is.

Avoiding going to Tribal Council in the tribal immunity stage is definitely possible if you are part of the right initial tribe and get a favorable swap if that occurs—this is part of the luck of *Survivor*. But there is a belief among a subsection of fans that going to Tribal Council can strengthen an alliance, and it may be beneficial to deliberately go to Tribal Council in the first stage of the game. This strategy gained the name "The Intentional Matsing" among the fan community. It is named after a tribe from *Philippines* (season 25, 2012), which began with three tribes of six, and the Matsing tribe lost the first four challenges, in the end leaving only Malcolm Freberg and Denise Stapley as the two remaining members. Denise and Malcolm were split onto the other two tribes, but both made it to the merge where they reformed as a very strong two-person alliance that made it all the way to the final four, where Malcolm was voted out. Denise would go on to win the season. A YouTuber who goes by the name Peridiam has a video breaking down the argument that players could try to recreate this intentionally. If using this strategy, a player would purposefully lose several times in the early part of the game, leaving only a small and loyal group. Because the tribe has fewer members than the other tribes, "When you do merge the other tribe or tribes view you as so non-threatening and powerless that you gain a little bit of leeway in the short term."[26] It may sound ridiculous, but there are many examples of players who appeared to be in the minority at the merge who would go on to win the season which makes speculation about an Intentional Matsing a diverting discussion.

Before the game reaches the individual stage, strategies are being implemented that will undoubtedly impact the latter half of the game. Most obviously, alliances that are formed within tribes can dominate the next part of the game. To keep players on their toes, several twists have been introduced to prevent a single strategy from becoming an obvious, safe path to follow. The most obvious of these is the tribe swap. If there is fear that a tight bond formed in the tribal stage will make for a boring latter half of the season, a remedy is to break up the groups and introduce new relationships.

With a tribe swap it is possible that players who were in a strong position in their original tribe suddenly find themselves in an unfavorable position. Among fans, this has become known as being "Swap-screwed."[27] One of the most obvious examples of this was in the fifth episode of *China*, when James Clement and Aaron Reisberger were swapped from the Fei Lang tribe to the Zhan Hu tribe. The four original members of Zhan Hu realized that if they lost the next challenge, they had the numbers to vote off an original Fei Lang member. During the next challenge, Peih-Gee Law and Jaime Dugan obviously sabotage their own tribe, and Aaron is voted out at Tribal Council. In general, throwing a challenge is frowned upon because any time you do not go to Tribal Council is guaranteed to improve your chances of winning the million dollars. However, due to how tribe swaps may shake out, some teams may be incentivized to lose when they have a definite target to vote out who was a member of another alliance.

For many viewers and players, the idea of throwing a challenge feels antithetical to the game of *Survivor*, but it has been used several times. The implication of throwing a challenge goes back to the second episode of season one, when B. B. Anderson suggested that it might not be a bad thing if his tribe had to vote someone out. Throwing a challenge has some strategic merit in limited circumstances. Almost never is it warranted before a tribe swap. But after a tribe swap—like in the *China* example discussed above— there are instances where losing may help an alliance in the long term. Of course, with so many seasons, strategic failures litter the landscape of *Survivor* gameplay. And one of the most amusing types of failures is when a tribe plans to throw a challenge, but fails.

In *Cagayan* (season 28, 2014), the season was divided into three tribes with members who were meant to represent Brains, Brawn, and Beauty. The Brains tribe performed very poorly at challenges. (And was incredibly awkward at camp too, but that's a separate issue. How a player can dump three-quarters of the rice out onto the fire because they're having a hyper-emotional moment and not be voted out immediately remains baffling on every rewatch.) Several members of the Brawn tribe, due to lies spread by Tony, thought that Cliff Robinson was targeting them. In the third episode, they chose to throw an upcoming challenge so that they could vote Cliff out. However, the entire tribe was not in on the plan, so only select members of the tribe would be struggling. Despite a herculean effort by Spencer Bledsoe to keep the Brains tribe in the competition and an equally herculean effort by Woo Hwang and Sarah Lacina to keep the Brawn tribe out of it, in the end it came down to a basketball-style game of shooting buoys into a floating hoop. Spencer did his best, but Cliff's eighteen years in the NBA had developed certain skills that proved useful in this instance. In the end, the Brains tribe lost again.

Successfully pulling off a challenge throw does not guarantee a player's plans will be successful. One of the most entertaining episodes in all of *Survivor* is "We're a Hot Mess," the fourth episode in *San Juan del Sur* (season 29, 2014). In this episode, Drew Christie decides that his tribe, which had been very successful in the challenges, needed to throw a challenge so that he could start eliminating the girls from his tribe. The episode is littered with poor choices and ironic quotes. Drew's blend of unearned confidence with a lack of self-awareness is instantly iconic for viewers. The editors clearly had a field day with the wealth of material that they were gifted by Drew in confessionals, around camp, and in his performance at the challenge. Whether it's Drew declaring that it's hard to do all the work around camp intercut with shots of him sleeping and other players complaining about his laziness, or his bold declaration that "Basically I'm a badass and the manipulator of this game" for scheming to throw a challenge, Drew's fall is so clearly set up it feels inevitable. But that makes it no less enjoyable to watch when he is voted out.[28]

THE MERGE

Near the midway point of the game, all of the remaining players are combined into one tribe. Originally this point in the game was called "the Merger," which is a term that feels more at home in a corporate boardroom than the return-to-nature adventure that the series promotes. A change was quickly adopted. The episode when the tribes combine in the first season titled "The Merger," but by the next season the episode at the same point is titled "The Merge."

The merge represents a shift in strategy. What had been a team game (in theory, at least), now becomes explicitly an individual game. Strategies change, what was a strength may now be a weakness, and what had been secure alliances often shatter. In the tribal phase of the game, often the cry is to "Keep the tribe strong" by voting off the weakest members. Once the merge hits, the overarching strategy often becomes "Vote off the threats." While 30 of the first 46 players voted out of the show have been women— often with some variation of "we need to keep the tribe strong" being a reason—28 of the first 46 players voted out at the merge have been men—often with the reason being that they're a threat to win individual challenges. After the merge, immunity challenges become individual contests leaving only the winner safe from being voted for. Occasionally, production may give both a man and a woman an immunity necklace after an individual immunity challenge.

Only once has there not been an official merge in a season. In *Palau*, the Ulong tribe was utterly dominated by Koror in terms of immunity challenges. While many results were close, Koror won eight consecutive immunity challenges and Ulong lost every member but Stephenie LaGrossa. The only member of Koror eliminated in this run, Willard Smith, was voted out on a night when both tribes had to attend a Tribal Council.

FINAL TRIBAL COUNCIL

The last stage of the game is called the Final Tribal Council. The players have been whittled down to the last two or three who will explain their game to the most recently voted out players who make up the jury. The jury then votes for a winner. Initially, there were two final players, but it became a final three during *Cook Islands*. There is a greater simplicity with a final two in several respects. The jury only has two choices, the rooting interest of fans is less diluted, and there is an added bonus for the winner in that they get to choose who they will sit next to in the end.

Though the winner of the last individual immunity chooses who they will be up against in the final two format, that certainly does not guarantee victory. In fact, interestingly, it isn't until *Thailand* (season 5, 2022), that the winner of the final immunity challenge, Brian Heidik, also becomes the sole survivor. In *Borneo*, Kelly Wiglesworth wins the challenge and brings Richard Hatch with her only to lose to him in the end. In *The Australian Outback*, Colby wins and brings Tina Wesson with him only to lose the million dollars to her in a 4–3 vote. This is widely considered one of the worst decisions in

Survivor history. While there are more iconically foolish choices that have been made, the fact that Colby would undoubtedly have won against Keith Famie but narrowly lost to Tina means that this was truly a million-dollar moment and he chose poorly. In *Africa*, Kim Johnson wins the final immunity and chooses to bring Ethan Zohn with her, and Ethan wins in a 5–2 vote. In *Marquesas* (season 4, 2002), Neleh Dennis wins final immunity and brings the eventual winner, Vecepia Towery, with her (losing in a 4–3 vote). In *Thailand*, Heidik is praised for his strategic game, but it should be noted that he barely defeated Clay Jordan in a final 4–3 decision from the jury.

Regardless of the outcome, the winner of the final immunity is incentivized to keep the weakest player with them, therefore a very strong player is often eliminated at this stage of the game. There is rampant speculation that after fan-favorite (and production-favorite) Terry Deitz gets voted out at this stage in *Panama* (season 12, 2006), the decision was made to end seasons with three contestants at Tribal Council rather than two.[29] The fact that the very next season introduces a final three fuels that idea for fans who try to deduce the reasoning behind changes to the game's format.

Survivor: Tocantins *(Season 18, 2009) Shown from left: J. T. Thomas Jr., Erinn Lobdell, Stephen Fishbach.* CBS / Photofest © CBS.

Players adjusted to the new final three, and soon began voting out the strongest players before the game reached that stage. In one of the constant adjustments between players and production, a new way of reaching the final three was created in *Heroes vs. Healers vs. Hustlers* (season 35, 2017). Rather than a vote where the other three players team up against the most likely winner, a Final Four Fire-Making Challenge was established. The Fire-Making Challenge has been a staple of the season finale ever since. At the final four, an immunity challenge is played. The winner gets to choose one other player to be safe. This player is guaranteed a seat at the final Tribal Council. The other two players face off, and whoever can build a fire that burns tall and hot enough to burn through a pre-set string of twine wins and goes on to the final Tribal Council. The losing player's torch is snuffed, and they are eliminated from the game without ever having been voted out.

Many fans feel this was introduced into the game to save season 35's winner, Ben Driebergen, from being voted out. And in a way it was, but it had been in the works before that season. Probst has explicitly stated that this twist was added to protect the strongest player from getting voted out at this stage of the game:

> This idea came about to solve a problem that has bothered me for years. If someone plays a great game and gets to the final four, it has always bothered me that the other three can simply say, "We can't beat him, so let's all just vote him out." So this year we decided to make a change. If you get to final four, you are guaranteed a shot to earn your way to the end. And if you are the one to win the final four challenge, you are in charge of who you take and who you force to fight for it in a fire-making showdown.[30]

This format change has been one of the most controversial that has become a staple in the show. For many fans, the vote-out and the attendant strategy is the core of the show. At one of the most critical junctures in the season, there is no vote. It upends the entire format of the show as it nears the finale. Additionally, for many fans, the core conceit of the show is that players vote each other out, but then have to convince a jury of the very people they voted out to give them a million dollars. The social politics of backstabbing a player and then asking for their vote is very different than someone losing a fire-making contest and blaming themselves for ending up on the jury.

However players reach the final Tribal Council, it is their last chance to argue why they should win the million dollars. It is impossible to know for certain how often the jury changes their vote based on what is said during Tribal Council. Some jurors likely come with their minds made up, some come with an inclination and find supporting evidence for why they should vote that way, and some may come truly open-minded.

Final Tribal Council is the grand finale of each season. At this point, as Probst is fond of saying, "The power shifts to the jury" and away from the players left in the game. As the first example players or viewers ever saw, *Borneo* set the tone for final Tribal Councils. No jury had ever asked questions before, and nobody—players or viewers—knew what to expect. Questions ranged from the inane to the bitter. Greg Buis asked the two players to pick a number between one and ten and insists that he only voted for Richard because his guess was closer (Richard only won by one vote, so every juror's choice was literally decisive to the final outcome). Sue gave one of the most-watched monologues in television history and eviscerated Kelly in a manner that left little doubt about where her vote was going. After slamming Richard—"your inability to admit your failures without going into a whiny speech makes you a bit of a loser in life"—Sue goes on to provide what remains one of the most bitter monologues in *Survivor* history,

> But Kelly, go back to a couple times Jeff said to you "what goes around, comes around." It's here. You will not get my vote. My vote will go to Richard. And I hope that is the one vote that makes you lose the money. If it's not, so be it. I'll shake your hand and I'll go on from here. But if I were to ever pass you along in life again, and you were laying there, dying of thirst, I would not give you a drink of water. I would let the vultures take you and do whatever they want with you with no ill regrets. I plead to the jury tonight to think a little bit about the island that we have been on. This island is pretty much full of only two things: snakes and rats. And in the end of Mother Nature, we have Richard the snake, who knowingly went after prey, and Kelly who turned into the rat, who ran around like the rats do on this island, trying to run from the snake. I feel like we owe it to the island's spirits that we have come to know to let it be in the end the way mother nature intended it to be . . . for the snake to eat the rat.[31]

While several subsequent players have been memorably angry at the finalists, this speech stands out and has become part of pop culture lore. There are many other memorable speeches from final juries. Lex's aggrieved lament that throws Boston Rob off-balance in *All-Stars*. Corinne Kaplan's extremely personal attack of Sugar Kiper in *Gabon*. Brenda Lowe's petty demand that

Dawn Meehan remove her false teeth in *Caramoan* (season 26, 2013). Reed Kelly's fairy-tale-inspired thrashing of Missy Payne in *San Juan del Sur*. All of these are memorable, but none have had the same impact as Sue's "Snakes and Rats" speech.

GAME THEORY AND STRATEGY

There are many identifiable strategies that have proven successful throughout the years. The first was to form an unbreakable alliance. Alliances have been a key part of the show since the first season, and the speed at which they form (and shift and reform) has sped up as players become more aware of what has worked in the past.

Borneo introduced the concept of alliances to the game. Richard, Sue, Kelly, and Rudy Boesch proved that a tight group of players could completely devastate outsiders as they marched from the merge to the final four with little resistance. Other players were caught off guard, and there was open debate about the morality of participating in an alliance in the game of *Survivor*. Of course, the fear that jury members will hold a grudge against players who form an alliance becomes a moot point when the only people they can vote for are members of the same alliance.

There is the issue that not all members of an alliance can make it to the end. Understanding when to turn on your alliance and how to jockey for a position within the alliance will become key bits of strategy in subsequent seasons. The cleverest bit of strategy in the first season came as the alliance had to turn on each other. At the final immunity challenge Richard, Rudy, and Kelly stood with a hand on an immunity idol while perched in an uncomfortable position. If a player lost contact with the idol, they were out. Richard had a final two agreement with Rudy, but knew that if Rudy made it to the finale, he would win the most jury votes. If Richard won and took Kelly, a bitter Rudy might poison the jury against him when he revealed that Richard broke his word. So Richard stepped down voluntarily, hoping that Kelly would win. Kelly, also knowing Rudy would win if he made it that far, would logically choose Richard. This gave Richard a much better chance to win the game than if he actually won the final immunity challenge and guaranteed himself a spot in the final two. By choosing to lose the challenge, Richard gave himself the best chance to win the game, which he did by a one-vote margin.

Survivor: Borneo *(Season 1, 2000)* Shown from left: Rudy Boesch, Kelly Wiglesworth, Richard Hatch. CBS / Photofest © CBS.

Boston Rob used fear to control his alliance in *Redemption Island* (season 22, 2011), never letting them speak or interact with players who weren't in his alliance. It made for an incredibly dominant but deeply boring season. In part, this was because as a fourth-time player Rob had no viable competition among the first-time players, who were simply outclassed in terms of strategic experience.

On the other side of the equation, Kim Spradlin ran a perfect alliance through friendship on *One World*. Seemingly every player believed Kim was their best friend on the island and was loyal to her (with exceptions from the men's tribe who were quickly voted out after the merge). Kim played perhaps the best first-time player game ever on *Survivor*. Her game was similarly dominant to Rob's—her alliance was never in danger of turning on her—despite the different methods they employed to navigate the game. However, both Rob and Kim gave viewers a similarly dull experience. *Redemption Island* and *One World* tend to be positioned in the lower half of season rankings.

In contrast, on *Cagayan*, Tony played an energetic, seemingly out of control game that led to his win. With a system of flipping on his alliance during odd-numbered votes then returning to them on even-numbered votes when they were more reliant on tight numbers he navigated his way to the end of the game. Then, with an unlikely manipulation of Woo that secured his spot in a final two, Tony became a runaway winner of the season as his strategy was viewed as more of a factor in the outcome than Woo's.

Because fans of the game are often cast as players, what happens in one season carries over into the following seasons. How alliances are formed in one season shape how they are formed in the next, both as examples of what works and what not to do. After viewers saw Boston Rob and Amber Brkich succeed together in *All-Stars*, new "couples" get voted out quickly. After the Black Widow Brigade—made up of women—led blindside after blindside on *Micronesia* (season 16, 2008), women alliances became feared. After Russell Hantz finds idols without clues and dominates two consecutive seasons (*Samoa* and *Heroes vs. Villains*—though losing both in the finale), anyone believed to be out idol hunting is considered a threat, even though everyone should be out searching.

For much of *Survivor*, a clear physical threat was considered the most dangerous type of player. But after John Cochran wins *Caramoan*, a new threat is seen. This is explicitly stated by Brad Culpepper—a former NFL player and current lawyer, in the alpha male mold often seen as a threat—in the first episode of *Blood vs. Water*. This season was the first after Cochran's perfect game with no votes cast against him and every jury member voting for him to win. Culpepper discusses this with Vytas Baskauskas, and says, "These days, the John Cochrans of *Survivor* are the big threats now. Because those are the people that win."[32] The most recent threats are either emulated or eliminated.

To avoid players copying the same formula too often, producers react to what has been working for the players and often try to throw a wrench in established strategies. In *Africa*, when a dominant alliance is taking shape within one of the tribes, a surprise swap shatters it and the lead figure is shortly sent home. When alliances formed on day one in large tribes run the game in *Redemption Island*, *South Pacific*, and *One World*, three smaller tribes are used in *Philippines*. The smaller initial tribes of six, rather than nine or ten, make it harder for a sub-alliance within the tribe to bond and cement plans for the post-merge game.

Analyzing *Survivor* for strategy can be fascinating and maddening at the same time. Barry Nalebuff, who taught courses on business management and game theory at Yale, became a go-to source for commentary about *The Australian Outback*. While he would make predictions for national publications, he noted that he can only make predictions based on what the players should do, not what they will actually do. There are too many personal variables from player to player to accurately know their motivations. But even when he was wrong, Nalebuff knew insight could be gained: "You have to ask why they did something so stupid, because they have a lot of time to think about these things."[33]

And that format simply works, because it forces the players to address competing, valid, internal motivations behind every decision they make. In the very first episode of every season, a losing tribe must vote someone off. Who gets chosen and why is generally the debate of the last act of the season premiere. Will it be the weakest member of the tribe, so that the tribe is kept strong and has a better chance of winning the next immunity challenge? Will it be the most annoying person at camp, because contestants have to live with tribemates twenty-four hours a day and the elements are already putting them on edge? Will it be the most likable person on the tribe, because they are the biggest threat to win the million dollars in the end? Will it be someone who is perceived to be playing too hard? All of these are reasons that are considered by contestants. And of course, the all-important "Anyone-but-me" mindset can snowball into a vote once a name has been thrown out.

But what is fascinating to watch is how players negotiate these concerns. It makes for compelling television as friendliness, strategy, emotions, and short-term and long-term goals are pressurized by the game's first step. As the game progresses and the million-dollar prize becomes more and more possible for remaining players to win, that pressure only increases.

The best fictional characters often have competing internal contradictions that give rise to inherent drama for viewers. While reality television contestants are not fictional characters, viewers are watching a mediated story that does present the action to them in familiar narrative beats. Characters struggling with competing impulses makes for an engrossing story. Players can legitimately say, "I like that person and don't want to vote them out," shortly before putting that person's name down on paper because that is in their best interest as game players. Or sometimes a player will say, "I know this move would be in my best interest, but I just can't vote them off because I really like them." And, in all likelihood, there will be a segment of fandom that is vocally upset either way.

Scholar Barbara Ann Schapiro argues that watching competitors navigate these contrasting impulses is at least a part of why *Survivor* is so captivating. She writes, "*Survivor*'s appeal lies in the psychological tension it creates," and fortunately for producers that appeal can translate across geographic locations, disparate casts, and generations of players. Schapiro highlights the contradictory impulses that dictate behavior on the show, because the premise of the show is "intensely intimate and intensely competitive" which forces players to display "trusting interdependence" and also "ruthless self-interest."[34] In the end, watching contestants try to balance those competing impulses is inherently fascinating television.

The contradictory requirements of the game have been enshrined by long-time reality TV commentator and podcaster David Bloomberg in his "Rules of Survivor." Bloomberg has been covering *Survivor* since its first season, first on the website Reality News Online and now on a podcast he co-hosts with former player Jessica Lewis (*Millennials vs. Generation X*) called *Why _____ Lost* that analyzes why the most recent contestant was voted off the island after each episode of *Survivor* airs. He codified his recommended strategy for winning the game into a set of rules that he's been refining across forty seasons of analysis. Rule #1 is "Scheme and plot" but rule #2 is "Don't scheme and plot too much."[35] The correct strategy at one point of the game may not be the correct strategy at another point of the game. Players are subject to so many competing and compelling stimuli and motivations that it can become very difficult for them to choose what to do next. And with so many variables, making the right choice does not guarantee a successful outcome.

Another fascinating aspect of the game is the assumption that every player has the same goal. This assumption can be completely false, and leads to poor decision making. On the face of it, everyone is on the island to win the million dollars. But for some players, looking like a good person on television for their friends and family is as important. For others, making a big memorable move is as important. Some insist that they're not there for the money or to play the game, but are there to have an adventure. Some of the most head scratching decisions from a strategy standpoint start to make more sense if you consider what other motives may be driving a participant's decision making.

Returning players offer an especially interesting avenue of exploration for player strategies because we have multiple data points. Examining how returning players adjust their games can reveal what they perceive to be their own strengths and weaknesses in terms of strategy. And with several seasons that pitted first-time players against returnees, we have several data points that reveal returning players are significantly better at playing the game than rookies. *Micronesia* featured a tribe of veterans versus super fans, and the final three were all returning players with Parvati Shallow winning the title of sole survivor. The next season with a similar format was *Blood vs. Water* in which the final three were again all returning players and Tyson Apostol won the season. The third time the series used one tribe of rookies against a tribe of veterans was *Caramoan*. In this season one rookie, Sherri

Biethman, did reach the final three, but the final tribal largely focused on the two returning players, Dawn Meehan and John Cochran. Cochran won that season in the end, with one of the most celebrated transformations from his first appearance on *South Pacific* as a superfan who struggled with his social game compared to his second time playing winning by unanimous vote.

There are two elements that can be seen influencing returning players' games. They tend to emulate the strategy of the winner from their original season to some degree, and they tend to react to the reception of their previous appearance on the show. Even returning winners will often alter their gameplay in response to fan reaction. While some of this analysis is speculation, some returnee's altered style of play is undeniable. Ben was seen as a selfish showboater in his first season, *Heroes vs. Healers vs. Hustlers*, and in *Winners at War* played a much quieter, almost martyr-esque game in which he essentially gave up at the end. Returning players often seem to be responding to criticisms of their past game.

Many *Survivor* fans imagine what it would be like to play the game, and this naturally leads to second-guessing the choices of those castaways who are playing the game. Debate around player's strategy takes place in conversations, on message boards, on podcasts, in online articles, and even in books. The stakes of the game are high, fans are invested in the outcome, and players' choices define the result of every episode. *Survivor* is a high-stress, high-stakes, high-reward game, that has millions of viewers reacting to the strategic choices of hungry, sleep-deprived players. Along with changes to the game from producers, player strategy has become more complex, and so has the depth of fan understanding of the game.

CHAPTER 4

TWISTS AND ADVANTAGES

There have been dozens of twists and advantages in the history of the show. Many had minimal impact and did not warrant a full write-up. Table 4.1 compiles the twists with a brief description and table 4.2 compiles the advantages with a brief description. Following the tables is an analysis of the most impactful twists and advantages in *Survivor*.

In the original *Survivor* era, there were very few surprises, twists, or advantages. The castaways were told the premise and let loose on the island. The game didn't deviate from the original plan, and only the player's choices came out of nowhere to disrupt the game. As fans of the show began to come prepared with strategies of how they would win the game, producers began to introduce wrinkles that introduced more uncertainty into the game. Some of these—like an individual immunity idol—have become so familiar to viewers, it almost feels odd to go back and watch seasons without them. Others—like Edge of Extinction—are accused of ruining the game. And others—like the Medallion of Power—are practically forgotten because they had so little impact they were abandoned mid-season.

Producers have a very challenging task in keeping the show fresh but retaining what has made it popular. In May 2021, a Twitter user asked people to share their most unpopular opinions about *Survivor*. Former player Rick Devens, knowing that many fans claim that twists are unnecessary, replied, "Production constantly adding new elements and twists to the show is the only reason it's been a success for going on 42 seasons."[1] Jeff Probst echoes this sentiment, stating, "One of the complaints I hear often from fans is, 'There's too many twists. You should really try a season with no twists.' Without that uncertainty, *Survivor* would not still be on the air. If it was

Table 4.1 Twists

Game Length	Typically, the game was 39 days (except for season 2, which was 42 days), until season 41 which has been 26 days.
Tribe Size and Number of Tribes	Tribe size varies with the number of players and the number of tribes—two tribes of eight, two tribes of nine, two tribes of ten, three tribes of six, four tribes of four, and four tribes of five.
Tribe Swap	A pre-merge event that mixes up the tribes in various ways, whether it be reshuffling the players into equal numbers on each tribe or dissolving one tribe into the other tribes.
Mutiny	Players from both tribes are offered the option to join the other tribe.
Rock Draw for Tie Breaker at Tribal Council	In the event of a tie at Tribal Council it goes to a revote. If the revote is still a tie, the players not receiving votes may discuss and come to a unanimous decision. If they cannot agree, the players with tied votes will be immune and the rest of the players must draw rocks. The player who draws the odd-colored rock is eliminated from the game.
Maroonings	This varies between seasons, sometimes players are marooned with supplies, no supplies, supplies you have to grab yourself, or barter for in a town, a hike to your campsite, or an immediate challenge.
Summit or Journey	A pre-merge event in which usually one or two members from each tribe meet in a new location and have to make a decision either for themselves or their tribe.
	Starting in season 41 this is called a Journey and has become a regular twist of the game which gives the players a chance to receive an advantage, or possibly lose their vote.
Kidnapping or Observing	The tribe that wins the challenge selects one member of the losing tribe to temporarily join them at their camp. The reverse is one member of the winning tribe temporarily joins the losing tribe to be able to observe.
Looting	The winning tribe of a challenge gets to send a player or multiple players to a losing tribe's camp and take an item.
Eliminated Contestants Return; Redemption Island; Edge of Extinction	Voted out players compete in a challenge to win their way back into the game.
Exile Island	A campsite away from tribe camps where one or two players gets banished to and often will contain advantages or clues to advantages.
Ghost Island	A variation of Exile Island, where a player from the losing tribe of the Reward Challenge is banished to Ghost Island and has a chance to obtain a *Survivor* relic as an advantage in the game.
Island of the Idols	Another variation of Exile Island in which players are banished to the island and meet with former players who share advice and challenge the players in a game of chance, risking their vote for a reward.

(Continued)

Table 4.1 (Continued)

Returning Players	Former contestants return to play the game. Sometimes to play against all former players, and sometimes a mixture of former and new players.
Double Tribal Council	Regardless of which tribe wins the challenge, both tribes must go to Tribal Council and vote a player out. Often a reward is given to the winning tribe, and get to sit in on the losing tribes Tribal Council to observe.
Joint Tribal Council	Two tribes both attend Tribal Council and vote as a group to eliminate one player.
Fire Making for Tie Breaker	In the final four Tribal council, if there is a 2–2 vote the tied contestants compete in a fire-making challenge and the winner stays and the loser is eliminated.
	In season 35 this was modified at the final four, the winner of the challenge selects one player to take with them to the final Tribal Council, and the remaining two compete in the fire-making challenge.
Final three instead of two	Initially it was a final two at the final Tribal Council. In *Cook Islands* for the first time there was a final three at the Tribal Council.
Haves vs. Have Nots	All the players build a furnished camp to then be divided into two tribes and compete in a challenge. The winning tribe went back to the furnished beach and the losing tribe were given very little to go build a new camp from scratch.
First Impression Vote Out	A player is voted out at the very beginning of the game, although not usually eliminated from the game, but rather does something separate from the rest of the tribe.
Do It Yourself Challenge	Challenges in which the players are given instructions and must run themselves. Jeff Probst is not present.
Tribal Leaders	Each tribe must vote for a tribe leader who makes various decisions for the tribe throughout the season.
Tribes Together in One Camp	The tribes live together at one camp.
Medallion of Power	Allows the tribe that possesses it to gain an advantage during a challenge. If the tribe chose to use it, the Medallion would then belong to the other tribe to use when they chose.
Blood vs. Water	Players compete against loved ones such as a significant other or relative.
Day Zero	A twist played on Blood vs. Water seasons, which has the pairs at different locations overnight leading them to believe they will be working together rather than competing against each other on different tribes.
Fire Tokens	Coins earned throughout the game that can be used to purchase luxuries or advantages.
Earn the Merge	Instead of going directly into the merge, remaining players are divided into two tribes and compete in the challenge. Players on the winning tribe make the merge and safe at Tribal Council. Players on the losing tribe do not make the merge until after the vote at Tribal Council.
Do or Die	The player who finishes last of a specific individual immunity challenge must play a game of chance at Tribal Council. If they lose, they are immediately eliminated.

Table 4.2 Advantages

Hidden Immunity Idol	An advantage that prevents the player from being voted out at Tribal Council. Must be played after voting, but before the votes are read. Only usable until there are five players left in the game.
Super Idol	An immunity idol that also prevents a player from being voted out at Tribal Council, but allows the player to play it after the votes are read.
Idol Nullifier	An advantage played at Tribal Council when the player is casting their vote. The player must write the name of their target on the back of the nullifier, which if done correctly, will render the target's immunity idol useless. If the target did not play an idol, the nullifier is wasted.
Extra Vote	Allows a player to vote twice at a Tribal Council.
Bank Your Vote	When used, a player must abstain from voting at a Tribal Council in order to then obtain an Extra Vote to be used at a later Tribal Council.
Steal a Vote	Allows a player to steal another player's vote and vote twice at Tribal Council.
Vote Blocker	Allows a player to prevent another player from voting at Tribal Council.
Juror Removal	At the final Tribal Council, allows one player to remove one of the jury members.
Safety without Power	Allows the player to leave Tribal Council before voting so they cannot be eliminated. However, this also means they cannot cast a vote.
Legacy Advantage	An advantage that can only be played at certain Tribal Councils. If the player in possession is voted out before one of the specific Tribal Councils, they must will it to another player. When played the advantage becomes an immediate immunity idol at that Tribal Council.
Reward Steal	Allows the player to steal a reward from another player.
Advantage Menu	Offers three potential advantages and allows the player to select one to use later in the game.
50/50 Coin	A coin with Safe on one side, and Not Safe on the other. The player must play it at Tribal Council and flip the coin. Whichever side is face up is their fate.
Extortion Advantage	A player on Edge of Extinction extorts a player in the game for Fire Tokens. The player who receives it must pay the amount of Fire Tokens requested or they cannot participate in the next immunity challenge, and lose their vote at Tribal Council.
Beware Advantage	An immunity idol or clue that comes with tasks that must be completed or else the player loses their vote at Tribal Council.
Shot in the Dark	A six-side die that each player is given at the start of the game. If desired, players can play their shot instead of the vote, and have a 1 in 6 chance of being safe from any votes against them.
Knowledge is Power	Allows the players to ask another player at Tribal Council if they have an immunity idol or an advantage. If they do, that player must give either to the asking player.

(Continued)

Table 4.2 (Continued)

Hidden Immunity Idol	An advantage that prevents the player from being voted out at Tribal Council. Must be played after voting, but before the votes are read. Only usable until there are five players left in the game.
Hourglass	Used along with the Earn the Merge twist, the Hourglass allows one player to reverse the results of the immunity challenge, making the winning team all vulnerable at Tribal Council, and the losing team all have immunity.
Advantage Amulet	A shared advantage in which the power of changes depending on the number of players in possession and still in the game. To use, the players must be on the same tribe and agree to play it together. When there is only one player left in the game still in possession, the amulet becomes an immunity idol.
Inheritance Advantage	A player secretly inherits all the advantages and idols played at one Tribal Council.

simple as, 'Hey, whoever has five people can vote out the group that has four,' this game would've died 15 years ago."[2] Fans and players are very quick to complain about new elements, but experimentation is vital to the longevity of the franchise.

Obviously, the producers are driven to create the best product possible, just as players are striving to play the best game they can imagine. Probst explains that changes are meant to force players to play the game, and not intended to frustrate players, stating, "Anybody who ever dreams of playing Survivor should always remember that our job as producers of this game is to keep you off balance. It's not intended to be cruel or even manipulative, it's only designed to force you to continue to adapt."[3]

However, player Malcolm Freberg (*Philippines*; *Caramoan*; *Game Changers*) argued after *41* (season 41, 2021) aired, that the amount of additional twists and advantages in the game has made it so *Survivor* is "losing some of the magic that made it our favorite show for two decades."[4] Andy Dehnart of *Reality Blurred* seems to agree when describing all the new advantages of the most recent seasons up to *44* (season 44, 2024), "What's disappointing, however, is to tune in and watch these contestants be played by *Survivor*, instead of letting them play *Survivor*."[5] Fan favorite Christian Hubicki (*David vs. Goliath*) argues that not even knowing what twists may happen in a game hurts gameplay, stating,

> I like the idea of everybody knowing the basic rules, and playing within that framework. I don't mind uncertainty in the game. There needs to be uncertainty to add interesting things to the game. But what [not knowing what twists are coming] creates is a scenario where players are encouraged to have some meta understanding of what production would do and would not do, and that's a little

weird for the show. You have to sniff out not just "Is this person telling the truth?" but "Can I get into the mind of Jeff Probst as to what kind of advantage he would allow?" And that's a level of meta-ness that doesn't make for good television when there's plenty of uncertainty about whether or not people are telling the truth.[6]

It's clear some twists and advantages are necessary. But there are so many advantages that production has begun adding a textual tally of advantages on screen when players are giving confessionals. Reporter Mike Bloom explains the significance of this:

There's been a proliferation of immunity idols, extra votes, a vote steal, an idol nullifier, to the point where the lower third—where people's occupations used to be—is now their advantages. I think that says a lot. It used to be about what someone did and how that informs who they are, now it's more reflective of the stuff they have in their pocket and how it can be played in the game.[7]

The fact that production needs to list who has what advantages points to there being too many in the game. And when a brand new twist is introduced, it can lead to a technical explanation that is often confusing, shifting the focus from the player to the twists and advantages.

Regardless of the number or type of twists and advantages, *Survivor* is a never-ending game of cat and mouse between producers and players. As soon as the contestants catch up to the way the game is being run and how to act and play accordingly, the producers add a new wrinkle. Twists include changes to the basic framework of the show. These changes affect everyone in the game, and everyone is aware of them. Advantages include individual, often secret, powers that players gain through various means. Both twists and advantages have been introduced to keep players and viewers from being able to predict what will happen in the game. Whether well-received or despised, it is useful to consider why producers may have introduced a twist or advantage. It is possible to track the logic and reasoning behind twists and advantages if we look for patterns that have developed in the gameplay that producers are trying to disrupt.

The first significant twist in game structure comes in *Africa* (season 3, 2001). After the first season saw the tribe with more members systematically eliminate every member of the opposing tribe after they merged together, the second season saw the tribes eyeing the merge as the key moment where the endgame could be decided. Due to Michael Skupin's injury from falling into a fire and being medevacked from the game, what looked like a probable majority for the Kucha tribe never occurred at the merge. The two opposing tribes merged with five members each, and the first vote out after the merge was a high point of drama for the season. But once the Ogakor tribe was able to vote off Jeff Varner, that dramatic tension dissipated as Ogakor dominated the post-merge game. Save for a detour to get rid of Jerri Manthey who was getting on Colby Donaldson's nerves, Ogakor voted off each Kucha member before they turned on themselves. A pattern had been set. In order to prevent a clearly predictable series of votes after the two tribes merged, something had to change. In *Africa*, the players were caught completely off-guard when the first tribe swap took place and players switched tribes before the merge. New strategy emerged as a result. This is now a standard and accepted twist of the game. It is not always used, but when it is it tends not to be controversial. Many fans may not even realize it is a twist in the first place as it has become so ingrained in the game. Probst pointed this out, stating, "There's a history on Survivor, every twist we've ever done people have hated in the beginning, going back to season three when we did the first [tribe] swap. Now, if tribes don't switch, they're upset!"[8]

There have, of course, been twists that have not been as well received. The Medallion of Power is a footnote in *Survivor* history because it had no impact on the game. It was introduced in *Nicaragua* (season 21, 2010) and would allow the tribe that possessed the Medallion of Power to gain an advantage during a challenge. If the tribe chose to use the Medallion, they would gain the advantage but the Medallion would then belong to the other tribe, which could deploy it whenever they chose. *Nicaragua* was a season with tribes divided by age, and it's likely that the hope was the Medallion could be used by the older tribe to level the playing field of any challenge they felt left them at a disadvantage. In the first four challenges the Medallion of Power was used twice, and each time the tribe that used it won the challenge. After four challenges, Probst announced that the Medallion of Power was being removed from the game. Dalton Ross from *Entertainment Weekly* sums up the issue with the Medallion of Power (besides its absurd name), "This is the one where you simply have to ask yourself: What were they thinking? . . . [E]ssentially, you ran the risk of no challenges actually being on a level playing field, or tribes ignoring it completely so that it never went over to the other team."[9] The Medallion of Power is more remembered for being an odd twist that seemingly was abandoned before becoming a major part of the game. But there are other twists that are hotly debated because of the impact they have on the game. Below are a few of the most impactful (and controversial) twists and advantages through the years that have not yet been explored in earlier chapters of this book.

GAME LENGTH

Between the first and second season, there were no twists introduced. However, the second season was the longest version of the game ever played, as three extra days were added to ensure extra episodes for the super-sized second season. The sense of exhaustion the players have at the end is notable. But, after this one super-sized season, filming returned to thirty-nine days until season 41. Reacting to COVID protocols that included two weeks of isolation for contestants before filming began, production shortened the gameplay to twenty-six days. This allowed two seasons to be filmed back-to-back in the same overall time frame as the previous thirty-nine-day seasons despite the necessary precautions undertaken due to the global pandemic.[10] As those restrictions eased, the choice was made to retain the twenty-six-day filming format.

The impact of this is interesting. In order to justify the shortening of the days on the island, production has tried to make the experience more difficult for players—such as no starting food, fewer supplies, fewer rewards, and more penalties for losing. The pace is also much quicker, which is more mentally exhausting for the players. Probst states,

> The pace is absolutely relentless. Faster than any other season. There is no time to sit back and contemplate even for a moment. You have to be assessing and reassessing your options on an hourly basis because you have no idea what is coming next. The game design has never been so dangerous.[11]

Probst has made no efforts to hide his feelings toward the 26 days compared to 39 days. On his podcast, when asked about 26 days vs. 39 days, he declared,

> As for the difficulty, I think it's pretty clear even just from this season, if anything, the new era—brace yourself, old time players—is more difficult. Because the physical demands of surviving with very, very little—or for some players, no food—is extremely punishing and it begins to break you down mentally. You can't think, you can't sleep, you can't trust. That leads to the emotional breakdown, which can be brutal.[12]

Probst calling out "old time players" (those who played thirty-nine-day seasons) directly is most likely due to many of those players being vocally negative about the constant claim the shorter season is more difficult than thirty-nine days. On his podcast, *The Pod Has Spoken*, Tyson Apostol often has a former player as a guest, and would ask them their thoughts on the twenty-six-day format vs. thirty-nine days. While the overall sentiment is understanding why production made this change, the frustration seems to come from the seemingly dismissal of the difficulty of thirty-nine days in the declarations of how challenging the show has made twenty-six days.

Xander Hastings from season 41 said on the podcast after playing the twenty-six-day season, "For me, I'd say it's on par with the 39 days season given the fact that there was a stretch of three days we didn't have food at all on Yase beach." Tyson countered, "I have seen 39 days where they have all not had food for a long time and stuff like that . . . can you imagine being on day 26 and realizing that you still have 33% of the game left to go?"[13] Tyson, in another episode, said, "I'm like, come on, I wasn't even hurting the 26 days, I felt great . . . [n]ot great, but like 26 wasn't the day where I was like, this is hard. It was past that." Multi-season player Cirie Fields charmingly said, "The 26 days, you know, kind of hurt my feelings because if I can do 39, they should 49, right?"[14] *China* winner Todd Herzog was asked by Tyson, "Can you replicate a 39 day feeling with a 26 day season?" Todd answered simply, "No, you cannot." He goes on to explain,

> You can starve these people as much as you possibly want. I was starving in China. I had limes. I had a tiny lime tree. So we didn't have food. So to hear these people bitch and moan about it, I'm like, yeah, we all starved. It's *Survivor*. That's part of the deal.
>
> But 26 days, I get it. The game is fast-paced and you're more paranoid and you have to jump back and forth and whatnot. Neat. But the way I look at it is day 30 was the family visit for us. Day 30. We still had nine days to go. Those were the hardest nine days. I'm sure you know exactly what it is because paranoia gets to you and then you just are literally mentally so gone. You still have to think and you still have to be on your toes. And so, those last nine days were just awful . . . [t]hat's just, I don't know. It makes me sick. I mean, okay, yeah, I get it. You're out there, you're playing for survival for 26 days. I know you want to pretend that it's as difficult, but you haven't played a 39 day season. You really cannot compare it.[15]

Todd's response lays out many of the arguments against dismissing the thirty-nine-day seasons as less difficult. Everyone can acknowledge that production has tried in every way to push the players as far as possible during the twenty-six-day season. But it is understandable that past players may feel as though their own experience is being invalidated by Probst and production not acknowledging the thirty-nine-day season was very difficult.

Regardless of fans or past players' opinions, Probst has made it clear that the twenty-six-day season is here to stay for now.[16] Until we have a player from the thirty-nine-day era play a twenty-six-day game (or vice versa), no one can declare with certainty one is harder than the other. Although no casting has been announced at the time of writing this book, it has been revealed that season 50 of *Survivor* will feature returning players, so it is possible we will get a direct comparison.[17]

RETURN OF VOTED-OUT PLAYERS

Every season Probst has declared, "In this game, fire represents your life. When your fire's gone, so are you." This is a fact of *Survivor*. Except when it comes to The Outcasts. Or Redemption Island. Or Edge of Extinction. The sense of the vote-off being a core concept of the series is one reason that some twists frustrate fans. The torch snuffing, some argue, should be final. The tribe has spoken and you're out of the game.

The first such twist that undid this was in *Pearl Islands* (season 7, 2003), where the first six players who had been voted out came back as the Outcast tribe. Wearing purple buffs, that tribe had the opportunity to compete against the two existing tribes, Morgan and Drake. If The Outcasts defeated one or both of the tribes in a challenge they could then vote one or two players back into the game, while the other tribes would have to vote someone off. The Outcasts defeated both Drake and Morgan, allowing two members of their tribe to return to the game. The Outcasts voted Burton Roberts and Lillian Morris back into the game and Probst reignited their snuffed torches.

Before the challenge between the three tribes, Probst states that the Outcasts have been deprived of nutrition just like the players on the island, to keep the game fair. However, in looking back on this choice, Probst has revealed that was not the case. In a 2015 interview with *TV Insider*, he said, "The Outcasts twist . . . was a bad call. It was unfair. People came back into the game who had been eating and sleeping, and that was bullshit."[18] And in 2020, Probst revealed that the entire twist was a spur of the moment decision.

> We did this thing where we brought back people. . . . We voted people out, they went to a hotel and ate and had a shower. And then Mark (Burnett) said, "We should just bring them back. That would blow their minds." And all of us were like, "That's fundamentally wrong." And we did it. And it was criticized. And I've said I'm no genius but I didn't think it was a good idea.[19]

It was a bad idea in the lack of preparation production put in before implementing it. It was not well received by viewers and players. One player directly impacted by the returning players was Andrew Savage on the Morgan tribe. In an interview in 2021, Savage admitted the effect it had on him, stating, "There was a long and difficult adjustment period. I was deeply haunted by the Outcast twist and the circumstances under which I left the game and how my adventure of a lifetime ended."[20]

Despite recognizing bringing players back in this was not a good idea, the show did an iteration of it less than a decade later. In *Redemption Island* (season 22, 2011), a new twist was introduced wherein every player voted out would go to Redemption Island and have a chance to duel the next player voted out in a typical *Survivor* challenge. The winner of the duel would remain on Redemption Island. Eventually, after several duels, the last player standing would reenter the game. Every player who lost the duels (or multiplayer battles) at Redemption Island would finally, actually be out of the game and burn their buff in the fire on their way out. Versions of Redemption Island also appeared on *South Pacific* (season 23, 2011) and *Blood vs. Water* (season 27, 2013).

The most loathed version of this twist is Edge of Extinction wherein every player voted out has the chance to stay on another island until there is one challenge for everyone who has stuck it out and the winner can reenter the game. This was first used in *Edge of Extinction* (season 38, 2019) and then again on *Winners at War* (season 40, 2020). In this twist, the player that eventually reenters the game has been living with the jury and forming bonds with them (and commiserating about how frustrated they are with everyone who voted them out). It feels immensely unfair to players who stay in the game the entire time. Even Probst has heard the fan discontent with the twist. When interviewed by Rob Cesternino before the fortieth season, Probst addressed fan backlash to the twist and said,

> I love this show. I love finding people who want to play. I love spending most of my year trying to figure out "What's something we could do, that would twist the game, so that when they get there they say 'Aw shit, now what am I gonna do?'" And I love watching it happen. I think it's fantastic watching all of these twists. And when people get so invested that they don't like it, that tells me, "Okay, we're in this together. You don't like it; I get it." I liked it, but I hear you. We're not going to do Edge [of Extinction] for a while. I've heard people; I got it. I'm not saying we won't do it again; we might . . . want to do it again.[21]

Ultimately, in season 38, after being the third player voted out, Chris Underwood returned from the Edge of Extinction on day thirty-five and won the game.

Notably for *Winners at War*, which featured former winners for the entire cast, Probst felt the Edge of Extinction was necessary in order to bring back twenty winners. In an interview with Ross, Probst explained, "The number one reason is that I did feel that when we called winners, that if they thought it was one and out—'I'm voted out and I'm done'—their chances of saying yes were not as high as if it would be if I said 'No matter what, you will have another shot at the prize.'" He continued, saying,

> It did make a difference because one player after another would say, "Are you doing something like Edge? Tell me you are." And I said, "I can't tell you what we're doing. I can only tell you you'll have a fair shot to win the game." And they all read between the lines, which is what I wanted them to do. It's fair. And so Edge of Extinction is really saying, in a season in which you are lucky enough to get these winners to come back and play again, give 'em a chance to play.

Ross goes on in his article to note when interviewing players before the season filmed that "several players told me unprompted before the game that they were not fans of Edge of Extinction and hoped it was not back."[22] Both can be true, that some players wanted a safety net like Edge, and others did not. *Winners at War* does have a better argument for having the Edge—to allow viewers to spend more time with favorite winners from past seasons. But, perhaps luckily for production, the winner of the season was not someone who had been voted out and returned to the game with the bonds of the jury. Tony Vlachos beat out Natalie Anderson and Michelle Fitzgerald in a 12–4–0 vote. Tony and Michelle played the full thirty-nine days of the game in the traditional style. In contrast, Natalie had been the first player voted out. We'll never know, but had Natalie won the season, we can assume there would have been immediate and very strong backlash from fans, as the results would have mirrored Chris Underwood's win.

IMMUNITY IDOLS

For ten seasons, *Survivor* was a standard game of play: a challenge, go to Tribal Council, vote someone out, repeat. In *Guatemala* (season 11, 2005), a new element was introduced—the individual immunity idol, hidden within the jungle. If the idol was played at Tribal Council, the player would be safe from elimination. Thus ushered in a new era of the game, where even just the threat of an immunity idol or any other advantage influences nearly every decision a player makes.

Scrambling to look for the immunity idol has become a day one activity for players in more recent seasons. But it took time for the immunity idol to become a staple of the series, and it took a few false starts before the correct balance of power for the advantage was found. There's a Goldilocks element to the immunity idol: at first it wasn't powerful enough, then it was too powerful, and finally it was just right.

The first Hidden Immunity Idol was found by Gary Hogeboom in the ninth episode of *Guatemala* on a night he was likely to have been sent home. The way the idol worked in this iteration was that before the tribe voted, someone who held the idol could announce that they had it and play it. At that point, nobody could cast a vote for that player. While this did protect an at-risk player, it did not fully disrupt the plans of a power alliance. Most likely, a pecking order of potential players to vote out was known, and a majority alliance could simply move on to the next name on their list. In usage, this version is essentially the same as the individual immunity necklace that can be won at a challenge, with the twist that players can arrive at Tribal Council not knowing that anyone has it.

A new version of the Immunity Idol appears in the next season, *Panama* (season 12, 2006), found on Exile Island by Terry Dietz, and could be played after the votes had been read by Probst. While the earlier version required a player to sense that they were in danger, with this variation a player could wait to know they had been voted out before playing the idol. Terry would go on a record-tying run of winning five individual immunity challenges, and never played the idol. In later seasons, producers would introduce a two-part idol that, if combined, would function the same way this idol does. Because that version of the combined idol is referred to on the show as a "Super Idol," any version of the individual immunity idol that can be played after votes are cast has become known as a Super Idol. In general, fans have complained that the Super Idol is too powerful.

The individual immunity idol that has appeared most frequently and which fans are most familiar with is generally called just a "hidden immunity idol." While this set of rules for the idol has the proper power balance and has largely left its rules for usage alone, it has hardly been static in its influence over the game. Players with the idol have passed the idol to other players in their alliance, pretended to play a fake idol to see how the other players react, and then decided to play their real idol, use the note from their real idol hidden with a fake idol in order to make another player believe they found a real idol, only to play it with no power. Just the existence of the idol can be enough to put seeds of doubt into players. Often, large alliances trying to vote out a specific player will split their votes onto two players, in case the intended target does play an idol, they can still successfully vote a player of their choosing. This, however, can be very tricky, and relies on every single member of an alliance voting correctly. There is a lot of room for error when splitting the vote. The effect the hidden immunity idol has had on the game is immeasurable given all the different reactions both players who have it and players who fear someone has it have had throughout the seasons.

In *David vs. Goliath* (season 37, 2018), the Idol Nullifier first appeared, although unannounced to players. A talisman that is played at Tribal Council as the player using it is casting their vote. The player must write the name of their target on the back of the nullifier. If that player plays an idol, the nullifier will prevent the idol from having any power and the player can be voted out. Amazingly, in the first season it appeared, the Idol Nullifier was played correctly by Carl Boudreaux against Dan Rengering who had no idea of its existence. Dan, who quite fairly assumed he was safe, was sent to the jury. The Idol Nullifier is not a given on every season. It has only appeared on *David vs. Goliath*, *Island of the Idols* (season 39, 2019), *Winners at War*, and *42* (season 42, 2022—although it was unaired, Omar Zaheer has confirmed that he did find an Idol Nullifier).[23]

In seasons from *41* on, finding an immunity idol has come with a set of stipulations for the player, and usually with a "Beware" warning indicating that if the task is not complete the player will lose their vote at Tribal Council. Rather than just having the idol once found, the player must follow the instructions in order to activate the idol or be given directions to the location of the idol. These instructions vary from season to season, but consist of tasks such as saying a specific phrase at a challenge, obtaining specific beads from their tribemates, going on a scavenger hunt to find the idol, melting wax that encases the idol, or finding a key to unlock the box containing the idol. While these tasks can be entertaining for viewers, it can also be confusing to watch. Denhart writes these types of advantages have changed the viewing experience while watching episodes, stating, "far too many episodes are like watching the producers drop the players into a pinball machine and whack them around for an hour."[24] There is a chaotic energy that comes with these newer seasons that can be fun initially with the fast pace, but it is drastically different than prior seasons. And the addition of Beware Advantages to obtain an immunity idol is a direct cause of this. However, despite any frustration of how idols now enter the game, this is easily one of the greatest twists added to the game.

Part III

THE SOCIAL EXPERIMENT

COURTING CONTROVERSY

For many, the genre of reality television is synonymous with trashy controversy. People yelling, people fighting, people revealing their worst selves in the name of entertainment. When every minute of a show that reaches television screens has been approved by editors, producers, and the network before the audience sees it, the question may be asked, why does anything controversial ever make it to air when it could be edited around or edited out entirely? Often, the controversy is the point. Scholars Anita Biressi and Heather Nunn argue that the commentary, debate, and coverage around controversial reality TV is essential to its success.[1] In a variation of the old adage that "There is no such thing as bad publicity," when it comes to reality TV, there is no such thing as bad buzz. Except there is substantial evidence that buzz does not mean long-term success. And there is, in fact, bad publicity.

In the early 2000s, as part of the wave of reality shows on American airwaves following the success of *Survivor*, several series seemed designed to court public outcry. *Extreme Makeover* saw ordinary people physically transformed through exercise, hairstyling, wardrobe changes, but also extensive plastic surgery. Academic Misha Kavka explains, "In its first series, the show sparked a great deal of controversy (and attendant publicity, averaging 11 million viewers per episode)."[2] Garnering significant pushback, *Extreme Makeover* ran for four seasons, from 2002–2007. By contrast, the spin-off series, *Extreme Makeover: Home Edition*, which saw families in need have their homes remodeled, was praised for showing "the softer side of Reality TV"[3] and ran for ten seasons from 2004–2012.

Fox chose an even more controversial version of the makeover concept with a show titled *The Swan* (2004). In this series, every episode sees two women who consider themselves ugly ducklings spend three months with personal trainers and cosmetic surgeons, and then one of them is judged as more attractive.[4] The show was immediately condemned by critics, and scholars have published substantial negative commentary about it. Academic Susan J. Douglas wrote that it "made all too explicit the narrow physical standards to which women are expected to conform, the sad degree to which women internalize these standards, the lengths needed to get there, and the impossibility for most of us to meet the bar without, well, taking a box cutter to our faces and bodies."[5] Other reality shows also used body transformations, whether through exercise—*The Biggest Loser* (2004–2020)[6]—or plastic surgery—*Bridalplasty* (2010–2011)[7]—or diet—*Supersize vs. Superskinny* (2008–2014)[8]—as a hook to create buzz.

There are many other examples of reality TV shows that courted controversy just with the announcement of their premise. There are so many unbelievably strange concepts that one is tempted to verify that these really aired. There are multiple dating shows where the audience is in on a lie that the contestants are not. *Joe Millionaire* (2003, 2022) saw women told the eligible bachelor they were all pursuing was an heir who just inherited $50 million, when he was a blue-collar construction worker.[9] *I Wanna Marry Harry* (2014) featured American women who were manipulated into believing they were trying to win the heart of Prince Harry, Duke of Sussex (this "Harry" was a look-alike actor named Matthew Hicks).[10] *Boy Meets Boy* (2003) saw a gay bachelor looking for love when he didn't know that many of the contestants were straight men pretending to be gay.[11] This is not to be confused with *Playing It Straight* (2004), where a woman isn't told that many of the contestants she can choose from are gay men pretending to be straight.[12] Notably, while many of these controversial shows generated media buzz, none have lasted nearly as long as *Survivor*, with many of them being pulled from the air before finishing their first and only seasons.

Survivor has some inherent level of controversy. In the lead-up to the premiere, one publication described the premise as "16 souls marooned on a deserted island, 'Lord of the Flies' style, of whom only one will remain to claim the prize,"[13] which sounds like a recipe for murder and betrayal. The show has still generated headlines throughout its entire run because of behaviors or moments that transgress societal norms. Various cast members going nude, the contestants eating rats and insects, killing pigs and chickens for food, sexual harassment, racist interactions, players treating each other terribly, and lies about personal tragedies have all aired and generated controversy.

Survivor has attempted to generate controversy at various points in its history. CBS president Les Moonves has acknowledged that in the early era of *Survivor*, there were times that casting was done "to build the most drama through personality." Moonves gives the example of the buzz that was built during the first season around Richard Hatch, "an outwardly gay man," sharing a beach with Rudy Boesch, "the original Navy Seal who was very anti-gay." Putting them on the same team was done to "see what happens" when they interacted. He gives another example of casting a player who "really didn't like being around Black people" who "wore her prejudice on her sleeve" and putting her on a tribe with an African American castmate because "it really was a game and a social experiment at the same time."[14] While Rudy did give the cameras plenty of homophobic commentary, he also had a long-term alliance with Richard that saw them both reach the final three. The player whom Moonves described as having racial prejudice never displayed any behavior during their season that would indicate a bias or discomfort with their African American tribemate, so the charged interactions Moonves was clearly hoping for never came about.

Moments that fans discuss, debate, and remember do not have to be problematic. *Survivor* has aired an incredible range of human moments. Across decades, with hundreds of players and cameras always rolling, a breadth of experiences have been captured. Burgeoning romances, personal revelations, comedic bumbling, and shocking twists are all part of viewers' expectations when watching *Survivor*. There are big, bold moves that are strictly part of the game play that become iconic for fans of the show. Whether it's the Black Widow Brigade convincing Erik Reichenbach to give up immunity and then immediately voting him out in *Micronesia*, Ben Driebergen finding and playing immunity idols for three consecutive Tribal Councils when the majority alliance planned to vote him out in *Heroes vs. Healers vs. Hustlers*, or production introducing a new game mechanism that allowed the third player voted out—Chris Underwood—to return to the game and win in *Edge of Extinction*, these moments can be celebrated or critiqued in discussions among fans. They fall strictly within gameplay, and don't involve any controversy about player's personal identities or mocking of a culture.

However, there are also hotly debated moments that fall outside strategy and gameplay. Often, these moments that break out of *Survivor* message boards or traditional watercooler talk and into wider news coverage involve issues of race, gender, and sexuality. Whether it's verbal harassment that is interpreted as misogynistic,[15] racist,[16] or homophobic,[17] a female contestant accusing a male contestant of grinding against her in the night,[18] instances of inappropriate touching,[19] or one contestant outing another as transgender in the hope that other players would view that as indicative of a deceptive nature,[20] there are many examples where poor choices by players made *Survivor* difficult to watch as simple popcorn entertainment. The "reality" of reality TV can become repellant to viewers when an ugly side of humanity is revealed.

There is an easily seen tension for producers when it comes to these moments. Having people talk about the show is desirable, but having them talk about how poorly a controversial moment was handled hurts the credibility of the show. There is also the fact that producers cannot control how fans react to any moment. Having players speak out about racism in an eloquent and moving way can be great television for some viewers, but a vocal portion of the fanbase prefers that the show give them obstacle course challenges and blindsides rather than what they deem to be "politics."[21] Even if producers were tempted to avoid airing some controversial behavior from players, for the sake of clarity, these so-called political moments sometimes must be shown. Decisions about whom to vote out—or who producers decide must be pulled from the game—can involve subjects that some viewers wish were not brought up on their TV shows.

A key aspect of *Survivor* is forming alliances. Thus, players inevitably look for what unites them with some players and also what divides them from others. What unites players could be style of gameplay or a particular strategic path. In *Redemption Island* (season 22, 2011), "Boston" Rob Mariano worries that some other players may be bonding over a shared religious background. In a confessional, Boston Rob says, "Look, I got nothing against God. I mean, I go to church on Sunday, but any time a group of individuals likes the same thing, I don't like that. It could be romantic comedies. It could be Oreo cookies. If they're all liking it together, I want that broken up."[22] Anything could unite a group and by the same token, commonly noted differences—gender, race, age, sexual orientation, religion, etc.,—could all disappear as the game begins.

At times it does. At times, players don't care who you are or about your background. They care if they can trust you or what you can provide to them. But everyone who plays *Survivor* is human and it is human nature to categorize, to spot differences, and to flock to commonalities. This is not to say that players only look to reward someone who looks like them. The winners of the show represent a spectrum of identities. The first winner was Richard Hatch, a thirty-nine-year-old gay man. The second winner was Tina Wesson, a forty-year-old Caucasian mother figure. The third was Ethan Zohn, a twenty-seven-year-old Jewish man. And the fourth was Vecepia Towery, a thirty-five-year-old African American woman. Subsequent winners have included Caucasians, African Americans, Asian Americans, Latino/a Americans, and members of the LGBTQ+ community. Winners have ranged in age from twenty-one to fifty-nine.

Because the game has been played for so long, *Survivor* is a reflection of our evolving society. Prominent social issues that are part of American life are present on the island and become part of what is edited down and relayed to audiences at home. In some instances, these become time capsules of behaviors society used to find acceptable, but are no longer commonplace. As an example, in *Borneo*, a homophobic slur is used several times in a manner that is treated as lighthearted and playful. It is unlikely the slur would even be aired today, and it is undeniable that various social issues have been treated differently by players, producers, and fans in different eras of the show.

AUDIENCE REACTION TO "POLITICAL" MOMENTS

There is a theory of media consumption called the Uses and Gratification Theory (UGT) which argues that media is a widely available product and while the media itself may be a static and stable creation, the individuals who make up the audience may have different purposes for seeking out and consuming that media. The exact same TV show viewed by different people will be received very differently.

UGT emerged in the 1940s when radio became the first mass medium that was simultaneously consumed in houses across the United States. It has been revisited as additional mediums of mass media have become prominent, like television and social media. While there were previous examples of mass-produced entertainment—newspapers, dime novels, and film for example—with radio the same media was available to be consumed simultaneously by a massive audience in ways that had never been seen before in any culture. UGT shifts focus away from the purposes of producers of media or the content of the media itself and onto the consumers of the media. UGT centers the agency of media consumers. The audience is not passively letting radio or television wash over them, but are actively seeking out certain types of media to fulfill their individual needs or wants. UGT focuses on how audiences use the media they consume more than how the media affects the audience.[23] In 1973, Elihu Katx, Hassah Haas, and Michael Gurevitch published "On the Use of Mass Media for Important Things" which argued that there are five different psychological needs that are gratified through media consumption: (1) Cognitive needs (educational), (2) Affective needs (aesthetic or emotional experience), (3) Integrative needs (understanding oneself or society through media models), (4) Social integrative needs (strengthening relationships through shared media), and (5) Tension-release needs (relaxation and escape).[24] When talking about *Survivor* and audience reactions, a viewer's negative response may come about because the particular psychological need they expected to be gratified by the show was not met. If a viewer turned on the thirteenth episode of *Marquesas* for a Tension-release need and watched a tense discussion about race between Paschal English, Sean Rector, and Vecepia Towery, that viewer may not feel like the episode was fulfilling the purpose they had for watching it.

The audience of *Survivor* is not a monolith, there are many varied reactions to every episode that airs. There is a portion of the audience who seem to argue that popular culture doesn't feel escapist if it is addressing issues of identity. On February 20, 2020, Matt Liguori, who has written blogs and podcasted about reality TV, tweeted out, "We're currently on a streak of 9 consecutive women getting their torch snuffed."[25] This was a voting streak that bridged *Island of the Idols* (season 39, 2019) and *Winners at War* (season 40, 2020). Former *Survivor* castaway Dan "Wardog" DaSilva responded, "Analyzing the best reality show on TV through the lens of gender is tiresome."[26] Choosing to not engage with issues like gender dynamics on a reality show is absolutely a valid way to watch television. Viewers can passively consume entertainment if they wish and there is value in using popular culture to check out from the stresses of life and recharge.

But when Jeff Probst constantly refers to *Survivor* as "one of the greatest social experiments ever created,"[27] his comment suggests that the show should be scrutinized in exactly the way Liguori did. When seasons begin by dividing the contestants according to age (*Panama*; *Nicaragua*; *Millennials vs. Gen X*), gender (*The Amazon*; *Vanuatu*; *Panama*; *One World*), occupation (*Worlds Apart*), or race (*Cook Islands*), the producers are inviting both the contestants and viewers to think about specific social identifiers. The producers have an implicit intent, but a portion of the fandom voices their explicit wish to avoid that intent. In 2020, CBS announced that all reality shows would feature at least 50 percent Black, Indigenous, and Other People of Color (BIPOC) representation in their casts. Christina S. Walker published an academic paper analyzing online responses to the first season of *Survivor* that aired after this initiative, and concluded that, "For many, this [initiative] was a step in the right direction. However, it also led to dissension and fallout amongst audiences. . . . Social media posts were often negative and critical."[28] CBS explained their intention to address a poor track record in terms of diversity in their casting, and some fans vocalized a negative reaction to this change.

Analyzing any TV show through the lens of gender (or race or age or sexuality) can indeed be tiresome, as Wardog noted. It requires earnest engagement rather than passive consumption. It can make you aware of implicit prejudices and biases that it is more comfortable to ignore. But putting in that work yields insights that would otherwise escape us. The entertainment and media we consume does inevitably have an effect on our worldview, our perceptions of others, and our sense of what the status quo for normal behavior is. Academic M. Brielle Harbin notes that, "Over six decades of research on cultivation theory has demonstrated that exposure to mass communications can influence the way that individuals perceive the world around them."[29] Cultivation theory argues that consumption of media, particularly regular television viewing, affects our perception of the real world. The content of our escapist entertainment can and does influence the individual viewer, which in turn has a real world impact. Doing a deep analysis denies us the option of passively consuming material without interrogating its implicit messages. However, when viewers seek the show for Tension-release gratification, they may offer criticisms when they feel that need is no longer being met. Among the social media posts about *41* (season 41, 2021) identified in Walker's study included posts like, "I watch this show for entertainment. It no longer is" or "I don't need a lesson on race relations or civics when I just want to be entertained" or "CBS has decided to turn it into a politically correct, race-driven series. . . . This is supposed to be an entertaining game, not a platform for political agendas."[30]

On occasions when moments from *Survivor* spark a larger cultural conversation, producers often capitalize on the press generated. This is particularly done when what occurs is perceived as having a positive outcome. *Survivor* is telling a story, and when the villain is voted out it's easy for fans and commentators to feel like justice has been served. Some sense of the moral scales being balanced provides a satisfying conclusion to a moment that provided heightened emotions. If a player makes statements at Tribal Council that are perceived as homophobic and gets voted out at that same Tribal Council, the emotional denouement is immediate for the viewer, as happens in the second episode of *Nicaragua*. But the storytellers in these instances are real people trying to win a million dollars, not writers trying to craft a satisfactory narrative. When the perceived villain survives one more week after a controversial moment, fan backlash can be swift and overwhelming.

Island of the Idols is seared into many fans' memories as the worst season of the show because of how the show handled issues of sexual harassment and inappropriate touching by Dan Spilo. But before the incidents with

Spilo completely took over discourse around *Island of the Idols*, there was an episode with a potentially racially charged exchange between Jamal Shipman and Jack Nichting. Jack had referred to Jamal's buff—the stretchy and adaptable piece of fabric that serves as the visual cue for tribe identity—as a durag. Jamal explained to Jack why that was a loaded term, and Jack was willing to listen and learn. They had a very open, honest, and in-depth conversation about race, stereotypes, and unconscious bias. Jamal explained,

> I can understand why someone might think, what's the big deal? Don't black men wear durags? The problem with it is the image that probably a lot of white America has about black men is the thug, the deadbeat father, the leech on social services, which is often, unfortunately, people wearing durags, tattoos, wife beaters, right? So this whole caricature is so ingrained in our culture, and so comfortable for mainstream white America to digest about the black male body, that for a sweet, well-intentioned boy like Jack, it flows off the tongue.[31]

Jack was very receptive to Jamal's feedback, and the entire episode was informative for audiences.

Production seemed eager to promote this scene as an important moment, with Probst stating in an interview,

> I rank it up there with the most compelling moments we've ever had on the show. A moment that in the hands of two other people could have led to more strife or an argument or hurt feelings, but in the hands of Jamal Shipman and Jack Nichting became a real teachable moment.[32]

This episode received positive responses from critics. Andy Dehnart wrote, "We need more of this: more conversations about the kind of ideas and biases that affect the actual game, and more conversations that give us deeper understanding of the people playing that game and what they must deal with, inside the game and out."[33] While Probst was happy with this teachable moment, the same season provides perhaps the most striking example of a negative controversy that rocked the show.

From the first episode of *Island of the Idols*, Kellee Kim voiced discomfort with how fellow contestant Spilo touched her and other women. During one confessional from Kellee, a producer's voice is heard from off-camera—a first in the history of the show—telling Kellee that if she thinks anything needs to be done about Spilo, she can "come to me and I will make it stop."[34] As TV critic Caroline Framke correctly points out, this is "a fine offer on the face of it, but one that ignores the fact that [Kellee] Kim was already doing as much in that very confessional."[35] Spilo's behavior became entangled with other player's strategy, as some players used Kellee's discomfort to make others believe they would align to vote Spilo out. Then those players blindsided Kellee and her allies, voting her out of the game.[36]

Near the end of the season, Spilo was pulled from the game unexpectedly, with no context provided to viewers during the episode that it occurred. At the end of the twelfth episode a black title card with white text appeared on-screen, informing viewers that "Dan was removed from the game after a report of another incident, which happened off-camera and did not involve a player."[37] Fans were, naturally, curious about what happened, but CBS and *Survivor* producers refused to say more. Probst simply said, "I've endeavored to be as forthcoming as possible with you regarding everything that has happened this season. In this situation, out of respect for privacy and confidentiality, I can't say anymore."[38] Writing for *People*, Steve Helling reported that after a challenge while getting into the boat that would transport the players back to camp, "Spilo allegedly touched" the leg of a woman on the crew. Spilo "insisted that the contact was inadvertent and accidental as he lost his balance while trying to get into the boat" but "the show's production team wasn't convinced that the contact was merely incidental. After consulting with the show's legal team, producers removed him from the show."[39] This is the first time a player was removed from the show for their behavior. Even when Brandon Hantz left the show in the fifth episode of *Caramoan* (season 26, 2013) due to his erratic behavior, there was an informal vote from his tribe to indicate they unanimously voted him out.

While the *Island of the Idols* had some excellent cast members and good gameplay, the inappropriate touching and what many deemed to be an insufficient response from producers overshadowed everything. After the episode in which Spilo was pulled from the game aired, he released a statement,

> I am deeply sorry for how my actions affected Kellee during the taping of this season of Survivor. . . . After apologizing at the Tribal Council when I first learned that Kellee still felt uncomfortable, I want to make sure I do so again, clearly and unambiguously. I truly regret that anyone was made to feel uncomfortable by my behavior. . . . In my life, I have always tried to treat others with decency, integrity and kindness. I can only hope that my actions in the future can help me to make amends and show me to be the kind of father, husband, colleague and friend that I always aim to be.[40]

Production would change the usual live finale of the season to a pre-taped finale. Kellee was given an extensive segment to discuss her experience and advocate for change. Probst announced that changes were going to be implemented in all future seasons of the show. Writing for *Variety*, Elaine Low reported that,

> Among the changes CBS is making, the company is adding an "on-site professional" to offer confidential means of reporting concerns, an "enhanced" preproduction orientation with anti-harassment, unconscious bias and sensitivity training for the cast, producers and production crew, and a new rule barring "unwelcome physical contact, sexual harassment and impermissible biases."[41]

Writer and podcaster Riley McAtee called it "the biggest crisis in the show's 20-year history."[42] While it is true that the handling of this incident leaves much to be desired, one thing that does stand out is how much has changed in society while *Survivor* has been on the air.

Regarding this season, TV critic David Bauder criticized CBS for fumbling a "#MeToo-era issue,"[43] but there is a problem with framing the season this way. *Island of the Idols* was not the first *Survivor* season with issues of sexual harassment. What had changed with the #MeToo-era was the response to the issue, not the existence of the issue. The #MeToo movement began in 2017, when Ashley Judd accused Harvey Weinstein of sexual harassment and then Alyssa Milano tweeted "If you've been sexually harassed or assaulted write 'me too' as a reply to this tweet." This tweet has been credited with starting a movement in which previously untouchable men faced consequences for their treatment of women.[44] The way that society addressed, considered, and reacted to sexual harassment and the objectification of women has been markedly different since the #MeToo movement. As Laura Bradley explains in a *Variety* article after producers removed Spilo from the game,

> The issue has hummed in the background of the season, seemingly bound to resurface in a bigger way—and when it did on Wednesday's episode, it got entangled with game strategy in a way that darkly mirrors the way these accusations can sometimes play out in the real world. For those who watch a lot of reality TV, the entire episode likely felt a little familiar—because more and more programs have begun publicly grappling with on-set issues just like this one, as the genre's viewers and contestants alike become more vocal about boundaries in the wake of #MeToo. And more often than not, these shows don't seem quite sure how to handle them.[45]

It is hard to cover all of the negative feedback that came at the show during this season. Scott D. Pierce, a well-known television critic wrote a column contending that "CBS and 'Survivor' failed [Kellee Kim], and failed all women. And Probst's promises that he and the production team have learned from this season ring hollow—they failed to act for weeks." Pierce also argued that Probst and other high level executives needed to be fired, stating, "at this point, heads should roll. The current management of the series—Probst is both host and showrunner—needs to be replaced, along with the network executives who signed off on a series of bad decisions."[46] After the season aired and the backlash was in full force, CBS issued this statement:

> Season 39 of *Survivor* has been unprecedented for all of us, with important social issues and inappropriate individual behavior intersecting with game play in complex ways that we've never seen before. During the course of the production, we listened to the players intently, investigated responsibly and responded accordingly, including taking the unprecedented step of removing a player from the game. At the same time, we are responsible for the final outcome of this season. We recognize there are things we could have done differently, and we are determined to do better going forward.[47]

Unfortunately, what happened isn't entirely unprecedented, just the public outcry was.

The demarcation of reaction can be seen in how earlier incidents in *Survivor*'s history were treated. Leigh Oleszczak said while writing about *Island of the Idols*, "*Survivor* has had uncomfortable moments like this in years past, but this was different from past events. We live in a society now where people are finally starting to realize that women go through this type of stuff every day, and a lot of the time, their stories aren't taken seriously."[48] That history goes back to the first season.

In *Borneo* (season 1, 2000), Richard wandered around naked and other players voiced discomfort with this. We hear Jenna Lewis say that when Hatch approached her "and sits like two inches from me, naked, I wanted to get away." This is accompanied by video of the moment, and Jenna is visibly uncomfortable with Richard's nudity and proximity to her. In the same episode, Richard gives a confessional where he says, "Colleen was particularly uncomfortable with my nakedness and when she saw me naked, she just made a funny face and put her hands over her face and who knows what that's intended to signal?"[49] Richard is being willfully obtuse here, as there is little doubt what Colleen wanted to signal. Richard's nudity was absolutely a conversation topic on the island and off, but the conversation was not about whether Richard's nudity constituted any form of sexual harassment. Richard's nudity was a memorable calling card that the show used to generate buzz.

Television critic Joyce Millman begins her 2001 review of *The Australian Outback* (season 2, 2001) with "Ah, you never forget your first fat naked gay guy."[50] She writes this even though *The Australian Outback* does not feature a nudist in the cast wandering around. But sex sells and a reference to a "fat naked gay guy" grabs attention. The association with *Survivor* and nudity remained strong after the first season, and would reappear occasionally throughout its run. While promoting the upcoming *All-Stars* season in 2004, *TV Guide*'s headline was "Three Tribes, 18 Seasoned Players, and Rich Is *Still* Naked."[51] That was seven seasons after Richard had first walked the beach, and the headline writer still called back to his penchant for nudity.

There is transgressive buzz around nudity and later reality shows centered the idea of nude players into the title and premise of their shows. In 2013, the Discovery Channel began airing *Naked and Afraid* (2013–present), in which survivalists are left with no clothes in inhospitable environments and must find food and shelter. Other cable channels began airing their own versions of "Naked" shows. In 2013, TLC aired the short-lived *Buying Naked*—in which a realtor tries to sell homes in clothing optional communities—and from 2014–2016 VH1 aired three seasons of *Dating Naked*—similar to *The Bachelor* but with nude contestants. Entire teams of editors have a day job of blurring out breasts and genitalia in these shows. John Koblin wrote a *New York Times* article about the team that edits *Naked and Afraid* and reports that they refer to themselves as the "Blur Man Group" and must go through various notes that include "Boobs blur insufficient" and "More opaque crotch blur" before an episode is ready for air.[52]

In 2013, an *Atlantic* article by James Parker examines why some shows have embraced nudity. "Awkwardness, things jiggling or flapping, the possibility of sex, privacy undone, the prying lens—reality TV has always thrived on these elements. So ask not 'Why is everybody suddenly naked?' Ask instead 'What took them so long?'"[53] After the #MeToo movement, the answer to that question for many reality TV producers was, "Oh. That's why." While the twenty-teens saw a wave of shows that embraced nudity more than ever before, *Survivor* has actually reversed course on nudity. While promoting season 40, Probst revealed that castaways will no longer be allowed to wander around nude on the island. "Today it wouldn't get past our producers for half of a second. . . . It speaks to the fact that 'Survivor' is always of the moment." In a likely reference to the #MeToo movement, Probst added, "whatever is happening in the culture is what's happening. No one thought anything in that first season, other than it was not that attractive to look at."[54] Of course it's not true that "no one thought anything" about Richard's nudity. Jenna and Colleen and other players shared their thoughts.

It's much more true to say that "Nobody thought anything about the women's discomfort." Richard's penchant for nudity is one of the worst parts of his strategic game. When the finale came down to a single vote, anything that bothered jury members could have cost him a million dollars.

In *Thailand* (season 5, 2022) a portion of the pre-merge story becomes dominated by Ghandia Johnson accusing another player, Ted Rogers Jr., of grinding against her in the night. This incident, which was first discussed in the third episode, was heavily promoted by CBS as a source of drama. A *USA Today* article notes that "In promo after promo, we've been promised an evening of escalating tension, capped by Ghandia repeating her now infamous accusation, 'He was grinding against me.'"[55] Viewer reaction was incredibly negative toward Ghandia. After ten seasons of *Survivor* had aired, Christopher J. Wright published a book about *Survivor* and included results of extensive polling done with fans of the show. Included was an "adjusted audience attitude index" which ranked all the players who had appeared on the show. Ghandia was ranked 149th out of 150, only Osten Taylor (who was the first player to quit the game) was ranked lower.[56] The headline for *Entertainment Weekly*'s article about Ghandia being voted out reads, "Why Ghandia should change her name to Gone-dia—The 'Denver Diva' has no one to blame but herself for her ouster in this week's sorta spiritless episode." In the article, Dalton Ross admits not being certain of what to make of the situation between Ghandia and Ted, but adds, "Even if you remove "Survivor"'s first sexual scandal, Ghandia still by almost all measures played a pretty horrible game."[57] It's a big ask for a player to separate out sexual harassment and focus on gameplay.

Even when there were months to process the incident, the way it was handled at the reunion is shocking by today's standards. Probst begins the segment of the reunion by saying nothing this season "raised more eyebrows or spawned more watercooler talk than the incident with Ted and Ghandia." Probst then grills Ghandia and asks if she encouraged Ted, and then highlights how the situation affected Ted's wife and Ghandia's husband. In the end, after the questioning from Probst, Ghandia says that she wishes she could "take back" hurting her husband and take back "hurting Ted and his family and his wife. You know, if I had a magic wand, I'd take it all away, that whole incident."[58] The framing of the entire incident places blame on Ghandia and no responsibility is assigned to Ted. In 2021, Ghandia appeared on a podcast with Rob Cesternino and opened up about the entire experience. She said that what happened with Ted was "one of the worst things that has ever happened to me in my whole entire life" and that how it was presented on television was "like getting slapped in the face over and over."[59]

Another incident occurs in *All-Stars* (season 8, 2004). Richard Hatch competed in multiple challenges completely nude. A challenge during the fifth episode requires players to pass by each other in close proximity. While crossing paths at a cross section of the planks Richard appears to rub his nude body against Sue Hawk, a player he knew well from their time together during *Borneo*. He clearly says, "Want some? You want some, honey?" as he appears to move his hips. The incident was only passingly addressed in the moment. Sitting from his viewing perch, Probst scolds Richard, saying, "Come on, guys. No one cares about that stuff." and Sue yells back, "Yeah we don't, Richard." From his point of view, Probst did not have the line of sight to see Rich appearing to rub up against Sue. Nothing else was said of the moment in the episode other than Sue saying, "I hope they vote Richard off 'cause what did to me was absolutely . . . that was disgusting."[60] Later in the episode Richard was voted out of his tribe for being considered a threat in the game. From the footage included in the episode, the incident with Sue never came up among his tribe.

In the next episode, the audience is shown Sue experiencing a much stronger emotional reaction. Having processed what happened, she is clearly shaken. Sue would later look back and explain, "That evening, when I had time to be by myself, I just kept reliving the incident. It just kept eating into me more and more like a cancer."[61] The next day, before a scheduled challenge, Probst says, "Before we get to today's challenge, I want to address something that happened yesterday. Richard Hatch, sort of being inappropriate. . . ." That phrasing of "sort of" will set Sue off. She responds, starting quietly but with emotion building, as Probst occasionally tries to unsuccessfully interject,

> *Sort of*, yeah. I was sexually violated. To have some guy come up . . . he passed a half dozen people on platforms and never touched them. And it went too far and he crossed the line, and he crossed the line with me. Okay, I know you don't know, and you didn't see it because his back was to you and he's too big of a [censored] slob to see around. I was violated, humiliated, dehumanized and totally spent, Jeff. It wasn't *"sort of,"* Jeff 'cause his back was to you, Jeff. That's all I'm saying and I'm [censored] spent. And I'm done with this [censored] game. There's no way I can continue with my emotions pushed to the ground that much.[62]

At Sue's request, a boat is called, and she leaves the game. After Sue quits, there is a brief acknowledgment that it's been an "odd" few days, but as a group, everyone seems to want to move on as quickly as possible. Colby Donaldson says, "Let's get back to some normalcy."

Richard, for his part, insists that CBS is at fault, that Sue "violated his space"[63] and that CBS edited the material to make him look as bad as possible. It is unknown how Sue and CBS handled things after she left the island. She did participate in the reunion show (with Rob Cesternino slid in between her and Richard even though everyone else was seated in the order they left the show). During press, Sue said, "I did consider, like, a lawsuit when it first occurred," and she further explained, "I decided I needed not to do something on that move, because that's emotionally draining also. And I decided to move forward, and CBS has been real nice about helping to deal with the situation."[64] This stands as one example of how social reactions have changed considerably. In the episode where Sue Hawk leaves, production seems uncertain what tone to strike, and largely portrays her as overly emotional and many of her tribemates as relieved that she is gone. If this were to air today, it is easy to imagine a much more sympathetic reaction toward Sue, as evidenced by the reception of Kellee Kim after *Island of the Idols* aired. She was in a high-tension moment with cameras rolling and a million-dollar prize on the line and spoke up for herself.

After this incident, there are still many examples of players choosing to be nude on *Survivor*, even during wrestling challenges. No lesson seems to have been learned until *Island of the Idols* and then new safety protocols that were put in place at that point. While it is impossible to know how hands-on CBS executive Les Moonves was in terms of the framing of these earlier incidents, it is worth noting that in 2018 Moonves was removed from his position as CEO at CBS due to sexual misconduct allegations.[65] Moonves was also denied a $120 million severance package in a decision that "capped the downfall of one of television's most influential figures, the biggest entertainment powerbroker to see his career derailed amid the #MeToo movement against sexual misconduct." While Moonves denies the accusations, there were "allegations from women who said he subjected them to mistreatment including forced oral sex, groping and retaliation if they resisted."[66] A man in a position of power who has been accused of abusing that power to mistreat women could have a vested interest in influencing how women's accusations of sexual harassment were presented. Such a man may wish to minimize the validity of women's claims and portray them as unserious emotional outbursts.

Sexual harassment should never happen, and it should certainly not be the responsibility of players to address it if it does occur. While producers do air these uncomfortable moments—some individual votes or even season-long storylines often would not make sense without such context—these incidents are not highlights for the show. We have direct evidence that the producers of the series do not consider these types of moments to be celebrated, because there were official hour-long highlight packages produced prior to the twentieth and fortieth seasons of the show. These specials highlighted dramatic gameplay far more than social aspects of the game. There are undeniably many factors that affect what is selected for an hour-long retrospective. Big dramatic finishes as challenges come down to the wire, or a reveal of a hidden immunity idol can be chopped up into ten-second highlights and packaged together as part of a montage much more easily.

Additionally, those specials were produced to be celebrations that reminded fans why they loved the series, not retrospectives that captured the lows as well as the highs of *Survivor*. Within the first minute of the special "*Survivor* at 40: Greatest Moments and Players," a clip of Oprah Winfrey can be heard intoning, "It was a social experiment made for TV that became a cultural phenomenon,"[67] but the highlighted elements mostly include the biggest players and the most surprising moments of gameplay. Personal attacks, problematic interpersonal interactions, and inappropriate moments were, understandably, not revisited. It was a necessary palate cleanser for fans to become excited about the series again, after the gross drudgery of watching *Island of the Idols*. Dalton Ross, in summing up *Island of the Idols*, said, "The ultimate feeling when it comes to this season is sadness. Watching *Survivor* should be fun! But nothing has seemed fun in light of the far more serious issue that clearly outweighed the final game result. Quite simply: It made the rest of the season impossible to enjoy." CBS used the anniversary special as a pivot point, shifting from the events of season thirty-nine to the fortieth season with beloved returning players.

Producers also notably exempted the first and most famous winner of the series, Richard Hatch, from *Winners at War*. While bringing the original winner—whose victory was one of the most-watched moments in television history—would make all the sense in the world from a promotional standpoint, Richard's history with Sue from *All-Stars* would bring up far too much baggage. Baggage of the type the show was desperate to leave behind after *Island of the Idols*. While there has never been a declarative statement from producers about why Richard was not invited back to *Winners at War*, Probst did say, "I didn't feel comfortable having him out on the show and representing a show that is for families."[68] Probst also added that in choosing which twenty winners would play in the fortieth season, "the bigger consideration was 'Where is the show now?' and 'Do these 20 winners represent the show today?' In that sense, we didn't feel that Rich fit into the equation."[69] In addition to the fallout from *All-Stars*, Richard spent fifty-one months in prison after being found guilty of tax evasion, in part due to "failing to report the money he had won in his 2000 tax return."[70]

With a show as long-running as *Survivor*, the earlier seasons will undoubtedly feel dated in many ways. The episodes are frozen in amber. What was once normalized behavior or an acceptable attitude may not be so twenty years later. New fans who discover the show and binge old seasons may find something to be controversial that wasn't when the season originally aired. *Survivor* is a constantly shifting product itself. Episodes from the forty-fifth season feel very different from seasons in the fifth season. Viewers cannot go back and view those episodes as they would have been seen twenty years ago, but also *Survivor* is not producing episodes like they were twenty years ago. Like society at large, *Survivor* is evolving and changing with the times.

CHAPTER 6

IDENTITY AND EVOLUTION

One inevitable facet of long-running entertainment is change. This can become one of the most fascinating parts of analyzing media, as what is produced and consumed both shapes and reflects society. What was considered standard in one decade may come to be considered problematic in another. Something that had not even been considered can become a new normal. How a production addresses issues of identity—in all its facets—is unlikely to remain static across time. Across multiple decades. *Survivor* has demonstrated the plasticity that makes entertainment so enlightening.

There is a field of analysis called New Historicism which attempts to explore the larger cultural network that is at work when a piece of literature or art or television is produced. In essence, the text—whatever it may be—is never created in a vacuum, but inherently is a construct of complex cultural networks that inform the final product. Closely reading or analyzing a text reveals assumptions, biases, ethics, ideals, fears, and other factors that informed the choices of the producer. With this type of analysis we can consider all the larger cultural factors that have influenced the text, rather than simply analyzing the text itself. There is a temptation to dismiss texts that are mass-produced entertainment as ephemera, as cultural detritus that will inevitably be forgotten. But that short-sightedness robs us of valuable insights into our cultural and social history. As Professor Peter Coon argues, the popular gives us insights into social history, political history, and the tastes of the culture at large.[1] Now that *Survivor* is into its third decade of popularity, it is possible to see evolution and change that reflects shifts in cultural norms and expectations.

In a 2024 podcast episode, Jeff Probst discussed why *Survivor* has
changed so much through the years. In his response, he cited changes in cultural attitudes that are reflected in the show itself. Probst explained,

> This gets overlooked, but *Survivor* has always been a reflection of our culture.
> If you go back and look at our last 23 years, you will see us reflected in every
> season. And you will see the shift and growth of our culture reflected in every
> season. Things that happened in those early seasons, they would never happen
> today. Things that are happening today, we couldn't have imagined happening
> 15 years ago.[2]

There are many facets of culture that have shifted in the decades *Survivor*
has aired, and the show itself is significantly different. Because *Survivor*
is heavily edited but entirely unscripted, that change can come from how
production presents the show or from how players act and speak. To highlight how both aspects are important in change, this chapter will examine
how foreign locales are framed for American viewers, a change that came
from production, and how issues of identity have been portrayed through
more than forty seasons, a change that has come from both players and
production.

CULTURAL EXOTICIZATION

Exoticization is a problematic trope wherein cultures and countries from
outside of the creator's and consumer's familiarity are presented as having
a heightened fantastical element. This increased "othering" of an unfamiliar
culture highlights difference, strangeness, and mystique. The scholars An
Kuppens and Jelle Mast write, "Being 'exotic' is not a quality inherent in
people or objects" and therefore "*exoticization* can be defined as the process
which produces the 'exotic'. More specifically, exoticization occurs in *discourse* about the Other, and in the *representation* of the Other."[3] *Survivor*
presents the "Other" of the local cultures in the descriptive language used to
describe the location, in the video images chosen to depict the culture, and in
the cultural interactions contestants experience.

When telling his own origin story with *Survivor*, Probst says, "I was
driving down the 101 freeway in Los Angeles. I heard this crazy British guy,
Mark Burnett, carrying on about this show called *Survivor*. And he didn't
give a lot of details, but it sounded exotic. It sounded far away."[4] If the allure
of the unknown is what piqued Probst's interest in becoming host of the
series, he clearly assumed it would interest fans as well. The language he

uses to tease new locations is replete with adjectives meant to convey a sense of the unfamiliar to American viewers.

Beginning with the first season, a macro-rhythm of production emerges. Air the season, host a reunion show, and then tease the next season. The exact nature of the reunion show has shifted through the years. Initially it was hosted by Bryant Gumble, then Rosie O'Donnell, and finally Probst took over. The reunion shows have served to recap the season and revisit the cast, but also allow the network to keep the audience invested in what would come next. A tease for the upcoming season has become a staple element of the reunion show. First, you let the audience look back at the season they enjoyed, then you invite them to look forward to what is next. A pattern of constant investment is created for the audience. In these teases, there are many examples of visual elements and verbal descriptions that exoticize the locales where the show has filmed. Similarly, until production settled into Fiji, *Survivor* seasons usually opened with a monologue from Probst that aired over footage of the location in which the season takes place. Examining the word choices in the teases and introductions for a season reveal language that highlights a sense of otherness about places outside the United States.

Wording that is used in several early seasons of the show captures a consistent tone used by production: "Mysterious Borneo."[5] "A land so vast, so remote, that large portions of it aren't even charted. Certainly majestic, stunning vistas, all sorts of exotic wildlife . . . a land that is really unlike any place on earth."[6] "A land of inherent dangers filled with exotic and deadly animals."[7] "A land virtually untouched by the modern world."[8] "The middle of the most remote place on earth."[9] "Home to some of the most exotic and dangerous sea life in the world."[10] "This fall, *Survivor* ventures into the mystical land of the ancient orient. . . . Far from civilization in the middle of the Andoman Seas, on a remote tropical rainforest . . . our survivors will be forced to work together to build a new world in an exotic land. . . . They will encounter an array of exotic wildlife."[11] "Exotic and deadly wildlife abound."[12] "One of the most mysterious places on earth."[13] "Without question, one of the most mysterious places on the planet." "In these Panamanian waters lurk some of the most exotic and dangerous marine animals anywhere in the Pacific Ocean."[14] All of these examples come from introductions and teases during the first seven seasons of the show. The word "exotic" is used seven times, essentially once for each season.

In the eighth season, *All-Stars* (2004), the focus is fully on the returning players, not the location, which is actually the same locale as the previous season's Pearl Islands in Panama. There is little exoticization in the promotion for this season of the show. But as the *All-Stars* season wrapped up and Probst began to promote season 9, the familiar exoticization begins anew. In the promo video of *Vanuatu* (2004), the monologue opens:

> In the remote waters of the South Pacific, near the tumultuous Ring of Fire, is an exotic land where ancient cultures thrive and nature makes its fury known. These are the islands of Vanuatu. In this land of volcanoes and ritual, sorcery is real, and the spirits of the dead are believed to have power over the living. More than 80 islands are home to over 100 languages and a diverse group of tribes and clans live out their history in today's world. Vanuatu is home to the famous land divers of Pentecost Island. Vanuatu is also a land with a fascinating history of cannibalism.[15]

The accompanying video footage would not look out of place in a King Kong film. References to cannibalism would recur in several seasons' openings. In *Fiji* (season 14, 2007), Probst's introduction would include flashing images of human skulls and scenery, while Probst says, "We are flying over the stunning water of the Fiji islands, a place once known for its cannibalism, uncharted reefs, and formidable warriors."[16]

When teasing *Guatemala* (season 11, 2005), Probst leaned into language about the lost wonders of Mayan civilization:

> These stunning cities of the past stand as clues to a mystery thousands of years old. While Europe was in the dark ages, it was the Maya who harnessed the knowledge of the stars and the celestial movements to create a mystical union of man, nature, and the gods. It was a world of great kings, elaborate ceremonies, fierce battles, and even human sacrifice. Eighteen survivors will be marooned within this mysterious and rugged terrain. For the first time the castaways will actually live within the ruins of a vanished civilization and they will be forced to embrace the ancient Maya lifestyle.[17]

During *Guatemala*'s season premiere, Probst used language about the animals that were present, too: "these jungles are home to exotic and dangerous wildlife—jaguars, poisonous snakes, and crocodiles that lurk in every body of water. It is an unforgiving environment, where extreme temperatures, high humidity, and torrential rainstorms bring even the strongest to their knees."[18]

One of the starkest examples of these descriptions comes in the introduction of *Gabon* (season 17, 2008). Over footage of skyscrapers, busy urban streets, a child on a bike delivering newspapers, a little league baseball game, a dad with a briefcase being hugged by children in front of a suburban home, and rural farm houses, Probst's voice narrates: "Every day, millions of Americans go about their familiar routines with friends and family in safe surroundings." Then, there is a CGI globe with a large yellow "USA" over North America that spins to reveal the same yellow font labeling the continent "Africa" as a red line connects from the USA to Gabon and Probst continues, "But this fall, 18 of them will be thrust into a land beyond their wildest imagination."[19] There are stock footage shots of gorillas roaring, dolphins leaping, hippos rising from the water, a native African performing a dance, a crocodile snapping its jaws, and an elephant trumpeting. Probst continues, as more shots of animals, uninhabited landscapes, and African tribal dances are presented in a video montage:

> This is Gabon, Earth's last Eden. Located in equatorial Africa, Gabon is one of the world's last remaining sanctuaries for pure, untouched wilderness. The culture of Gabon reflects the beauty of this ancient land, with rituals and dances as pure today as they were generations ago. Gabon is the only place on the planet where surfing hippos ride the waves and elephants roam with gorillas as leopards keep watch. 18 Americans will be caught in the midst of nature's fierce battle for survival as they live among some of the world's most dangerous animals.[20]

This video presents a point of view that contrasts the safe and familiar experiences of Americans with the wild and unknown existence that takes place in Gabon. Of note, the paperboy, little league players, and family shown in the footage to represent America are all white.

Survivor's fourth season was set to be in Jordan, but after 9/11 occurred filming in the Middle East was deemed logistically unfeasible. Producers quickly switched gears and Marquesas was chosen as the new location. Part of the allure of *Survivor* is the illusion of the contestants being in the middle of nowhere, and the presentation of that false reality is maintained at high cost. As reported by anthropologist Kathleen C. Riley, for *Marquesas* (season 4, 2002), a seventy-four-year-old man named Daniel's "house, dock and plumbing system were bulldozed to make the valley look uninhabited" and he was relocated to a prefab house provided by production.[21] The beaches where they filmed were used by local Marquesans, but production strove to make them appear completely uninhabited.

The Tribal Council sets are often meant to evoke ancient ruins, but are usually modern, freshly built sets. In *China* (season 15, 2007), production built a "three-story temple" that "took 57 workers seven weeks of 12-hour days in sweltering humidity to build. Not to mention 20 tons of steel framing, 8 tons of concrete and 400 sheets of timber shipped in from Russia and milled in Shanghai before being driven seven hours to the remote building site."[22] Elements for that set, like the marker used to cast a vote being modeled after an opium pipe or the dragon-shaped torch-snuffer, were chosen to evoke a sense of otherness for the American players.

The third season being called *Africa* is another example of framing that harkens back to the European and American concept of the unknown in Africa. The previous season had been called *The Australian Outback* to highlight that the players were not in the tourist-friendly, urbanized parts of Australia, but the entire continent of Africa stands in for the unknown and exotic in the third season. Production would return to the continent again for *Gabon*.

One recurring example of the exoticization in the early seasons that has largely disappeared is a challenge that production calls "Bug Off" but is more colloquially known as the "Gross Food Challenge." There are variations to this challenge—whether it's an individual or team challenge, whether the food is blended into a smoothie or just set on a plate, etc.—but the essence is always for American contestants to eat "native food" that is presented as gross, disgusting, and nearly inedible. The exact food itself varies, but Probst almost always introduces it with some form of the phrase "local delicacy" and insists that it is eaten regularly in the country where they are filming. Examples of this challenge include *Borneo* where they ate butok (bug larvae), *The Australian Outback* with a mangrove worm, *Africa* with a glass of cow's blood, *Marquesas* with farfaru (fermented fish), or *Thailand* with a tarantula.

There are versions of this challenge that are more problematic than others. In *Borneo*, when the finale of the challenge is to eat Balut (fertilized duck eggs that are boiled or steamed and eaten from the shell), it is pointed out over and over again how this is really eaten by the people here. This commentary explicitly others the people being referred to. There's a tone of "Can you believe there are people who eat this gross thing?" which ends up highlighting a sense of difference between the cultures. Acknowledging differences between cultures is not inherently problematic, but the gross food challenge implies a value judgment about the people who would eat the "gross" food as a delicacy. When they were filming in China, Probst says that the Chinese government had a representative who could look at their tapes to make sure "we were portraying China in a positive light." When they had a gross-food eating challenge, the representative said, "This is not gross, this is our normal everyday lunch" and Probst "had to explain that it's a cultural thing we (Americans) don't eat."[23]

In contrast, in *Samoa* (season 19, 2009), the gross food challenge featured Probst making raw seafood smoothies that players had to drink. There is no commentary about the food they have to eat being a delicacy from another country. The idea of drinking recently blended raw seafood mixed with salt water is stomach-churning by itself, and this variation avoids the problematic othering that was present in the previous incarnations. However, the series would return to the potentially insulting "local delicacy" version of the challenge when it was reused in *Caramoan* (season 26, 2013), *Blood vs. Water* (season 27, 2013), *Cambodia* (season 31, 2015), and *Ghost Island* (season 36, 2018), but has not been used since.

Another recurring, but not consistent, feature of *Survivor* is the opportunity to win a reward that includes local experts who come and teach the contestants how to live off the land. Sometimes these rewards result in a "noble savage" stereotype being perpetuated about the native people from wherever *Survivor* is filming that season. The noble savage is a character type from fiction that presents people with "less civilized" life experiences as being more in touch with nature than those who have been corrupted by modern life and civilization. While this may, on the surface, appear to be an example of a positive stereotype meant to ennoble people who had their lands colonized by Europeans, it does carry with it several problematic assumptions. The Noble Savage stereotype stands in contrast to the Brutal Savage stereotype, but as scholar Helen Gardner explains, both "are fantasies of the European mind that kept Indigenous peoples in a suspended state of either elevated purity or perpetual evil."[24] Both stereotypes serve as a type of "othering" that, historically, excused European and American colonization.

The exoticization of the locations where the show films and the people who live where they film has lessened as the series has aged. There are several possible reasons for this change. We know that the governments in some locales had concerns about how their land would be shown. For example, *China* begins with shots of skyscrapers and high-speed trains, and Probst saying the contestants "are beginning the adventure of a lifetime in ultramodern Shanghai. But as their journey continues, these sixteen strangers are being transported back in time."[25] It seems likely that a stipulation of filming in China was to show the modern city before filming the show away from urban infrastructures. If other countries expressed similar concerns about how the show represented their culture, producers may have become more careful through the years.

Additionally, creative choices may be different because the storytellers who produce, direct, and edit the show have changed. Yes, there are some of the crew who have worked on the show since day one, but with any show that runs for decades there will naturally be new voices who are brought in. Similarly, there could have been an evolution in how the producers wish to present the locales if they received criticism about exoticization and therefore altered how they presented the cultures of locations they visited.

Another factor may be that the series has become more reliant on twists and contestant identity rather than in location for marketing purposes. The focus of *Millennials vs. Gen X* (season 33, 2016) or *Winners at War* (season 40, 2020) is going to be very different from *The Amazon* (season 6, 2003).

A key aspect of exoticization is unfamiliarity, so as the shooting location becomes more familiar to viewers, the presentation of "the other" is less likely. The series settled into a production schedule that included filming in the same location for back-to-back seasons starting with season 19 in order to save money. But the series truly settled into one consistent location beginning with season 33. When the same location is used and has become familiar to the audience, the sense of the strange unknown that is part of exoticization is inevitably dulled. As academic Tzvetan Todorov explains, "The best candidates for the role of exotic ideal are the peoples and cultures that are most remote from us and least known to us. . . . Knowledge is incompatible with exoticism."[26] In using the same shooting locations, the producers—most likely unintentionally—lessened the exoticization of the setting for the show. The marketing for the earlier seasons was heavily rooted in where the survivors would be playing, and the producers leaned into presentational elements and word choices that highlighted how different those locations were than what American viewers would be most familiar with. Through the forty-six seasons that have aired at the time of this writing, the level of exoticization on display has diminished considerably.

ISSUES OF IDENTITY

Maryanne Oketch, who won season 42 of *Survivor*, gave an eloquent speech during a memorable tribal council. Speaking about the experiences of players of color on the show, Maryanne said, "We all technically have a 1 in 18 shot for a million, but because we all come with our burdens and . . . privileges, that 1 in 18 might be bigger or smaller for some people."[27] While anyone who is familiar with a concept like unconscious bias combined with the fact that *Survivor* has cast far more White contestants than contestants of color could likely intuit that Maryanne is correct, there have been several studies that objectively confirm Maryanne's assertion. Erin O'Mara Kunz, Jennifer L. Howell, and Nicole Beasley published a study titled "*Surviving* Racism and Sexism: What Votes in the Television Program *Survivor* Reveal About Discrimination." This article analyzed all the first forty seasons of *Survivor* and considered every vote that took place. Their statistical analysis—which was far more in depth than simply tracking who was voted out first—concluded that Black, Indigenous, and People of Color (BIPOC) women were "voted off the show significantly earlier than White women and male contestants, and White men [lasted] significantly longer than White women and BIPOC contestants."[28]

Of note, this study only analyzes the first forty seasons of *Survivor*. In that era, almost three-quarters of all participants were White. In several seasons, there was only one player of color on a starting tribe, which immediately created an out-group dynamic. In 2020, George Cheeks—"CBS's first Black, biracial, and gay president"[29]—announced a massive change that would occur before season 41. Beginning with the 2021–2022 seasons, CBS would aim to "diversify its unscripted shows by setting a target to make the casts of all such shows at least 50% Black, Indigenous, and People of Color (BIPOC)."[30] This followed requests from the Black Survivor Alliance, a group of former players who had specific concerns with *Survivor*. Ramona Amaro, who appeared on *Borneo* and was concerned that her portrayal made her "one of the first Black people stereotyped by *Survivor*," was part of the group who made specific requests to CBS and *Survivor* producers. These included,

> Hire more people of color to work behind the scenes as casting executives, editors and producers to improve portrayals. Enforce a zero tolerance policy for racist acts. Avoid creating storylines for non-white contestants that play to racial stereotypes. And issue a public statement acknowledging systemic racism in the franchise, with a concrete plan for addressing it.[31]

Including a more diverse group behind the scenes is important, as many players of color feel that their stories are marginalized because the people who edit, package, and tell the story are not diverse enough.[32] Producers who are from similar backgrounds and experiences may lean into tropes and stereotypes they are familiar with, even if it is unintentional and not meant to be harmful.

Increasing diversity in terms of the players is also important. Julia Carter, who played on *Edge of Extinction* (season 38, 2019), wrote in detail about her *Survivor* experience. She was the only player of color on her initial tribe nine-member tribe. She revealed that on her first day on the island, one of her white castmates used the n-word when quoting a movie. She recounts her reaction: "'Wow,' I thought. On day one, really? A social game, and we're out here dropping racial slurs?" Julia continues, " I did not think I was going to have to hit the beach and fight against racism and bias. I do that enough in my daily life." She goes on to explain that the word was said again soon after, as the same player quoted an episode of *South Park*. At that point, Julia's fellow contestant, Ron Clark, told the player that they could not say that word. Julia further recounts that she then noted "repeated instances of racial slurs and negative racial references being used at camp. The tribe ended up having a very healthy dialogue about race, each person contributing a different perspective."[33] While none of that made it on air, it added to Julia's burden as a player. This not only affected her experience; it likely affected her ability to play the game. Beginning a season as a clear social outlier due to race was a position unique to Julia compared to her tribemates. Seasons that include a more diverse starting position shift that position considerably.

While the likelihood of a player may experience conscious or unconscious bias based on their race increases when they are in the minority, there is also a different burden they may place upon themselves. Cheeks notes that "contestants felt pressure to represent entire races because they were the only people of color in the cast."[34] Increasing diversity can help to relieve external and internal pressure on players of color.

As a result of the Diversity Initiative from CBS, all the casts from season 41 onward have been notably racially diverse. Of significance, the two most diverse previous seasons of the show were *Cook Islands* (season 13, 2006), which saw Yul Kwon become the first Asian American winner in the show's history, and *Fiji*, which saw Earl Cole become the first African American man to win the show. At the time of this writing, there have been six seasons that followed the casting initiative. Four of the six winners have been BIPOC, including Erika Casupanan—the first player of Filipino descent to win, Maryanne Oketch—the second Black woman to win the show, Yamil "Yam Yam" Arocho—the first Puerto Rican to win the show, and Dee Valladares—the first player with Cuban ancestry win.

Probst is excited about the change that has come about in this new era. He declared that the order from CBS "will go down as one of the most positive and significant changes ever in 'Survivor.'"[35] One of the strengths of the seasons that have come after the break in filming that resulted from COVID has been the casting. Excellent players from more diverse backgrounds have brought exciting gameplay to the island.

One area where *Survivor* may have felt ahead of its time in representation was in terms of LGBTQ+ identity. The first season was groundbreaking for its representation of homosexuality on broadcast television in the year 2000. Homosexuality had been addressed on broadcast television before. For example, 1982's "Boys in the Bar" episode of *Cheers* (1982–1993) won accolades from GLAAD for how Sam and Diane support a former baseball player coming out of the closet, but the same episode portrays Norm and Cliff as homophobic. Later in the series, Norm will comfortably pretend to be gay in order to secure work as an interior designer, a secret talent of his. In the 1990s, *Frasier* (1993–2004) would use homosexual characters to transform love triangles into quadrangles or more complex shapes in farcical fashion. But those *Frasier* storylines were most often contained to single episodes. Series that centered homosexual characters in the late 1990s include *Ellen* (1994–1998), which saw the titular character played by Ellen DeGeneres come out in 1997, and 1998's *Will & Grace* (1998–2006) on NBC. Nonetheless, it could still be controversial to even acknowledge homosexuality on television. A reality TV show with a gay player talking about themselves is inherently different than a pre-written performance by an actor on a sitcom. *Survivor* was reaching a different audience than adult-targeted sitcoms and had an inherently different tone in how Richard Hatch discussed his life. On the one hand, the unlikely friendship between an elderly no-nonsense army veteran and a proudly gay business consultant was a highlight of season one. Rudy Boesch, the seventy-two-year-old veteran, was shown saying homophobic things that were received with a general tone of "how lovably out of touch the old guy is." When Richard Hatch won the first season of *Survivor* it clearly established that a member of the LGBTQ+ community could win a million dollars in a contest that came down to votes from peers who had played the game.

Richard is an indelible part of pop culture history. He won $1 million at a time when a prize of that magnitude was a shocking amount, and he did it on one of the most watched events of this century. A gay man was presented somewhat nefariously, but also his homosexuality was presented as a matter of fact. There was even an exchange where he made clear it was not a choice, but part of his inherent makeup. It may feel trite to say this decades later, but at the time this was a significant step in representation on television.

Changes in how homosexuality is perceived were highlighted in *Millennials vs. Gen X*. In the season, Zeke Smith is part of the millennials tribe and an out and proud gay man. Bret LaBele is a part of the Gen X tribe and is a police officer from Boston. In what Dalton Ross calls "one of the most unexpectedly delightful moments in the history of *Survivor*," Bret and Zeke have a one-on-one conversation during a reward. "Bret LaBelle—a loud, beer-drinking, sports-loving police officer who at first blush appeared to be a seemingly stereotypical bro's bro" leans over to Zeke and reveals he is also gay. Bret calls this his proudest moment on the show:

It was a long time coming. I had an internal struggle with myself with coming out and being gay for years. When I mentioned it on the show, it was like a huge weight off my shoulders, and I found that it really helped me in my personal life going forward. The support I received from family, friends, and co-workers was amazing. I wish I had come out sooner.[36]

In the episode, Bret explains that he hadn't told his tribe because they were "a big macho group." Zeke says, "I never thought about not saying anything" and Bret replies, "I've lived with not saying anything."[37] Bret, who was not out to everyone in his life, has said he received an outpouring of messages and "still gets messages about it to this day."[38] It is hugely important to note that Bret Labelle chose the moment to come out, knowing what it would mean for his game and also his personal life back home. There is a massive difference between Bret coming out and what will happen the very next season when Jeff Varner will choose to out Zeke as transgender. Varner was a popular three-time contestant whose final tribal council forever changed his reputation. The thirty-fourth season, *Game Changers* (2017), featured entirely returning players as contestants. Varner had originally appeared in *The Australian Outback*, and in *Cambodia* (season 31, 2015) as well. In both those previous seasons, he just missed making the merge and becoming, at the very least, a member of the jury. In *Game Changers*, as the merge neared, Varner was clearly in danger of being voted out, which may be why he pursued such a desperate course of action to attempt to stay within the game.

At tribal council, Varner announced, "There is deception going on right here, and you guys are the victims of it." Varner continued telling Probst, "Deceptions on levels, Jeff, that these guys don't even understand." When Probst prompts Varner to continue, Varner turns to Zeke and says, "Why have you not told anyone you're transgender?" There is a pause, and shots of various players looking shocked and uncomfortable, and then Varner continues, "What I'm showing is a deception." Then every other player at tribal—Andrea Boehlke, Ozzy Lusth, Tai Trang, Debbie Wanner, and Sarah Lacina—turns on Varner and condemn what he has just done. Varner attempts to defend himself, saying, "I argue for the rights of transgender people every day in the state of North Carolina. I would never say or do anything to hurt anyone here. Jeff, I'm arguing for my life. I feel like I've got to throw everything at the wall."[39]

Varner has argued that his actions at Tribal Council were misperceived. The deception he was referring to, Varner claims, was a secret alliance between Zeke, Ozzy, and Andrea, not Zeke's personal identity. In an interview after the episode aired, Varner said, "So when I go back to camp and am talking to everyone about deception, I wasn't thinking at all about trans. . . . I was arguing to everyone at tribal that there was this secret alliance and that they were all being deceived."[40] While it is true that the Tribal Council we consume at home is a heavily edited and condensed version of a much longer affair that occurs on the island, the reactions we see in the moment do not conform with Varner's telling. It is clear that Probst and the other players are equating Varner's accusations of deceptions with Zeke's transgender identity. Probst and Varner have an exchange about this.

Probst: When you say by revealing that Zeke is transgender, you're proving that he's deceptive . . .

Varner: I'm not saying, Jeff, that transgender people are deceptive.

Probst: No, you're saying by him not revealing it that he's capable of deception. That is a giant leap of logic.

Varner tries to say that he assumed Zeke was out and proud about being transgender, but Probst argues that essentially "either you can say he's out and it's okay, or you can say it's deception, but it can't be both."[41] Probst confers with all the other players at tribal council stating, "I think I know the answer to this question, but there's no question who's going home tonight, right?" After the players give verbal agreement, Probst says, "We don't need to vote. Just grab your torch. Varner, the tribe has spoken. Time for you to go." In his final words, when contestants who have been eliminated provide a monologue to camera, an emotional Varner said through tears:

I don't even know what I was thinking. It was a horrible move. It was me wrapped up in this game trying to do everything I possibly could, but nobody on the planet should do what I did tonight. Ever. And I'm so sorry to anyone I offended, especially Zeke and his family and his friends. I can't even talk. I'm sorry.[42]

After the episode aired, Varner was understandably vilified. With months of reflection to prepare for the airing of the episode he wrote, "Until I die, I am that gay guy who outed that trans guy on international television. There's no escaping it. It is a mess of my own making that doesn't allow a day to pass without remorse and regret. A colossal mistake that has neither excuse nor defense."[43]

CBS released a statement saying that they had consulted with Zeke and with the Gay & Lesbian Alliance Against Defamation (GLAAD) prior to the episode airing, and they had prepared media releases addressing the Tribal Council. After the episode aired, GLAAD released a statement saying, "Zeke Smith, and transgender people like him, are not deceiving anyone by being their authentic selves, and it is dangerous and unacceptable to out a transgender person. It is heartening, however, to see the strong support for Zeke from the other people in his tribe."[44] Zeke wrote a lengthy piece that appeared in *The Hollywood Reporter* explaining his life experiences and personal reaction to being outed. "I'm not wild about you knowing that I'm trans." He explained that he had imagined after his season, "I'd return home, laugh at my misadventure, and go about my life, casually trans in the same way that Zac Efron is casually Jewish." He also highlights how what happened to him was fundamentally different than Bret coming out,

> Many gay people consider coming out a moment of liberation, because sharing their sexual orientation with the world causes them to be seen more authentically. Often, the opposite is true for trans people. When we share our gender history, many see us less authentically—doubting, probing or denying our identities. . . . A person's gender history is private information and it is up to them, and only them, when, how and to whom they choose to disclose that information. Keeping your gender history private is not the same as a gay person being "in the closet."[45]

But after this episode aired, Zeke's gender history was known to millions. It has been pointed out that for the audience at home, "Varner didn't out Zeke to the world. CBS did."[46] It would have been awkward, but the show could have edited around Varner's accusation.

It's hard to know what it would have looked like had they chosen that path, but *Island of the Idols* (season 39, 2019) did reveal one way production could address a player removed from the game with no footage being shown to the audience. A title card appeared saying Dan Spilo was pulled from the game at the end of the episode, without showing any video to provide context. For the superfans, that was not enough information and reporters and fans dug to find out what had happened. Likely a similar quest would have resulted had a title card appeared simply stating, "Varner was pulled from the game." But it is likely that far more viewers see an episode than seek out additional information online, so even if the reason for Varner's departure had been discovered in this hypothetical scenario, it would not have been broadcast to millions and then also become a permanent part of the streaming library of *Survivor*.

Years later, in *42* (season 42, 2022) the show would cast its first transgender player who was out, Jackson Fox. Jackson would tell his tribe about his transition on his first night, and his experience became part of an edited package revealing a player's backstory. Jackson said, "I wanted to put it out there because I wanted my message to get out that anybody can do this. You can be in one of the worst places in your life, which I was. For 40 years, I was a miserable person. And then I found who I was supposed to be and started living my life for the first time and I enjoyed everything around me."[47] Unfortunately, Jackson was pulled from the game for medical reasons before the first tribal council and his *Survivor* story was cut short.

While these stories are all about individuals and how they approached certain aspects of identity, they are also indicative of shifts in the culture at large. A show like *Survivor* reflects where society is at, but can also lead to increased empathy and understanding in viewers who watch the show.

CHANGE

These uncomfortable and problematic interactions happened. They are part of *Survivor*'s history, and they are preserved in DVD sets and on streaming services to be discovered by new audiences. It is key to remember that change may have happened for the participants of those moments. Probst has argued that change and evolution is key to enduring interest in the show. In the reunion episode for the thirty-fifth season, Probst proudly argued that, "One of the things that I think keeps *Survivor* relevant is that, you know, we have new people playing every year and their stories are of the moment. They're current. And sometimes their stories bring to light something important that is going on in the culture right now."[48] With a show that began in 2000, the fact that it reflects what was current necessarily means some aspects have become dated. *Survivor* commentator Shannon Guss argues that producers have "evolved and grown, as everyone else has. Every show from the early 2000s is cringe now. You watch *Friends* (1994–2004), and it's my favorite show, but there are things that do not hold up." Because of the nature of *Survivor*, many of the moments that have sparked change in how production approaches matters are core parts of the show itself. Guss continues, "*Survivor* is ongoing. It's had decades, it's always learning. There are things that go wrong and you have to course correct, but it's extremely unfortunate to be the example that forces them to course correct."[49] Looking back to early seasons more than a decade later it is easy to find moments that have not aged well.

The Amazon can be remembered for Rob Cesternino innovating strategy by bouncing between alliances in a way that hadn't been seen before. But that is overshadowed by the particularly libidinous way some members of the women's tribe are talked about by the men's tribe. The objectification is certainly not limited to the men's tribe. In the third episode, when Heidi Strobel, Jenna Morasca, and Shawna Mitchell go to rinse in the Amazon River, production not only spends an extended edited sequence on the event with lingering shots of their bikini-clad bodies, they flew in a helicopter to provide aerial footage of the three women bathing. As much as the objectification of the women is problematic, it must be acknowledged that in *The Amazon*, Heidi and Jenna in particular talked openly about using their bodies and sexuality as part of their strategy in the game. Both women went on to appear in *Playboy* magazine together, indicating their comfort and willingness to embrace how men perceived their physical appearances.

Despite Jenna and Heidi's willingness to use their bodies and sexual appeal to manipulate the men around them, some instances in the show where their bodies are exploited definitely deviate from in-game strategy. A notable instance comes during the seventh episode which production titled "Girls Gone Wilder." During an endurance challenge, Heidi and Jenna ask Probst if he will give them peanut butter and chocolate if they strip completely naked. During endurance challenges, Probst often does tempt players with food if they give up. This serves as a way of revealing which players feel safe, which can be valuable information for the other players and has a place within in-game mechanics. But in this instance, it is not Probst tempting players with food, it is two young women tempting Probst and the crew with nudity for food. It's removed from the gameplay and comes across as manipulative by the women and more than a bit lecherous by the production crew. The women do strip down and are rewarded with a plate of peanut butter and chocolate cookies. While the women are obtaining food they want, the nudity seems to exist solely to satisfy the male-gaze of production and home viewers. Given Probst's pronouncement that after *Island of the Idols* players will not be allowed to be nude on the island, it would be impossible for anything like this to happen in modern *Survivor*. The leering edit from 2003 is an artifact that can ruin the season for some viewers. It was from an era when, in some aspects, the island was treated more like a frat house. Guss argues that production, after decades, has realized that the island "is a workplace, so workplace parameters have been put in. . . . We shouldn't be naked around our coworkers, because that's essentially what we are."[50]

There has been rapid transformation in the last twenty years in how issues like race, gender, and sexuality are addressed. This has shifted what the acceptable reactions would be in given situations. As part of reviewing old seasons, it is worth considering offering grace to players whose past actions have not aged well. Particularly when there is evidence of change on the player's part.

One instance that stands out where we know that a player has evolved in their thinking comes from Cesternino. While *The Amazon* is dripping with sexism and misogyny that feels best relegated to an earlier era, there is a moment of interaction based around race that is worth noting. This season, which was filmed in 2003, Dan Lue complained that as the only Asian American in the tribe he felt excluded and left out by the rest of the group, who were all Caucasian. "I'm one Asian guy versus seven other white guys. Even though I was born and raised in the U.S., you know, just, even before I speak, I stand out from the rest, and sometimes that makes me an outcast." Cesternino jumped in and said:

> That is completely false. I don't think for one second any of us said that we're going to treat Daniel any differently because his relatives are from a different country than our relatives may be from. We're all from different places and from different backgrounds, and we all realize that everybody's different and that's what makes us unique.[51]

Almost twenty years later, Cesternino rewatched this season and offered commentary on his podcast network, and admitted he was wrong in how he responded to Dan. Speaking about what it was like to view his younger self on TV, Cesternino said,

> Watching it back now, I'm like "Eff you, Rob. How dare you speak for what he is feeling. Also there's things that are happening that you don't even know about." . . . That's something that I really just look back on and cringe. And I know I say a lot of dumb stuff this season, but that is something that really bothered me when I went back for this rewatch.[52]

Cesternino owns what he said at the time, and acknowledges he had no right to say it and that he was in the wrong. His reaction that was captured while filming that tribal council in *The Amazon* is static, but Cesternino himself is a dynamic, changing individual. His views have evolved and matured.

Undoubtedly most viewers of the show can look back at some things they did or said a decade or more ago with some twinge of regret. But for most of us, those moments are not available to watch on DVDs or streaming services and being discovered by new viewers. The social interactions on *Survivor* may be products of their time, but with new fans discovering the series every year, those artifacts of earlier eras are pulled into the present whether they should be or not. For some players, moments from long ago are constantly rehashed on their social media timeline even if it was a different time for them.

Because *Survivor* is beloved, older seasons are constantly being watched and rewatched. What is being produced now may feel natural and normal to us, but in another twenty years viewers may cringe at something that was aired in 2024. How the producers and players on the show addressed aspects cultural and personal identity for entertainment purposes has been problematic at times. How unquestionably those choices were received by viewers reflects cultural norms at the time. Change is essential to the ongoing health of the show. Producers, players, and viewers are all changing, even as the episodes remain static once they air. As *Survivor* is approaching its fiftieth season, we shouldn't be surprised if it feels different than everything that has come before. And that can be a good thing.

CONCLUSION

Survivor is one of the entertainment properties where there is a before and after. Before *Survivor*, "reality TV" wasn't a recognized genre. After *Survivor*, it is an immediately known part of the entertainment landscape. Before *Survivor*, a few cable channels had a handful of unscripted shows with regular people as the cast; after *Survivor* all the broadcast channels aired reality TV and entire channels created brand identities around reality shows and personalities. Before *Survivor*, getting "voted off the island" would be a nonsense phrase; after *Survivor* that and other associated phrases became part of the cultural vernacular. To be culturally literate in the twenty-first century requires familiarity with *Survivor*.

In trying to explain what makes *Survivor* so compelling, there are many parallels that can be drawn to other popular media. Undoubtedly, there are many different parts of the show that different fans find interesting, but identifying some of the connections with other media can help to explain *Survivor*'s long-term popularity and the depth of its fandom.

Sports are one of the most-consumed entertainment products in the world today. The Superbowl has become the most-watched event in American entertainment every year. *Survivor* definitely has elements of sports entertainment that draw in viewers. Every episode there is challenge with players competing against each other to try and claim a prize. The result is unscripted, underdogs might win, and viewers can have rooting interests as their favorite players struggle to win. At the end of the season, like the playoffs in major sports, only one player is declared champion after all other players have been defeated.

One of the most popular media franchises to debut during *Survivor*'s time on television has been Suzanne Collins's young adult novels and the subsequent film adaptations of *The Hunger Games* (2008).[1] In the dystopian Hunger Games, an annual television broadcast of children who have been chosen at random hunting each other until only one survives is the most popular entertainment. Without very much squinting, it is possible to see the reality TV show *Survivor* and the classic short stories "The Lottery" (1948)[2] and "The Most Dangerous Game" (1924)[3] as building blocks that helped inspire this story. In Shirley Jackson's "The Lottery" a small town lottery leads to the person who is picked being killed. Richard Connell's "The Most Dangerous Game" tells the story of a man being shipwrecked on an island, only to be hunted for sport by its sole inhabitant. Audiences have found the concept of amateurs engaged in a winner-takes-all style competition to be a compelling narrative hook. Each season of *Survivor* offers that promise, without the life-or-death stakes of Collins' fictional world. Audiences can take comfort that eliminated players are taken to nice meals and comfortable beds after they are voted off the island while still enjoying the battle of wits that takes place on the island.

There are also many stories of romantic adventure that *Survivor* seems to draw on. Academic Richard J. Gerrig points out *Gilligan's Island* and *The Swiss Family Robinson* as cultural touchstones that *Survivor* evokes with its island theme. Of course, *Survivor*'s social politics and players' efforts to "assume overt or covert control over their tribemates"[4] also invites comparisons to *Lord of the Flies*. Comparisons to gladiator games in ancient Rome don't feel out of place.

But the cultural allusions don't have to be so serious. If you like sitcoms, every season of *Survivor* has laugh-out-loud moments. Mario Lanza has curated a list of "The Funny 115,"[5] detailing the funniest moments in the show's history. Some iconic episodes of the series are remembered for the comedy. In *Tocantins*, editors leaned into the absurd in presenting Benjamin "Coach" Wade's time on Exile Island in an episode titled "The Martyr Approach." In the *San Juan del Sur* episode titled "We're a Hot Mess," Drew Christie gives comically overconfident confessionals as he describes his plan to throw a challenge so his tribe can vote out Kelley Wentworth, only for Drew to be voted out at that tribal council. Viewers can find elements of romantic comedy, drama, adventure, tragedy, and more on *Survivor*. *Ghost Island* even leans into horror in its editing.

For academic analysis, *Survivor* also offers a wealth of possible interpretations. As seen in this book, it can serve as a vehicle to discuss the history of popular culture, or game theory, or issues of identity. Richard J. Gerrig's essay collection *The Psychology of Survivor* examines the show through the lens of psychological principles.[6] Christopher J. Wright's *Tribal Warfare: Survivor and the Political Unconscious of Reality TV* uses semiotics to examine social hierarchies and class politics as presented on the show.[7]

Matthew J. Smith and Andrew F. Wood's *Survivor Lessons* has chapters that apply the academic fields of communication studies, political science, psychology, and sociology.[8] *Survivor* can be used in the classroom to explain cultural theories like postmodernism in an accessible way. There is more to be said in all these areas of analysis, and there also remain unexplored areas of study.

Conversation around *Survivor* will broaden and deepen as future seasons are produced, new fans become invested in the show, and academics continue this discourse. The good news for fans is that the show does not appear to be going anywhere. In an interview in June 2024, Jeff Probst said, "I can't just be worried about this season. I have to go, 'How are we going to get to 50?' And then, 'What's 51? How do we get to 60?' So, I'm always taking a big picture view."[9] When *Survivor* was first announced, there was doubt that it would have a second season. Now, Jeff Probst is able to confidently discuss the sixtieth. *Survivor* has become an institution, one that will endure for some time.

APPENDIX

One reason *Survivor* still thrives is deep fan engagement. Fans love lists. Fans love arbitrary rankings. Here are our lists and arbitrary rankings.

THE *SURVIVOR* MOUNT RUSHMORE

If one were to try to build a Mount Rushmore of *Survivor* contestants—and production was halfway there in *Island of the Idols* (season 39, 2019)—there would be dozens of contestants debated for the final four spots. But in the end, we've selected Sandra Diaz-Twine (*Pearl Islands*; *Heroes vs. Villains*; *Game Changers*; *Winners at War*), "Boston" Rob Mariano (*Marquesas*; *All-Stars*; *Heroes vs. Villains*; *Redemption Island*; *Winners at War*), Tony Vlachos (*Cagayan*; *Game Changers*; *Winners at War*), and Cirie Fields (*Panama; Micronesia; Heroes vs. Villains, Game Changers*).

Survivor: Marquesas *(Season 4, 2002) Shown: "Boston" Rob Mariano.* CBS / Photofest © CBS, Photographer: David M. Russell.

They are solid strategists, charismatic characters, and masters of the sound-bite in confessionals. Being good storytellers is key to receiving screen time from the editors, and more screen time is key to being memorable to fans. This is an underrated part of the audience's reaction to players. How well can they explain their strategy? Can they describe events in an entertaining way? Can they land a barb about another player that makes the audience smile but doesn't cross a line? Some of these skills are learned, and with sixteen seasons between them (and also one season of *Australian Survivor*) these four characters have become experts.

Survivor Mount Rushmore	
Sandra Diaz-Twine	One of only two players who have won twice, and she did it in her first two seasons.
Tony Vlachos	The other two-time winner, and his second win came against nineteen other winners.
"Boston" Rob Mariano	He has played in more seasons—five—than any other player.
Cirie Fields	The best player to never win.

ICONIC PLAYERS

Casting, casting, casting. For all the twists and turns that have been introduced into *Survivor*, the key component for a successful season is the cast. Among the hundreds of players, here are some of the most iconic to ever play the game.

Player	Strengths
Tyson Apostol	Sardonic tone, physical challenges
Yamil "Yam Yam" Arocho	Charisma, charm
Rupert Boneham	Survival elements, on-screen charisma
Aubry Bracco	Student of the game, transformation
Janet Carbin	The brightest spot in all of *Island of the Idols*
Rob Cesternino	Iconic confessionals, founder of a large online fan community
James Clement	Strong, fascinating
John Cochran	"Nerd" archetype, dominated a season
Rick Devens	Good confessionals, oozes affable dad energy
Colby Donaldson	Challenge beast,[1] charismatic narrator
Stephen Fishbach	Superfan with the strategy to back it up
Malcolm Freberg	Big moves, pretty good at everything
Abi-Maria Gomes	A wild card with no filter
Russell Hantz	Finding idols, losing to women he does not respect
Richard Hatch	Understood game strategy before anyone else
Sue Hawk	Monologues, toughness
Wendell Holland	Solid at challenges, won a tie vote
Christian Hubicki	Confessionals, analytical strategy
Amanda Kimmel	Quiet strategy, uninspiring tribal council performances
Adam Klein	Successful super-fan, fun idol play
Yul Kwon	Strategic genius, physical threat
Sarah Lacina	Physical game, loves advantages
Stephenie LaGrossa	Physical strength, perseverance
Jesse Lopez	Strategic game, blindsides
Ozzy Lusth	Survival elements, physical challenges

(Continued)

Player	Strengths
Jerri Manthey	"Black Widow" archetype
"Chaos" Kass McQuillen	Causing chaos
Dawn Meehan	Emotional connections, "maternal" archetype
Maryanne Oketch	Social and emotional game
Jonathan Penner	The best narrator in the show's history
Parvati Shallow	"Flirt" archetype, strategic game
Kim Spradlin	Social game, options
Denise Stapley	Underdog win, incredibly tough
J. T. Thomas	If you could bottle whatever charisma J. T. was oozing in *Tocantins* you could be a millionaire too
Benjamin "Coach" Wade	Gloriously absurd confessionals
Kelley Wentworth	Strong, idol play
Tina Wesson	Social game, positive energy
Carolyn Wiger	Purely, 100 percent herself
Courtney Yates	Just great TV, sound bites
Ethan Zohn	Overall game, likable winner

[1] In his first appearance.

ERAS

Fans love to categorize. Breaking down *Survivor* into eras is something of a fan pastime. There are numerous threads on the *Survivor* subreddit debating the topic, and several websites have posted their own take on the eras. Unsurprisingly, there is significant variation in these lists, and even the number of eras is debated. For example, in 2018 Jacob Rausch wrote an article for *Surviving Tribal* that presented six different eras—The Classic Era, The Transitional Era, The Golden Age, The Dark Ages, The Revival Era, and The Meta Era.[1] In 2020, Matthew Storrs presented nine different eras in an article for Inside Survivor—The Golden Age, The Silver Age, The Era of Experimentation, The Era of Exile, The Hantzian Age, The Survivor Renaissance, The Laurel Year, The Big Moves Era, and The Big Twists Era.[2] In 2024, Jason P. Frank and Nic Juarez broke the franchise down into eight eras for *Vulture*—The Golden Age, The Identity Crisis, The Renaissance, The Dark Ages, The Re-Renaissance, The Worst Themes, The New Era 1.0, and The New Era 2.0.[3]

For our breakdown, we did our best to set aside the existing and conflicting analyses that we came across. In considering what united consecutive seasons by a distinctive theme, we settled on five distinct eras: (1) The Original Era, (2) Classic Era, (3) The Personality Era, (4) The Advantage Era, and (5) The Beware Era. Effort has been made to avoid labels that age poorly. For example, production and fans have called the seasons after the

COVID pandemic "The New Era" but, assuming the show continues on for any significant amount of time, that is the type of label that loses meaning. To define an era, we attempted to consider several factors. What unites a group of chronological seasons together? What is a turning point to a new set of criteria and when does it happen? How are the seasons remembered looking back across the years? As with all such divisions, there are some frayed edges where what we have identified as the unifying factor may start to appear before we've drawn a dividing line, and could also continue after. This is unavoidable in any ex post facto attempt to organize a large and sprawling subject. The producers and players were, generally speaking, not creating a show to fit into a specific era when the season was produced. As observers, we are trying to organize dozens of seasons into recognizable periods. Others have chosen to be more granular when tackling this subject, and that may certainly be preferable for some fans as they think back on their favorite series. For our list, we believe limiting *Survivor* to five eras serves to create a manageable and memorable breakdown.

Original Era (*Borneo – Palau*)

The series began with two tribes competing for tribe immunity, then a merge after which individuals played for immunity, and then two players at Tribal Council pleading their case head-to-head in front of the jury. This simplest version of the game was the mold that was largely followed for the first ten seasons. There was some variation in how the game started—schoolyard pick for tribes, tribes split by gender, three initial tribes of All-Stars—but the basic gameplay remained the same.

After this era, twists become more common, gimmicks are added and then abandoned, and returning players will appear more frequently. The game necessarily had to change and adapt, but there is something ideal in the simplicity of the Original Era. Strategy is more straightforward, but with that comes the danger of a dominant alliance running the game without a real danger of their plans being thwarted (so long as the alliance members are loyal). This famously happened in the very first season, and gave rise to the fan-verb "Pagonging" to describe a tribe with fewer members at the merge being systemically taken out one-by-one at the merge. A pagonging can lead to a predictable string of episodes if it becomes apparent that the larger tribe is unlikely to vote out any of their own number.

The Classic Era (*Guatemala – Gabon*)

While Original Era *Survivor* is appealing in its simplicity, there are elements that are missing. The individual hidden immunity idol is so iconic it has become a staple part of player strategy and audience expectations. Going back to rewatch the earliest seasons feels like there is a hidden-immunity-sized hole in the game being played. The first version of the idol comes into play during *Guatemala* and since then has significantly altered strategy and allows players who are not part of the dominant alliance the chance to upend the game. This era features the immunity idol, but few other advantages are added to the mix.

Personality Era (*Tocantins – Worlds Apart*)

The end of the Classic Era is with *Tocantins*, and particularly one player: Benjamin "Coach" Wade. The producers and editors leaned into his more outlandish qualities, particularly during his stay on Exile Island, and viewers and future players learn that an individual can become a breakout star by being esoteric and odd rather than dominant at any particular facet of the game. When Coach is invited back two more times in the next five seasons, the lesson will be fully learned by subsequent players. Soon other players will be interested in coming on to the show and create a character who "is more personality than contestant," as journalist Josh Wigler describes Phillip Sheppard who first appears on *Redemption Island*.[4] This era is replete with big personalities. Russell Hantz was an incredible force that took over two seasons in a row with his big personality, offensive confessionals, and salt-the-earth gameplay. NaOnka Mixon dominates airtime in *Nicaragua* (season 21, 2010) even though she is part of the immensely hated and controversial double-quit. Subsequent seasons in this period will have cast members who feel more present for their big personalities than for their likelihood of excelling at strategy.

The show also began to use more big-name stunt casting in this era. These included famous athletes like Olympian Crystal Cox (*Gabon*), NFL players Steve Wright (*Redemption Island*), Grant Mattos (*Redemption Island*), and Brad Culpepper (*Blood vs. Water, Game Changers*), MLB players Jeff Kent (*Philippines*) and John Rocker (*San Juan del Sur*), and NBA player Cliff Robinson (*Cagayan*).There is one professional athlete in an earlier era (NFL quarterback Gary Hogeboom [*Guatemala*]) and more will play after this era. But there is a notable trend in these seasons for celebrity casting. Other celebrities in this era include NFL coach and commentator Jimmy Johnson (*Nicaragua*), singer Taj Johnson-George (*Tocantins*), and TV star Lisa Whelchel (*Philippines*).

Additionally, producers leaned on returning players more than in previous eras. In the Original Era, the only season to feature returning players was *All-Stars*. In the Classic Era, only two seasons had returning players. In the Personality Era, six of the seasons—fully half of this era—have returning players. In this era, players were cast who had appeared on other reality shows, including Nadiya and Natalie Anderson (*San Juan del Sur*) who had appeared on two seasons of *The Amazing Race*, and Hayden Moss (*San Juan del Sur*) who had won the twelfth season of *Big Brother*.

Advantages Era (*Cambodia – Edge of Extinction*)

No moment of the Advantages Era is more symbolic of how many items have been added to the game than "Advantage-geddon." In the twelfth episode of *Game Changers* (season 34, 2017) Cirie Fields, a beloved player who has never won the game, ended up eliminated despite no votes being cast for her. Every other player in the game had an advantage. At the final six Tribal Council after votes are cast, Probst asks if any players would like to play an immunity idol. Brad Culpepper has the immunity necklace from winning the challenge. Tai Trang plays an idol for himself and a second idol for Aubry Bracco. Sarah Lacina plays a Legacy Advantage that makes her immune. Troyzan Robertson plays an idol for himself. Cirie, sitting alone with no advantage to play, is eliminated without a vote against her at that Tribal Council.

This period sees a large number of advantages introduced. Some appear only once, some become semi-recurring. In some ways it feels as though producers are throwing spaghetti against the wall to see what sticks. Hidden immunities at tribal challenges. A vote steal. Idols that can be combined to form a super idol. An extra vote. The power to remove a jury member from the final Tribal Council. A legacy advantage. A reward steal. An advantage menu (with a reward steal, an extra vote, or individual immunity). A joint Tribal Council. A right to abstain from voting in one Tribal Council to gain a vote at a future Tribal Council. Immunity idols with timers that become powerless after a certain point in the game. Edge of extinction. Safety without power. Idol nullifiers. It can become difficult to track, and to help viewers there are times editors add information in the lower third of the screen about what advantages players have.

This is, bluntly, a problem. Much of the enjoyment of *Survivor* comes from understanding the strategy. Being unable to track what advantages exist, who has them, when they need to be played and why, makes understanding player motivations a chore. Just understanding what gameplay is happening can become confusing when there are too many advantages in play.

The Beware Era (*Island of the Idols* – present)

In the most recent iteration of *Survivor*, producers have become invested in the idea of "dangerous fun." In discussing *41* Probst said, "When you combine dangerous fun with a dilemma that forces a player to make a risk-vs-reward decision, then you have a great *Survivor* game element."[5] The clearest form this takes is that many advantages are now labeled with the word "Beware." Often, players must complete a task in order to claim the advantage, and there is a stipulation that they cannot vote until that task is completed. Players losing their vote has become a staple of the beware era, indicative of the new stakes introduced. While it is tempting to make a line of demarcation between seasons 40 and 41, we have chosen to start the Beware Era with season 39. In many of the episodes, players had the opportunity to win an advantage, but faced consequences if they failed. This is the exact mindset from production that leads the advantages being labeled as Beware Advantages in season 41. As this era encompasses the most recent seasons, it is difficult to identify when or if a new era is beginning. Some distance is needed to look back at *Survivor* to identify when new eras are formed, but if the show continues, as it seems it inevitably will, there will be some new era to be identified that comes after this Beware Era.

SEASON TIERS

For our season rankings, we're not going straight through from top to bottom. Rather, we are slotting the seasons into five tiers, from one-star seasons that are hard to watch to five-star seasons that are truly excellent. In our first run-through of ranking the seasons, we worried we had been overly generous with too high of a percentage of seasons being ranked as five-stars. We adjusted to increase the rigor of our ratings. It is worth noting that outside of the one-star seasons, every season is enjoyable. Even the one-star seasons have some silver linings that could be found, but some very dark clouds overshadow the seasons so much that it is hard to recommend those three. Within tiers, seasons are presented in chronological order.

One-Star Seasons—Hard to Watch	
Thailand (2002)	A case of sexual harassment that was handled poorly casts a shadow over the season.
All-Stars (2004)	The Richard Hatch and Sue Hawk incident is unpleasant, and the bitterest jury ever removes some fun from the season.
Island of the Idols (2019)	The entire season feels like a slow crawl to a tragic end, despite some solid casting and interesting game play.

Two-Star Seasons—OK	
Marquesas (2002)	While Vecepia is an underrated winner, there are late-game debates that come across as racially insensitive.
The Amazon (2003)	Splitting the tribes by gender does not inherently have to lead to the objectification of the women by the men's tribe (and the host, cameramen, editors, and production as whole). But it does here.
Vanuatu (2004)	Some good players, but on the whole this is an unremarkable season.
Fiji (2007)	The question of whether a team with an abundance of food, luxury items, and shelter will perform better than a starving team with no shelter doesn't need to be asked, but this season asks it. The results are as predictable as they are unenjoyable.
Gabon (2008)	This season is light on strategy, high on chaotic energy, and Bob Crowley is one of the least strategic winners ever.
Nicaragua (2010)	This season is marred by two quits that come late in the game. Also, Jud "Fabio" Birza gives Bob Crowley a run for his money as the least strategic winner.
Redemption Island (2011)	Boston Rob finally gets a win in his fourth time playing but his game is so dominant this results in one of the most boring seasons ever produced.
Worlds Apart (2015)	The premise of this season—White Collar vs. Blue Collar vs. No Collar—is a bit strained and there is too much misogyny in the air.
Kaoh Rong (2016)	Players are mean and the climate is harsh.
Game Changers (2017)	Jeff Varner is awful, Zeke Smith is amazing. Bit of a mess of a season.
Edge of Extinction (2019)	The defining twist of the season makes the finale unsatisfying.
41 (2021)	There are so many new twists and advantages even super fans had trouble tracking it all, and the editing makes it hard to celebrate the winner.

(Continued)

Two-Star Seasons—OK	
43 (2022)	Largely the same notes as above for 41.

Three-Star Seasons—Solid	
Africa (2001)	Solid winner and satisfying gameplay, even if it is a hot, dry, uncomfortable-looking season.
Guatemala (2005)	There are some underrated characters that keep the season fun.
Samoa (2009)	Russell Hantz is a camera-time vacuum, but he is fascinating to watch in his first appearance.
South Pacific (2011)	The returning captains are an odd pair, but there are several memorable new players.
One World (2012)	Kim Spradlin's excellence elevates what would otherwise be a two-star season.
Philippines (2012)	A good underdog story is always satisfying.
Caramoan (2013)	John Cochran's win is one of the most remarkable evolutions from where a player begins to where they end.
San Juan del Sur (2014)	Natalie Anderson is a compelling protagonist for the season.
Heroes vs. Healers vs. Hustlers (2017)	Surprises abound, even if fans don't love all the twists.
42 (2022)	Maryanne Oketch bursts with energy, and there is strong strategic gameplay.
46 (2024)	A slow start is overcome at the merge and leads to an unexpected finale.

Four-Star Seasons—Very Good	
The Australian Outback (2001)	Season 1 was a phenomenon, season 2 ensured Survivor was a franchise. Great casting and gameplay.
Pearl Islands (2003)	This season had some of the greatest breakout characters playing the game—most notably the hero Rupert Boneham, the villain Jonny "Fairplay" Dalton, and the icon Sandra Diaz-Twine—but also had an excellent pirate theme.
Palau (2005)	Shocking pre-merge and a satisfying winner.
Panama (2006)	Some of the best chaotic energy mixed with brilliant strategy overcomes a lackluster finale.
Cook Islands (2006)	Notwithstanding the awkward premise, this results in one of the most satisfying come-from-behind victories for the Aitu Four.
China (2007)	Beautiful location and fun players. Todd Herzog's final tribal council performance is a textbook example of what to do.
Tocantins (2009)	Incredible cast. Benjamin "Coach" Wade on Exile Island is a five-star episode. Several players come back multiple times.
Blood vs. Water (2013)	Tyson Apostol is a satisfying winner and this is the best variation of returning players vs. new players.
Cambodia (2015)	Jeremy Collins is an emotionally and strategically satisfying winner of the season.
Millennials vs. Gen X (2016)	The premise creates clear divides, and the season as a whole is excellent.
Ghost Island (2018)	Good gameplay and alliances throughout, and the tie vote for the winner at the end is thrilling to watch.
David vs. Goliath (2018)	Great cast, fun gameplay, and clear alliances make this one of the best seasons with all-new players.
44 (2023)	The Tika three are a delight to watch survive to the end.
45 (2023)	Dee Valladares played one of the best strategic games in recent memory.

Five-Star Seasons—Outstanding	
Borneo (2000)	One of the most impactful seasons of any show ever.
Micronesia (2008)	The Black Widow Brigade convincing Erik Reichenbach to give up his immunity is *Survivor*'s most iconic moment in a great season.
Heroes vs. Villains (2010)	This season had one of the best top-to-bottom casts ever assembled for the show and allowed characters and gameplay to be front and center.
Cagayan (2014)	Great casting and unforgettable fireworks. From the Brains tribe meltdown to Tony Vlachos's chaotic energy, this season never slows down.
Winners at War (2020)	Twenty winners were back. Every player is memorable. The family visit was the culmination of the shared community the show has built.

NOTES

PREFACE

1. Peter White, "'Survivor': CBS Planning 'Year-Long' Celebration for Season 50." *Deadline*, June 11, 2024. https://deadline.com/2024/06/survivor-cbs-season-50 -1235970491/.

2. Alison Herman, "'Survivor' Is the Quintessential TV Show." *The Ringer*, May 12, 2020. https://www.theringer.com/tv/2020/5/12/21255075/survivor-legacy-40th -anniversary-reality-tv.

3. Shannon Guss. Zoom interview with Joseph J. Darowski. April 2024.

4. Michael Schneider, "100 Most-Watched TV Series of 2023–24: This Season's Winners and Losers." *Variety*, May 28, 2024. https://variety.com/2024/tv/news/most -popular-tv-shows-highest-rated-2023-2024-season-tracker-survivor-1236015844/.

5. Rick Porter, "TV Ratings 2023–24: Final Numbers for (Almost) Every Network Series." *The Hollywood Reporter*, June 11, 2024. https://www.hollywoodreporter.com/tv/ tv-news/tv-ratings-2023-24-primetime-network-show-rankings-1235919819/.

6. Katie Campione, "'Survivor' Season 45 Boasts Renewed Ratings Success for CBS As Younger Audiences Flock to Long-Running Competition Series." *Deadline*, December 20, 2023. https://deadline.com/2023/12/survivor-season-45-ratings-cbs -1235678298/.

CHAPTER I

1. Christopher Rivera, "Cast of 'Survivor' Season 1: Where Are They in 2024!" After Buzz TV, May 22, 2024, https://www.afterbuzztv.com/cast-of-survivor-season-1 -where-are-they-in-2024/.

2. Christopher Kuhagen, "Survivor 40: Wisconsinites Who Have Played in the Hit Reality TV Show," *Milwaukee Journal Sentinel*, February 12, 2020, https://www.jsonline .com/picture-gallery/communities/2020/02/11/survivor-sue-hawk-andrea-boehlke-among -wisconsin-players-tv-show/4668113002/.

3. Time Cover, *Time*, June 26, 2000, https://content.time.com/time/covers/0,16641 ,20000626,00.html.

4. The Internet Movie Database, *The Weakest Link*, episode aired January 6, 2002. https://www.imdb.com/title/tt0744761/.

5. Rivera, "Cast of."

6. Jeff Jensen, "Bawdy and Sole: What's Up with That Reebok Ad?" *Entertainment Weekly*, August 11, 2000, https://ew.com/article/2000/08/11/bawdy-and-sole-whats -reebok-ad/.

7. CBS News, "Bush Appears with Regis," *CBS News*, September 21, 2000, https:// www.cbsnews.com/news/bush-appears-with-regis/.

8. Annette Hill, *Reality TV: Audiences and Popular Factual Television* (New York: Routledge, 2005), 2.

9. Anita Biressi and Heather Nunn, *Reality TV: Realism and Revelation* (London: Wallflower Press, 2005), 10–11.

10. Sean Brenton and Reuben Cohen, *Shooting People: Adventures in Reality TV* (New York: Verso, 2003), 8.

11. Hill, *Reality TV: Audiences and Popular Factual Television*, 55.

12. Martin Holmes, "Birth of a Phenomenon—An Oral History of Survivor Borneo," Inside Survivor, May 29, 2020, https://insidesurvivor.com/birth-of-a-phenomenon-an-oral -history-of-survivor-borneo-43932.

13. Martin Holmes, "Birth of a Phenomenon."

14. Leslie Moonves, "Leslie Moonves Discusses 'Survivor' - EMMYTVLEGENDS. ORG," FoundationINTERVIEWS, YouTube video, January 23, 2013, https://www .youtube.com/watch?v=fQhrILJW6yU.

15. Veronica Rose, "'Roar': A Throwback to Heath Ledger's Irish Prince Stint," *The Series Regulars*, July 13, 2020.

16. Bill Carter, "CBS Is Surprise Winner in Ratings Contest," *New York Times*, August 24, 2000.

17. Joe Flint, "CBS's Hit Show 'Survivor' Ends Summer Run with Huge Ratings," *The Wall Street Journal*, August 25, 2000.

18. Lisa De Morales, "ABC Aims at 'Survivor,'" *The Capital Times*, June 6, 2000.

19. Chicago Tribune, "'Survivor' Finale Posts Ratings Even Larger Than Show's Hype," *Chicago Tribune*, August 25, 2000, https://www.chicagotribune.com/2000/08/25/ survivor-finale-posts-ratings-even-larger-than-shows-hype/.

20. Tom Shales, "Summer of Silliness, *Electronic Media*, July 3, 2000.

21. Bill Carter, "TV Notes; Vicarious Thrills," *The New York Times*, May 24, 2000.

22. Bill Carter, "Survivor of the Pushiest." *New York Times Magazine*, January 28, 2001.

23. Tom Shales, "Reality Faked Out," *Electronic Media*, June 4, 2001.

24. Quoted in Susan Murray, "'I Think We Need a New Name for It': The Meeting of Documentary and Reality TV," in *Reality TV: Remaking Television Culture* (New York: New York University Press, 2009), 66.

25. Hill, *Reality TV*, 15.

26. Annette Hill and Gareth Palmer, "Big Brother," *Television and New Media* 3(3) (August 2002): 251.

27. Misha Kavka, *Reality TV* (Edinburgh: Edinburgh University Press, 2012), 2.

28. See James Friedman (6), Misha Kavka (76), Annette Hill (3), Annette Hill and Gareth Palmer (251), Laurie Oullette and James Hay (8), and Jon Dovey (135).

29. Judy Berman, "Reality TV Has Reshaped Our World," *Time*, August 4, 2022. https://time.com/collection/reality-tv-most-influential-seasons/6199108/reality-tv-influence-on-world/.

30. Bill Carter, "CBS's 'Survivor' Is Winner for Network; Real-Life Show Pulls in Younger Viewers," *The New York Times*, June 2, 2000.

31. Richard M. Huff, *Reality Television* (London: Praeger, 2006), 1.

32. Scott D. Pierce, "'Survivor' Changed TV as We Know It," *Deseret News*, December 22, 2009. https://www.deseret.com/2009/12/22/20360166/scott-d-pierce-survivor-changed-tv-as-we-know-it/.

33. Emily Yahr, Caitlin Moore, and Emily Chow, "How We Went from 'Survivor' to More Than 300 Reality Shows: A Complete Guide," *The Washington Post*, May 29, 2015. https://www.washingtonpost.com/graphics/entertainment/reality-tv-shows/.

34. Sallie Tisdale, *The Lie about the Truck: Survivor, Reality TV, and the Endless Gaze* (New York: Gallery Books, 2021), 14.

35. Steve Clarke, "How 'Survivor' Has Outplayed Its Competition for 25 Years," *Variety*, October 14, 2022. https://variety.com/2022/tv/global/survivor-25-years-anniversary-charlie-parsons-1235402539/.

36. Jessica Tucker, "After More than 40 Seasons on Air, How Much Does Survivor Rake in for CBS?" *TheThings.com*, March 29, 2023. https://www.thethings.com/how-much-money-does-survivor-make-for-cbs/.

37. B. J. Sigesmund, "The Tribe Has Spoken," *Newsweek*, September 5, 2001. https://www.newsweek.com/tribe-has-spoken-152053.

38. Scott Donaton, "Real Bad: The Backlash Begins Against Exploitative Tube Trend," *Advertising Age*, vol. 71, no. 41 (October 2, 2000).

39. Marc Peyser et al. "'Survivor' Tsunami," *Newsweek*, vol. 136, no. 9 (August 2000), p. 52.

40. Jason Mittell, *Television and American Culture* (Oxford: Oxford University Press, 2009), 90.

41. Mittell, *Television and American Culture*, 91.

42. Moonves, "Leslie Moonves discusses 'Survivor.'"

43. Jennifer Maas, "Reality TV Exec Who Launched 'Survivor' Sues CBS for Wrongful Termination, Discrimination," *The Wrap*, November 25, 2019. https://www.thewrap.com/survivor-exec-ghen-maynard-sues-cbs-wrongful-termination-discrimination/.

44. Holmes, "Birth of a Phenomenon."

45. Bill Carter, "Britons Revamp American TV," *The New York Times*, July 18, 2000.

46. Maas, "Reality TV Exec."

47. Moonves, "Leslie Moonves Discusses 'Survivor.'"

48. Martin Holmes, "Birth of a Phenomenon."

49. Mark Burnett, "Mark Burnett on Creating Survivor - EMMYTVLEGENDS. ORG," FoundationINTERVIEWS, YouTube video. June 8, 2011. https://www.youtube.com/watch?v=jle_s0wZYOA.

50. Alicia Ault, "Turning a Camera, Stress, and the Wild into a Sudden Hit," *The New York Times*, July 23, 2000.

51. Burnett, "Mark Burnett on Creating Survivor."

52. Moonves, "Leslie Moonves Discusses 'Survivor.'"

53. Jason Mittell, *Television and American Culture*, 90–91.

54. Becky Ebenkamp, "Return to Peyton Placement." *Brandweek*, June 6, 2001.

55. Steve Helling, "'Survivor' Contestant B.B. Anderson Dead at 77," People.com, November 1, 2013. https://people.com/tv/survivor-contestant-b-b-andersen-dead-at-77/.

56. ABC News, "Original Survivor Claims Show Was Rigged," *ABC News*, February 6, 2001.

57. *Chicago Tribune*, "'Survivor' Finale."

58. Michael Schneider, "100 Most-Watched TV Series of 2023–24: This Season's Winners and Losers," *Variety*, May 28, 2024. https://variety.com/2024/tv/news/most -popular-tv-shows-highest-rated-2023-2024-season-tracker-survivor-1236015844/.

59. Mario Lanza, *When It Was Worth Playing For* (Scotts Valley, CA: CreateSpace Independent Publishing, 2015), 272–80.

60. Mike Bloom (reporter), Zoom interview with Joseph J. Darowski, December 2021.

61. Linda Hutcheon, *A Theory of Adaptation, second edition* (New York: Routledge), 120–28.

62. Holly Fournier, "Ex-'Survivor' Star Gets up to 4 Years for Child Porn," *The Detroit News*, December 27, 2016, https://www.detroitnews.com/story/news/local/oakland -county/2016/12/27/ex-survivor-sentenced-child-porn-possession/95867296/.

63. Snejana Farberov, "Fearless 'Survivor' Winner's Heartbreak after Her Son, 25, Is Killed in Car Accident 'Because He Wasn't Wearing a Seat Belt,'" *The Daily Mail*, December 11, 2013. https://www.dailymail.co.uk/news/article-2522095/Survivor-winner -Tina-Wessons-heartbreak-son-killed-car-accident.html.

64. Emlyn Travis, "Keith Nale, Two-Time Survivor Contestant, Dies at 62," *Entertainment Weekly*, April 19, 2023. https://ew.com/tv/keith-nale-dead-survivor-contestant/.

65. Kimberly Nordyke, "Caleb Bankston, 'Survivor' Competitor, Dies at 26 in Railway Accident," *The Hollywood Reporter*, June 25, 2014. https://www.hollywoodreporter .com/news/general-news/caleb-bankston-dead-survivor-competitor-714851/.

66. Tilo Hartman and Charlotte Goldhoorn, "Horton and Wohl: Revisited: Exploring Viewers' Experience of Parasocial Interaction," *Journal of Communication*, 61(6) (December 2011), 1004.

67. Dong-Hee Shin, "Do Users Experience Real Sociability Through Social TV? Analyzing Parasocial Behavior in Relation to Social TV," *Journal of Broadcasting & Electronic Media*, 60 (2016), 140.

68. The Supreme Court recently stated a ruling in a case that for the sake of clarity it would refer to it as Twitter as most of the posts in the case were from when it was known as Twitter instead of X. We will follow the same standard throughout this book.

69. TMZ, "'Survivor' Contestants Violate NDA: $5 Million Fine on the Line," *TMZ*, May 15, 2018. https://www.tmz.com/2018/05/15/survivor-season-37-contestants-out -themselves-5-million-dollar-nda/.

70. Alyssa Norwin, "'Survivor' Finale Reunion: Why Is Alec Merlino Missing from the Live Show?" *Hollywood Life*, December 19, 2018. https://hollywoodlife.com/2018/12 /19/where-is-alec-survivor-david-vs-goliath-reunion-finale/.

71. Marc Peyser with B. J. Sigesmund, Suzanne Smalley, and Devin Gordon. "'Survivor' Tsunami," *Newsweek*, 136(9) (August 8, 2000), p. 52.

72. ABC News, "Did Network Reveal 'Survivor' Champ on Web?" *ABC News*, July 18, 2000.

73. James Poniewozik, "Aaargh! CBS Is Playing 'Survivor' Mind Games," *Time*, August 3, 2000.

74. Henry Jenkins, *Convergence Culture: Where Old and New Media Collide* (New York: New York University Press, 2006), 25.

75. Thiago Oliveira Santos, Abel Correia, Rui Biscaia, and Ann Pegoraro, "Examining Fan Engagement through Social Networking Sites," *International Journal of Sports Marketing and Sponsorship* (October 2018).

76. Beverley Skeggs and Helen Wood, "Introduction," in *Reacting to Reality Television: Performance, Audience and Value* (New York: Routledge, 2012), 1–2.

77. Inside Survivor, https://insidesurvivor.com/.

78. Reality Blurred, https://www.realityblurred.com/realitytv/topic/survivor/.

79. True Dork Times, https://www.truedorktimes.com/index.htm.

80. Survivor Stories, FanFiction, https://www.fanfiction.net/community/Survivor-Stories/76449/.

81. Mario Lanza, "All-Star Survivor: Hawaii, A Fictional Serial Novel," Funny 115, http://www.funny115.com/hawaii/hawaii.htm.

82. SirNiceGuy, "Follow/FavPokémon Survivor: South Hoenn," FanFiction, August 1, 2020. https://www.fanfiction.net/s/13660255/1/Pokémon-Survivor-South-Hoenn.

83. SurvivorOnCBS, https://www.youtube.com/@survivor/videos.

84. Land of Survivor, https://www.youtube.com/@landofsurvivor/videos.

85. Idoled Out, https://www.youtube.com/@IdoledOut.

86. Peridiam, https://www.youtube.com/@Peridiam/videos.

87. Survivor Geek, https://www.youtube.com/@SurvivorGeek.

88. Once Upon an Island, https://www.youtube.com/@OnceUponAnIsland.

89. "5 Times Survivor Players Hacked Challenges," *Peridiam*, YouTube video, July 29, 2020. https://www.youtube.com/watch?v=cKsKUPlAMlk.

90. "Survivors Falling Over For 17 Minutes," *Eager Tortoise*, YouTube video, February 12, 2021. https://www.youtube.com/watch?v=bBMK9sV_YLA.

91. Dalton Ross, "Survivor Host Jeff Probst Says Mike White Helped Get Rid of Redemption Island," *Entertainment Weekly*, November 13, 2014. https://ew.com/article/2014/11/13/survivor-jeff-probst-mike-white/.

92. Mike Holmes, "Mike White Responsible for Survivor Ditching Fire Tokens Twist," Inside Survivor, September 9, 2021. https://insidesurvivor.com/mike-white-responsible-for-survivor-ditching-fire-tokens-twist-50592.

93. Dalton Ross, "Jeff Probst Reveals the Survivor Concept Season We Never Saw," *Entertainment Weekly*, April 13, 2023. https://ew.com/tv/survivor-jeff-probst-concept-season-we-never-saw/.

94. Daniel George, "Survivor's Jeff Probst: 'I Hear You. We're Not Gonna do Edge (of Extinction) for a While,'" *Surviving Tribal*, February 11, 2020. https://survivingtribal.com/2020/02/11/survivor-jeff-probst-no-edge-extinction/.

95. Dalton Ross, "'Survivor: Cagayan': Jeff Probst Weighs in on the Latest Blindside," *Entertainment Weekly*, April 17, 2014, https://ew.com/article/2014/04/17/survivor-cagayan-jeff-probst-blindside/.

96. Dalton Ross, "Survivor Quarantine Questionnaire: Jolanda Jones on Being Portrayed as the 'Bitch' in Palau," *Entertainment Weekly*, October 2, 2020. https://ew.com/tv/survivor-palau-jolanda-jones-quarantine-questionnaire/.

97. Dalton Ross, "Survivor Quarantine Questionnaire: Crystal Cox on Why Survivor Needs More Minority Editors," *Entertainment Weekly*, October 22, 2020. https://ew.com/tv/survivor-gabon-crystal-cox-quarantine-questionnaire/.

98. John Scalzi, *Red Shirts* (New York: Tor Publishing Group, 2012).

99. *Survivor: Blood vs. Water*, Season 37, episode 7, "Swoop in for the Kill," aired October 30, 2013. https://www.paramountplus.com/shows/survivor/.

100. *Survivor: 46*, Season 46, episode 1, "This Is Where the Legends Are Made," aired February 29, 2024. https://www.paramountplus.com/shows/survivor/.

101. Martin Holmes, "Survivor Edgic – An Introduction," Inside Survivor, September 13, 2015, https://insidesurvivor.com/survivor-edgic-an-introduction-3094.

102. Mike Bloom, "Outwit, Outplay, Out-cut: How the Editing Team Has Kept the 'Survivor' Tribe Together Through 40 Seasons," Cinemontage.org, February 11, 2020, https://cinemontage.org/cbs-survivor-editors-editing/.

103. Dalton Ross, "Survivor Quarantine Questionnaire: Kelly Shinn Talks about Her Infamous 'Purple Edit' in Nicaragua," *Entertainment Weekly*, September 8, 2020, https://ew.com/tv/survivor-nicaragua-kelly-shinn-purple-quarantine-questionnaire/.

104. Brian Lowry, "Decade's Big 'Survivor,'" *Variety*, December 18, 2009, https://variety.com/2009/tv/columns/decade-s-big-survivor-1118012985/.

105. John Koblin, "'Survivor' Defies Gravity to Hang on as CBS Ratings Stalwart," *The New York Times*, September 30, 2015. https://www.nytimes.com/2015/10/01/business/media/survivor-defies-gravity-to-hang-on-as-cbs-ratings-stalwart.html.

106. Dalton Ross, "Meet the Cast of Survivor 41," *Entertainment Weekly*, August 30, 2021. https://ew.com/tv/survivor-41-cast-photos-bios/.

107. Brennan Carley, "Jeff Probst Is the Ultimate 'Survivor': Despite Many Changes to the Reality Show over the Last 21 Years, He Has Been a Constant," *The New York Times*, September 18, 2021. https://www.nytimes.com/2021/09/18/style/jeff-probst-survivor.html.

CHAPTER 2

1. Jeff Probst, "Jeff Probst on Fighting to Become Host of 'Survivor' - EMMYLEGENDS.ORG," FoundationINTERVIEWS, September 17, 2013, YouTube video, https://www.youtube.com/watch?v=3_ojDBrkx8k.

2. Brennan Carley, "Jeff Probst Is the Ultimate Survivor," *The New York Times*, September 19, 2021, https://www.nytimes.com/2021/09/18/style/jeff-probst-survivor.html.

3. Mark Burnett, "Mark Burnett on Casting Jeff Probst - EMMYTVLEGENDS.ORG," FoundationINTERVIEWS, June 8, 2011, YouTube video, https://www.youtube.com/watch?v=aOUvpJeSsP4.

4. Carley, "Jeff Probst."

5. John Koblin, "'Survivor' Defies Gravity to Hang on as CBS Ratings Stalwart," *The New York Times*, September 30, 2015. https://www.nytimes.com/2015/10/01/business/media/survivor-defies-gravity-to-hang-on-as-cbs-ratings-stalwart.html.

6. Nicole Bitette, "Jeff Probst on 'Survivor's Ability to Outlast," *Paramount*, February 26, 2024, https://www.paramount.com/news/jeff-probst-on-survivors-ability-to-outlast.

7. Carley, "Jeff Probst."

8. Mara Reinstein, "Through Two Decades and 40 Seasons, the Tribal Council Remains the Heart of 'Survivor,'" *The Ringer*, May 12, 2020, https://www.theringer.com/tv/2020/5/12/21254206/survivor-tribal-council-evolution-behind-the-scenes.

9. Probst, "Jeff Probst on Fighting."

10. Andrew Barker, "Jeff Probst: Strong 'Survivor,'" *Variety*, June 20, 2013. https://variety.com/2013/tv/awards/jeff-probst-strong-survivor-1200498658/.

11. *Survivor: Borneo*, Season1, episode 3, "Quest for Food," aired June 15, 2000, on CBS. https://www.paramountplus.com/shows/survivor/.

12. Bitette, "Jeff Probst."

13. Reinstein, "Through Two Decades."

14. David Canfield, "Jeff Probst on a Survivor Season of Triumphs, Breakthroughs, and Quits: 'I Was Shocked,'" *Vanity Fair*, December 13, 2023, https://www.vanityfair.com/hollywood/jeff-probst-survivor-45-successes-quits-emmys-interview-awards-insider.

15. Carley, "Jeff Probst."

16. Jeff Probst, "Jeff Probst REVEALS His Favorite Moments From 20 Years of 'Survivor' | Full Interview," *Entertainment Tonight*, February 15, 2020, YouTube video, https://www.youtube.com/watch?v=biN72tLAN6E.

17. Dalton Ross, "Jeff Probst Addresses His Future as Survivor Host," *Entertainment Weekly*, December 7, 2022, https://ew.com/tv/jeff-probst-future-survivor-host/.

18. Dalton Ross, "How to Get on Survivor: Behind the Scenes of Casting Season 45," *Entertainment Weekly*, September 18, 2023, https://ew.com/tv/survivor-45-behind-the-scenes-casting-cover-story/.

19. Ibid.

20. Andy Dehnart, "Best Survivor Contestants 'Have Really Strong Opinions, They Know Who They Are,'" *Reality Blurred*, December 24, 2008, https://www.realityblurred.com/realitytv/2008/12/survivor-samoa-spillman_casting/.

21. Mark Burnett, "Mark Burnett on Casting Survivor- EMMYTVLEGENDS.ORG," FoundationINTERVIEWS, YouTube video, June 8, 2011, https://www.youtube.com/watch?v=9Q2ncu_iHwo.

22. Mike Bloom, "Outwit, Outplay, Out-cut: How the Editing Team Has Kept the 'Survivor' Tribe Together Through 40 Seasons," Cinemontage.org, February 11, 2020, https://cinemontage.org/cbs-survivor-editors-editing/.

23. Andy Dehnart, "Why Survivor Stopped Recruiting Players, and How Casting Has Changed Recently," Reality Blurred, October 27, 2020, https://realityblurred.com/realitytv/2020/10/survivor-casting-changes-recruits/.

24. Andy Dehnart, "Bob Crowley: 'I'm Not Playing the Game, I'm Here to Have a Good Time,'" Reality Blurred, September 3, 2008, https://www.realityblurred.com/realitytv/2008/09/survivor-gabon-bob_crowley/.

25. Dehnart, "Why Survivor."

26. Dehnart, "Best Survivor."

27. Ross, "How to."

28. Dehnart, "Why Survivor."

29. Martin Holmes, "Casting Director Lynne Spiegel Spillman 'Let Go' from Survivor," Inside Survivor, July 1, 2018, https://insidesurvivor.com/casting-director-lynne-spiegel-spillman-fired-from-survivor-34504.

30. Dehnart, "Why Survivor."

31. Peter White, "CBS Sets Diversity Targets for Reality Casts; 50% of Talent Must Be BIPOC & Commits 25% of Unscripted Development Budget to BIPOC Creatives," *Deadline*, November 9, 2020, https://deadline.com/2020/11/cbs-diversity-targets-reality-casts-bipoc-commits-unscripted-development-budget-1234611548/.

32. Carley, "Jeff Probst."

33. Bitette, "Jeff Probst."

34. Martin Holmes, "Jeff Probst Says There Will Be No More Villains on Survivor," Inside Survivor, February 26, 2024, https://insidesurvivor.com/jeff-probst-says-there-will -be-no-more-villains-on-survivor-56582.

35. Lynette Rice, "'Survivor' Issues Rare Statement to Viewers," *Deadline*, May 30, 2024. https://deadline.com/2024/05/survivor-issues-statement-to-viewers-consider -embracing-kindness-1235945399/.

36. Bitette, "Jeff Probst."

37. Dalton Ross, "Jeff Probst Says Survivor Quitters Will No Longer Get Torch Snuffed," *Entertainment Weekly*, November 15, 2023, https://ew.com/survivor-jeff-probst -quitters-no-longer-get-torch-snuffed-8402222.

38. Jeff Probst, "Jeff Probst Won't Snuff Out the Torch for Survivor Quitters," Live-KellyandMark, November 15, 2023, YouTube Video, https://www.youtube.com/watch?v =MQh5O9mQOlc&t=51s.

39. Todd Garner with Jeff Probst, *The Producer's Guide*, podcast audio, September 13, 2018. https://podcastone.com/episode/Jeff-Probst.

40. Dalton Ross, "Jeff Probst Wants Survivor to Stay in Fiji Permanently," *Entertainment Weekly*, September 12, 2017, https://ew.com/tv/2017/09/12/survivor-jeff-probst -fiji/.

41. Dalton Ross, "*Survivor* Quarantine Questionnaire: David Wright Buried a Fake Idol . . . before the Season Even Began!" *Entertainment Weekly*, June 1, 2021. https:// ew.com/tv/survivor-david-wright-millennials-vs-gen-x-edge-of-extinction-quarantine -questionnaire/.

42. Ross, "Jeff Probst Wants."

43. Dalton Ross, "Survivor Considered Filming in Georgia and Hawaii Due to COVID," *Entertainment Weekly*, September 1, 2021, https://ew.com/tv/survivor-41 -georgia-hawaii-covid-jeff-probst/.

44. Ross, "Jeff Probst Wants."

45. Dalton Ross, "Survivor's 35 Best Challenges Ever," *Entertainment Weekly*, August 22, 2022. https://ew.com/tv/survivor-the-35-best-challenges-ever/.

46. Jeff Probst, with Brittany Crapper and Jay Wolfe, *Designing Challenges: On Fire with Jeff Probst: The Official Survivor Podcast*, podcast audio, March 22, 2023.

47. Andy Dehnart, "Did Survivor's Flirting, Furtive Foraging, or Puzzle Prep Pay Off?" *Reality Blurred*, March 8, 2023. https://www.realityblurred.com/realitytv/2023/03/ survivor-44-episode-2-two-dorky-magnets-recap/.

48. Probst, *Designing Challenges.*

49. Probst, *Designing Challenges.*

50. Kaila Yu, "I Worked on 'Survivor.' We Tested Challenges before Contestants, Stayed in Island Resorts, and Got Front-Row Seats for Filming," *Business Insider,* September 29, 2022, https://www.businessinsider.com/survivor-dream-team-job-test-challenges -before-cast-contestants-2022-9.

51. Probst, *Designing Challenges.*

52. Ross, "Survivor's 35 Best."

53. Dalton Ross, "All Hands on Deck: Behind the Scenes of a Survivor Marooning," *Entertainment Weekly*, February 20, 2019, https://ew.com/tv/2019/02/20/survivor-edge-of -extinction-marooning/.

54. Mike Bloom, Zoom interview with Joseph J. Darowski, December 2021.

55. Bloom, "Outwit."

56. Dalton Ross, "'Survivor': Jeff Probst on 'the Most Frightened I've Been in All My Time' on the Show," *Entertainment Weekly*, March 10, 2016, https://ew.com/article /2016/03/10/survivor-jeff-probst-kaoh-rong-caleb-alecia-debbie-episode-4/.

57. Bloom, "Outwit."

58. *Survivor: 44*, Season 44, episode 1, "I Can't Wait to See Jeff," Aired March 1, 2023, on CBS. https://www.paramountplus.com/shows/survivor/.

59. *Survivor: 44*, Season 44, episode 13, "Absolute Banger Season," Aired May 24, 2023, on CBS. https://www.paramountplus.com/shows/survivor/.

60. Bloom, "Outwit."

61. *Survivor: Worlds Apart*, Season 30, episode 13, "It's A Fickle, Fickle Game," Aired May 21, 2015, on CBS. https://www.paramountplus.com/shows/survivor/.

62. Emily Yahr, "'Survivor' Changed Television Forever and It Still Endures. What's the Secret?" *Washington Post*, May 29, 2015, https://www.washingtonpost.com /news/arts-and-entertainment/wp/2015/05/29/survivor-changed-television-forever-and-it -still-endures-whats-the-secret/.

63. Bloom, "Outwit."

64. Ibid.

65. Misha Kavka and Amy West, "Temporalities of the Real: Conceptualizing Time in Reality TV," in *Understanding Reality Television* (New York: Routledge, 2004), 146.

66. Lauren Thomas, "Sears, Mattress Firm and More: Here Are the Retailers that Went Bankrupt in 2018," *CNBC*, December 31, 2018. https://www.cnbc.com/2018/12/31/ here-are-the-retailers-including-sears-that-went-bankrupt-in-2018.html.

67. Roger Conrad, "T-Mobile US: The Sprint Merger So Far," *Forbes*, June 28, 2021. https://www.forbes.com/sites/greatspeculations/2020/06/23/t-mobile-us-the-sprint -merger-so-far/.

68. Bloom, "Outwit."

69. Dalton Ross, "Jeff Probst on Tony's Three Days of Survivor Dominance," *Entertainment Weekly*, April 23, 2020, https://ew.com/tv/survivor-jeff-probst-winners-at -war-tony-vlachos-episode-11-interview/.

70. Meghan Cook, "'Survivor' Players Reveal What It's Really Like to Compete on the Show," *Business Insider*, March 11, 2022, https://www.insider.com/what-its-like -being-on-survivor-contestants-reveal-2021-6.

71. Colby Donaldson, "Commentary," Disc 1, *Survivor: The Australian Outback*, Season 2, episode 1, DVD.

72. Cook, "'Survivor' Players."

73. ABC News, "Some 'Survivor' Scenes Were Reenactments," *ABC News*, May 10, 2001, https://abcnews.go.com/Entertainment/story?id=105494&page=1.

74. SurvivorQuotesX (@SurvivorQuotesX), "I'm Saying to You, Heart to Heart, Friend to Friend, Human Being to Human Being . . .," Twitter, April 23, 2024. https://x. com/SurvivorQuotesX/status/1782776979214704805.

75. Kass McQuillen (@KassMcQ), "This Had to Be Redone Because Trish's Mic Wasn't Working . . .," Twitter, April 24, 2024. https://x.com/KassMcQ/ status/1783124800522641682.

76. Davie Rickenbacker (@WheresDavie), "Lol since We Talking about Reshoots . . .," Twitter, April 24, 2024. https://x.com/WheresDavie/status/1783177491546316857.

77. Jeff Probst, with Brittany Crapper and Jay Wolfe, *Shooting Survivor: On Fire with Jeff Probst: The Official Survivor Podcast*, podcast audio, May 3, 2023. https:// podcasts.apple.com/us/podcast/shooting-survivor/id1673596832?i=1000611662379.

CHAPTER 3

1. *Survivor: Vanuatu*, Season 9, episode 14, "Spirits and the Final Four," aired December 12, 2004. https://www.paramountplus.com/shows/survivor/.

2. *Survivor: Borneo*, Season 1, episode 12, "Death of an Alliance," aired August 16, 2000. https://www.paramountplus.com/shows/survivor/.

3. Andy Dehnart, "Survivor Rules: The Contract that Details Pay, Tie-Breakers, Prohibited Behavior, and More," *Reality Blurred*, May 31, 2010, updated October 12, 2021. https://www.realityblurred.com/realitytv/2010/05/survivor-cast-contract/https://www.realityblurred.com/realitytv/2010/05/survivor-rule-book/.

4. James Poniewozik, "Survivor's Rulebook Leaks Out," *Time*, June 1, 2010. https://entertainment.time.com/2010/06/01/survivors-rulebook-leaks-out/.

5. Dehnart, "Survivor Rules."

6. Ibid.

7. *Survivor: All-Stars*, Season 8 episode 5, "I've Been Bamboozled!" aired February 26, 2004, on CBS. https://www.paramountplus.com/shows/survivor/.

8. Michael Starr, "He Was Robbed! - Wrong Team Won 'Survivor' Challenge," *New York Post*, March 4, 2004. https://nypost.com/2004/03/04/he-was-robbed-wrong-team-won-survivor-challenge/.

9. Andy Dehnart, "'Survivor: Samoa' Rises to New Season of Challenges," *NPR*, September 16, 2009. https://www.npr.org/2009/09/16/112850247/survivor-samoa-rises-to-new-season-of-challenges.

10. Kellie Boyle, "'Survivor' Winner Kenzie Addresses Heated Q Exchange & Why Liz Could've Won," *TV Insider*, May 23, 2024. https://www.tvinsider.com/1137331/survivor-finale-season-46-winner-kenzie/.

11. Brian Anthony Hernandez, "*Survivor* Season 46 Winner Kenzie Talks Season 50 Cast Wish List, Jury Votes, Q-Skirt and 'Mermaid Dragon' (Exclusive)," *People*, May 23, 2024. https://people.com/survivor-46-winner-kenzie-talks-season-50-cast-jury-votes-husband-baby-exclusive-8653352.

12. Andy Dehnart, "Answers to Survivor 46's Burning Questions," *Reality Blurred*, May 24, 2024. https://www.realityblurred.com/realitytv/2024/05/survivor-46-questions-answers/.

13. Associated Press, "Piercing Error Leads to More Prize Money for 2 'Survivor' Contestants," *Cleveland 19 News*, February 20, 2002. https://www.cleveland19.com/story/672757/piercing-error-leads-to-more-prize-money-for-2-survivor-contestants/.

14. *Survivor: Africa*, Season 3, episode 14, "The Final Four: No Regrets," aired January 10, 2002, on CBS. https://www.paramountplus.com/shows/survivor/.

15. Don Kaplan, "'Survivor' 'Screw-Up' Costs CBS $200G," *New York Post*, February 20, 2002. https://nypost.com/2002/02/20/survivor-screw-up-costs-cbs-200g/.

16. Mary Catherine Bateson. "It's Just a Game, Really," *New York Times*, vol. 149, no. 51493, August 27, 2000, p. 15.

17. *Survivor: Heroes vs. Villains*, Season 20 episode 15, "Reunion," aired May 16, 2010, on CBS. https://www.paramountplus.com/shows/survivor/.

18. Dalton Ross, "'Survivor' Host Jeff Probst on the Pair that Dropped Out and a Possible Final Two." *Entertainment Weekly*, September 8, 2014. https://ew.com/article/2014/09/08/survivor-jeff-probst-san-juan-del-sur-final-2/.

19. Dalton Ross, "How to Get on Survivor: Behind the Scenes of Casting Season 45," *Entertainment Weekly*, September 18, 2023. https://ew.com/tv/survivor-45-behind-the-scenes-casting-cover-story/.

20. For clarification of when back-to-back sitting out was allowed, see Andy Dehnart, "Why Sandra Sitting Out Back-to-Back Challenges Is Allowed," *Reality Blurred*. For clarification about the most recent rules for sitting out, see Dalton Ross, "Jeff Probst Explains Why *Survivor* Just Made a Huge Rules Change," *Entertainment Weekly*.

21. Dalton Ross, "Survivor Recap: Dumbest. Tribe. Ever," *Entertainment Weekly*, February 27, 2015. https://ew.com/recap/survivor-one-world-episode-4/.

22. Charlotte Walsh, "Survivor's Jeff Probst Explains Why the Hourglass Twist Has Been Voted Off the Island," *Yahoo Entertainment*, September 14, 2022, https://www.yahoo.com/entertainment/survivor-jeff-probst-explains-why-191900876.html.

23. Lee Whitten, "Survivor 42: Why the Hourglass Twist Is a Creative Failure," Screenrant, April 17, 2022. https://screenrant.com/survivor-42-hourglass-twist-creative-failure-jeff-probst/.

24. Emily Longeretta, "Jeff Probst on His Future on 'Survivor,' the Format Change He Was Told Would 'Kill the Franchise' and Already Planning for 51," *Variety*, June 18, 2024. https://variety.com/2024/awards/features/jeff-probst-survivor-format-changes-season-51-1236040161/.

25. Mara Reinstein, "Through Two Decades and 40 Seasons, the Tribal Council Remains the Heart of 'Survivor,'" *The Ringer*, May 12, 2020. https://www.theringer.com/tv/2020/5/12/21254206/survivor-tribal-council-evolution-behind-the-scenes.

26. Peridiam, "The 'Intentional Matsing' Strategy in Survivor," YouTube video, January 24, 2018. https://www.youtube.com/watch?v=jXtOj32Tx4U.

27. Jeff Pittman, "Doing Their Best, Despite . . . ," *True Dork Times*, November 29, 2020. https://www.truedorktimes.com/s17/recaps/e3.htm.

28. *Survivor: San Juan del Sur*, Season 29, episode 4, "We're a Hot Mess," aired October 15, 2014, on CBS. https://www.paramountplus.com/shows/survivor/.

29. Dalton Ross (@DaltonRoss), "The 1 Big Bummer Is that Panama Was the Last Season with a Final 2 (with rare injury exceptions). Producers Then Changed to Final 3 after Watching Terry Not Make It . . ." Twitter, June 15, 2021. https://twitter.com/DaltonRoss/status/1404826841660243969?s=20.

30. Dalton Ross, "Survivor Finale: Jeff Probst Explains Reason behind Controversial Twist," *Entertainment Weekly*, December 21, 2017, https://ew.com/tv/2017/12/21/survivor-finale-jeff-probst-twist/.

31. *Survivor: Borneo*, Season 1, episode 13, "The Final Four," aired August 23, 2000, on CBS. https://www.paramountplus.com/shows/survivor/.

32. *Survivor: Blood vs. Water*, Season 27, episode 1, "Blood Is Thicker than Everything," aired September 18, 2013, on CBS. https://www.paramountplus.com/shows/survivor/.

33. Alex P. Kellogg, "A Game Theory for 'Survivor,'" *Chronicle of Higher Education*, 46(32), (April 20, 2001): A8.

34. Barbara Ann Schapiro, "Who's Afraid of Being Kicked Off the Island?" in *The Psychology of Survivor: Overanalyze, Overemote, Overcompensate* (Dallas: Benbella Books, 2007), 4.

35. David Bloomberg, "What Survivor Players Should Have Learned," Rob has a Website, September 14, 2021. https://robhasawebsite.com/blog/survivorrules/.

CHAPTER 4

1. Rick Devens (@Rick_Devens), "Production Constantly Adding New Elements and Twists to the Show Is the Only Reason It's Been a Success for Going on 42 Seasons," Twitter, May 24, 2021, 9:38 a.m., https://twitter.com/Rick_Devens/status /1396868205252128768.

2. David Canfield, "Jeff Probst on a Survivor Season of Triumphs, Breakthroughs, and Quits: 'I Was Shocked,'" *Vanity Fair,* December 13, 2023, https://www.vanityfair.com /hollywood/jeff-probst-survivor-45-successes-quits-emmys-interview-awards-insider.

3. Dalton Ross, "Survivor Host Jeff Probst Explains the Show's New Intro," *Entertainment Weekly*, October 3, 2019, https://ew.com/tv/2019/10/03/survivor-jeff-probst -island-of-the-idols-episode-2/.

4. Malcolm Freberg, "'Survivor' Was Anyone's Game When I Played It, But Twists and Advantages Are Ruining What Makes the Show Special," *Business Insider*, December 1, 2021, https://www.businessinsider.com/former-survivor-player-whats-wrong-with-the -show-new-season-41-2021.

5. Andy Denhart, "How Jeff Probst Made Me Fear for Survivor's Future," Reality Blurred, May 23, 2023, https://www.realityblurred.com/realitytv/2023/05/survivor-jeff -probst-podcast-fear/.

6. Rob Cesternino with Christian Hubicki, *Survivor* All-Time Top 40 Rankings | #9: Cambodia with Christian Hubicki, Rob Has a Podcast, podcast audio, July 28, 2021, https://robhasawebsite.com/survivor-season-rankings-9-cambodia/.

7. Mike Bloom, Zoom interview with Joseph J. Darowski, December 2021.

8. ENews, "A History of Survivor's Most Controversial Twists," Eonline.com, September 22, 2021, https://www.eonline.com/photos/33298/a-history-of-survivors-most -controversial-twists.

9. Dalton Ross, "The Best and Worst Survivor Twists Ever," *Entertainment Weekly*, June 18, 2019, https://ew.com/tv/2019/06/18/survivor-best-and-worst-twists/.

10. Dalton Ross, "Jeff Probst Says Survivor May Never Go Back to 39 Days," *Entertainment Weekly*, September 7, 2021, https://ew.com/tv/survivor-41-jeff-probst-26 -day-game-instead-of-39/.

11. Ross, "Jeff Probst Says."

12. Jeff Probst with Jay Wolff and Dee Valladares, Play or Get Played: On Fire with Jeff Probst: The Official *Survivor* Podcast, podcast audio, May 16, 2024, https://podcasts .apple.com/us/podcast/play-or-get-played/id1673596832?i=1000655737413.

13. Tyson Apostol and Riley McAtee with Xander Hastings, The Pod Has Spoken: 'Survivor' Season 43, Episode 8, podcast audio, November 10, 2022, https://www .theringer.com/2022/11/10/23451086/survivor-season-43-episode-8.

14. Tyson Apostol and Riley McAtee with Cirie Fields, The Pod Has Spoken: 'Survivor' Season 41 Finale, podcast audio, December 16, 2021, https://www.theringer.com /2021/12/16/22839726/survivor-season-41-finale.

15. Tyson Apostol and Riley McAtee with Todd Herzog, The Pod Has Spoken: 'Survivor' Season 43, Episode 9, podcast audio, November 17, 2022, https://podcasts .apple.com/us/podcast/the-ringer-reality-tv-podcast/id1580146037?i=1000586556150.

16. Dalton Ross, "Jeff Probst Explains Why They Are Sticking with 26-Day Survivor Seasons," *Entertainment Weekly*, May 15, 2024, https://ew.com/survivor-jeff-probst -explains-not-going-back-to-39-day-seasons-8649115.

17. Jeff Probst (@jeffprobst), BREAKING NEWS Get ready to see returning players on #Survivor: 50!, April 27, 2024, https://www.instagram.com/reel/C6SheDqLLVy/?utm_source=ig_web_copy_link&igsh=MzRlODBiNWFlZA==.

18. Rob Moynihan, "30 Seasons of Survivor: An Oral History of the Reality Competition That Changed the Game," TV Insider, September 18, 2015. https://www.tvinsider.com/1458/30-seasons-of-survivor-epic-blindsides-machiavellian-maneuvering-icky-bug-bites/.

19. Jeff Probst, "Jeff Probst | A Peek Behind the Scenes of Survivor's 20-Year Success," Talks at Google, February 20, 2020, YouTube video, https://www.youtube.com/watch?v=azzJur0cukc&t=2905s.

20. Dalton Ross, "Survivor Quarantine Questionnaire: Andrew Savage Was 'Deeply Haunted' by the Outcast Twist," *Entertainment Weekly*, February 8, 2021, https://ew.com/tv/survivor-pearl-islands-cambodia-andrew-savage-quarantine-questionnaire/.

21. Rob Cesternino, "Survivor 40 Premiere Red Carpet Interviews," Rob Has a Podcast, February 11, 2020, YouTube video, https://www.youtube.com/watch?v=f2rMdTJ-BUI&t=1s.

22. Dalton Ross, "Jeff Probst Explains Why They Brought Edge of Extinction Back on Survivor: Winners at War," *Entertainment Weekly*, January 24, 2020, https://ew.com/tv/2020/01/24/survivor-winners-at-war-jeff-probst-edge-of-extinction/.

23. Dalton Ross, "Omar Zaheer Reveals Unseen Idol Nullifier that Led to His Survivor Demise," *Entertainment Weekly*, May 19, 2022, https://ew.com/tv/survivor-42-omar-zaheer-interview/.

24. Denhart, "How Jeff Probst."

CHAPTER 5

1. Anita Biressi and Heather Nunn, *Reality TV: Realism and Revelation* (London: Wallflower Press, 2005), 11–12.

2. Misha Kavka, *Reality TV*, Edinburgh University Press (2012), 129.

3. Felicia R. Lee, "'Home Edition' Shows the Softer Side of Reality TV," *New York Times*, November 4, 2004.

4. Emma Kelly, "Remembering the Swan—the Noughties' Most Controversial and Offensive Reality TV Series," *Metro*, October 22, 2019. https://metro.co.uk/2019/10/22/remembering-swan-noughties-controversial-offensive-reality-tv-series-10962780/.

5. Susan J. Douglas, *The Rise of Enlightened Sexism* (St. Marin's Press, 2010), 223.

6. Sophie Gilbert, "The Retrograde Shame of *The Biggest Loser*," *The Atlantic*, January 29, 2020. https://www.theatlantic.com/culture/archive/2020/01/the-retrograde-shame-of-the-biggest-loser/605713/.

7. The Week Staff, "'Bridalplasty': A New Low for Reality TV?," *The Week*, January 8, 2015. https://theweek.com/articles/490971/bridalplasty-new-low-reality-tv.

8. Ed West, "The Reality Show that Supersizes Cruelty," *Spiked*, March 6, 2009. https://www.spiked-online.com/2009/03/06/the-reality-show-that-supersizes-on-cruelty/.

9. Maggie Shiels, "Women's Group Attacks Reality Show," *BBC*, January 17, 2003. http://news.bbc.co.uk/2/hi/entertainment/2668029.stm.

10. Alessandra Stanley, "So Rowdy, They Discomfit the Royal Hell-Raiser," *New York Times*, May 19, 2014. https://www.nytimes.com/2014/05/20/arts/television/i-wanna -marry-harry-a-reality-series-on-fox.html.

11. Nicholas Fonseca, "Details on the 'Bachelor'-Style Gay Reality Show," *Entertainment Weekly*, June 6, 2003. https://ew.com/article/2003/06/06/details-bachelor-style -gay-reality-show/.

12. Reality TV World Staff, "Fox Releases Details of 'Playing It Straight''s Unaired Conclusion," *Reality TV World*, July 28, 2004. https://www.realitytvworld.com/news/fox -releases-details-of-playing-it-straight-unaired-conclusion-2782.php.

13. Gavin McNett, "The Wacky World of Television," *Salon*, March 13, 2000. https://www.salon.com/2000/03/13/wackytv/.

14. FoundationINTERVIEWS, "Leslie Moonves Interview part 4 of 5—EMMYT-VLEGENDS.ORG, YouTube video, September 9, 2009. https://www.youtube.com/watch ?v=uALSVBYHKP4&t=1191s.

15. *Survivor: Borneo*, Season 1, episode 6, "Udder Revenge," aired July 5, 2000, on CBS. https://www.paramountplus.com/shows/survivor/.

16. *Survivor: Samoa*, Season 19, episode 2, "Taking Candy from a Baby," aired September 24, 2009. https://www.paramountplus.com/shows/survivor/.

17. *Survivor: Nicaragua*, Season 21, episode 2, "Fatigue Makes Cowards of Us All," aired September 22, 2010, on CBS. https://www.paramountplus.com/shows/survivor/.

18. *Survivor: Thailand*, Season 5 episode 3, "Family Values," aired October 3, 2002, on CBS. https://www.paramountplus.com/shows/survivor/.

19. *Survivor: Island of the Idols,* Season 39, episode 8, "We Made it to the Merge," aired November 13, 2019, on CBS. https://www.paramountplus.com/shows/survivor/.

20. *Survivor: Game Changers,* Season 34, episode 6, "What Happened on Exile, Stays on Exile," aired April 12, 2017, on CBS. https://www.paramountplus.com/shows/ survivor/.

21. M. Brielle Harbin, "'Don't Make My Entertainment Political!' Social Media Responses to Narratives of Racial Duty on Competitive Reality Television Series," *Political Communication*, 40(4), March 30, 2023, 464–83.

22. *Survivor: Redemption Island*, Season 22, episode 8, "This Game Respects Big Moves," aired April 6, 2011, on CBS. https://www.paramountplus.com/shows/survivor/.

23. Arthur Asa Berger, *Media and Society: A Critical Perspective* (New York: Rowman & Littlefield, 2012), 213.

24. Elihu Katz, Hadassah Haas, and Michael Gurevitch, "On the Use of the Mass Media for Important Things," *American Sociological Review* 38, no. 2 (1973): 164–81.

25. Matt Liguori (@mattliguori), "We're Currently on a Streak of 9 Consecutive Women Getting Their Torch Snuffed," Twitter, February 20, 2020, https://twitter.com/ mattliguori/status/1230692951614988288.

26. Dan "Wardog" DaSilva (@IAmTheWardog), "Analyzing the Best Reality Show on TV through the Lens of Gender Is Tiresome," Twitter, February 20, 2020, https://twitter .com/IAmTheWardog/status/1230874836664123393.

27. *Survivor: Ghost Island*, Season 36, episode 1, "Can You Reverse the Curse," aired February 28, 2018, on CBS. https://www.paramountplus.com/shows/survivor/.

28. Christina S. Walker, "'I'm So Sick of This Race Talk. Boo Hoo': Perceptions of Race on 2021-22 CBS *Survivor*," *Howard Journal of Communication*, April 5, 2023. https://www.tandfonline.com/doi/pdf/10.1080/10646175.2023.2195058.

29. Harbin, "Don't Make."

30. Walker, "'I'm So Sick of.'"

31. *Survivor: Island of the Idols*, Season 39, episode 6, "Suck It Up Buttercup," aired November 6, 2019, on CBS. https://www.paramountplus.com/shows/survivor/.

32. Dalton Ross, *"Survivor* Host Jeff Probst Weighs in on Jamal and Jack's Racial Incident," *Entertainment Weekly*, October 31, 2019. https://ew.com/tv/2019/10/31/survivor-jeff-probst-island-of-the-idols-episode-6/.

33. Andy Dehnart, "Survivor: An Honest, Vulnerable Discussion of Race and Privilege Was Just One Part of an All-Time-Great Episode," *Reality Blurred*, October 30, 2019. https://www.realityblurred.com/realitytv/2019/10/survivor-island-of-the-idols-episode-6-suck-it-up-buttercup-recap/.

34. *Island of the Idols*, Season 39, episode 8.

35. Caroline Framke, "'Survivor' Mishandling of Sexual Harassment Is Irresponsible and Infuriating," *Variety*, November 21, 2019. https://variety.com/2019/tv/news/survivor-island-idols-sexual-harassment-1203411590/.

36. *Island of the Idols*, S39E8.

37. *Survivor: Island of the Idols*, Season 39, episode 12, "Just Go for It," aired December 11, 2019, on CBS. https://www.paramountplus.com/shows/survivor/.

38. Dalton Ross, *"Survivor* Host Jeff Probst Talks about First Player Ever Ejected from the Game," *Entertainment Weekly*, December 11, 2019. https://ew.com/tv/2019/12/11/survivor-host-jeff-probst-dan-spilo-removed-episode-13/.

39. Steve Helling, "'Survivor' Contestant Dan Spilo Was Uninvited from Live Finale After His Removal from Show," *People*, December 12, 2019. https://people.com/tv/survivor-contestant-dan-spilo-was-uninvited-from-live-finale-after-his-removal-from-show/.

40. Steve Helling, "'Survivor''s Dan Spilo Breaks Silence on His Behavior on the Show: 'I Am Deeply Sorry,'" *People*, December 17, 2019. https://people.com/tv/survivors-dan-spilo-breaks-silence-on-his-behavior-on-the-show-i-am-deeply-sorry/#:~:text=%22I%20am%20deeply%20sorry%20for,again%2C%20clearly%20and%20unambiguously.%22.

41. Elaine Lowe, "'Survivor': CBS Adds New Guidelines Following Misconduct Allegations," *Variety*, December 17, 2019. https://variety.com/2019/tv/news/survivor-cbs-policy-change-dan-spilo-alleged-misconduct-1203446825/.

42. Riley McAtee, "'Survivor' Ejected Dan Spilo—but the Show's Harassment Crisis Is Far from Over," *The Ringer*, December 12, 2019. https://www.theringer.com/tv/2019/12/12/21012988/survivor-dan-spilo-removed-harassment-season-39-episode-9.

43. David Bauder, "Television's 'Survivor' dealing with #MeToo-era issues," *AP Top News Package*, December 18, 2019.

44. Joseph J. Darowski and Kate Darowski, *Cheers: A Cultural History*, New York, Rowman & Littlefield, 2019, p. 147.

45. Laura Bradley, "Will Reality Television Ever Learn How to Handle Misconduct Allegations?" *Vanity Fair*, November 15, 2019. https://www.vanityfair.com/hollywood/2019/11/survivor-dan-spilo-kellee-kim.

46. Scott D. Pierce, "Despite #MeToo, 'Survivor' and CBS Failed Women and Heads Should Roll," *The Salt Lake Tribune*, December 15, 2019. https://www.sltrib.com/artsliving/2019/12/15/scott-d-pierce-despite/.

47. Jennifer Drysdale, "'Survivor': How the Dan Spilo Controversy Was Addressed on 'Island of the Idols' Finale," *Entertainment Tonight*, December 18, 2019. https://www

.etonline.com/survivor-how-the-dan-spilo-controversy-was-addressed-on-island-of-the-idols-finale-138260.

48. Leigh Oleszczak, "Survivor: Production Steps in for First Time Despite Past Issues," *Surviving Tribal*, November 17, 2019. https://survivingtribal.com/2019/11/17/survivor-island-idols-production-steps-in/.

49. *Survivor: Borneo*, Season 1, episode 9, "Old and New Bonds," aired July 26, 2000, on CBS. https://www.paramountplus.com/shows/survivor/.

50. Joyce Millman, "I Survived 'Survivor: The Australian Outback,'" *Salon*, May 3, 2001. https://www.salon.com/2001/05/03/last_survivor2/.

51. Shawna Malcolm, "Three Tribes, 18 Seasoned Players, and Rich Is Still Naked," *TV Guide*, January 17-23, 2004.

52. John Koblin, "Fully Clothed and Barely Afraid," *The New York Times*, April 11, 2016.

53. James Parker, "Race to the Bottom: Why There Are So Many Naked People on TV These Days," *The Atlantic Monthly*, October 2015.

54. Marcus James Dixon, "'Survivor' Nudity No Longer Allowed, Confirms Jeff Probst: 'Today It Wouldn't Get Past Our Producers for Half a Second,'" *Gold Derby*, February 12, 2020. https://www.goldderby.com/article/2020/survivor-nudity-jeff-probst-richard-hatch/

55. Robert Bianco, "Sold on Sex: Voyeuristic Views Can't Get Enough, So Reality . . ." *USA Today*, October 10, 2002.

56. Christopher J. Wright, *Tribal Warfare:* Survivor *and the Political Unconscious of Reality Television* (New York: Lexington Books, 2006), 151.

57. Dalton Ross, "Why Ghandia Should Change Her Name to Gone-dia," *Entertainment Weekly*, October 11, 2002. https://ew.com/article/2002/10/11/why-ghandia-should-change-her-name-gone-dia/.

58. *Survivor: Thailand*, Season 5 episode 15, "Reunion," aired December 19, 2002, on CBS. https://www.paramountplus.com/shows/survivor/.

59. Rob Cesternino with Ghandia Johnson and Teresa Cooper, Talking with T-Bird: Ghandia Johnson, Rob has a Podcast, podcast audio, February 1, 2021. https://robhasawebsite.com/survivor-ghandia-johnson-interview-thailand-tbird/.

60. *Survivor: All-Stars*, Season 8 episode 5, "I've Been Bamboozled," aired February 26, 2004, on CBS. https://www.paramountplus.com/shows/survivor/.

61. Rome Neal, "Hawk and Hatch: Getting Past It," *CBS News*, March 4, 2004. https://www.cbsnews.com/news/hawk-and-hatch-getting-past-it/.

62. *Survivor: All-Stars*. Season 8 episode 6, "Outraged," aired March 4, 2004, on CBS. https://www.paramountplus.com/shows/survivor/.

63. Tamara Grant, "'Survivor' Winner Richard Hatch Claims CBS Is Responsible for Controversial Incident," *Showbiz Cheatsheet*, February 8, 2020. https://www.cheatsheet.com/entertainment/survivor-richard-hatch-claims-cbs-is-responsible-for-incident-with-sue-hawk.html/.

64. Neal, "Hawk."

65. Ronan Farrow, "Les Moonves and CBS Face Allegations of Sexual Misconduct," *The New Yorker*, July 27, 2018. https://www.newyorker.com/magazine/2018/08/06/les-moonves-and-cbs-face-allegations-of-sexual-misconduct.

66. Alexandra Olson, "CBS Denies Former CEO Les Moonves $120 Million Severance," *Associated Press*, December 18, 2018. https://apnews.com/television-arts-and-entertainment-general-news-7858ff2dc8044b139c99a20aed18c502.

67. *Survivor at 40: Greatest Moments and Players*, aired February 5, 2020, on CBS. https://www.paramountplus.com/shows/survivor/.

68. Alex Rees, *"Survivor*'s New Season Brings Back Many of the Show's Most Influential Winners. Where Is Original Champion Richard Hatch?" *Time*, February 12, 2020. https://time.com/5781331/survivor-winners-season-richard-hatch-harassment/.

69. Mara Reinstein, "Jeff Probst Reveals Why Richard Hatch Is Not Part of 'Survivor' Season 40," *US Weekly*, January 15, 2020. https://www.usmagazine.com /entertainment/news/jeff-probst-why-richard-hatch-is-not-on-survivor-winners-at-war/.

70. Daniel Bukszpan, "And the Oscar for Not Paying Taxes Goes to . . ." *NBC News*, March 22, 2012. https://www.nbcnews.com/id/wbna46800653.

CHAPTER 6

1. Peter Conn, *Great American Bestsellers: The Books that Shaped America* (The Teaching Company, 2009) (audiobook).

2. Jeff Probst with Jay Wolfe and Dee Valladares, What's Up, Jeff? On Fire with Jeff Probst: The Official Survivor Podcast, podcast audio, April 10, 2024. https://podcasts .apple.com/us/podcast/whats-up-jeff/id1673596832?i=1000652089872.

3. An Kuppens and Jelle Mast. *"Ticket to the Tribes*: Culture Shock and the 'Exotic' in Intercultural Reality Television," *Media, Culture & Society*, 34(7) (October 2012): 799–814.

4. "Survivor: Inside the Phenomenon," *Survivor - The Complete First Season*, DVD, 2004.

5. *Survivor: Borneo*, Season 1, episode 1, "The Marooning," aired May 31, 2000, on CBS. https://www.paramountplus.com/shows/survivor/.

6. *Survivor: Borneo*, Season 1, episode 14, "The Reunion," aired August 23, 2000, on CBS. https://www.paramountplus.com/shows/survivor/.

7. *Survivor: The Australian Outback*, Season 2, episode 16, "Reunion," aired December 15, 2001, on CBS. https://www.paramountplus.com/shows/survivor/.

8. *Survivor: Africa*, Season 3, episode 1, "Question of Trust," aired October 11, 2001, on CBS. https://www.paramountplus.com/shows/survivor/.

9. *Survivor: Africa*, Season 3, episode 15, "Reunion," aired January 10, 2002, on CBS. https://www.paramountplus.com/shows/survivor/.

10. Ibid.

11. *Survivor: Marquesas*, Season 4, episode 15, "Reunion," aired May 19, 2002, on CBS. https://www.paramountplus.com/shows/survivor/.

12. *Survivor: Thailand*, Season 5 episode 1, "The Importance of Being Eldest," aired September 19, 2002, on CBS. https://www.paramountplus.com/shows/survivor/.

13. *Survivor: Thailand*, Season 5 episode 15, "Reunion," aired December 19, 2002, on CBS. https://www.paramountplus.com/shows/survivor/.

14. *Survivor: The Amazon*, Season 6, episode 15, "Reunion," aired May 11, 2003, on CBS. https://www.paramountplus.com/shows/survivor/.

15. *Survivor: All-Stars*, Season 8 episode 18, "America's Tribal Council," aired May 13, 2004, on CBS. https://www.paramountplus.com/shows/survivor/.

16. *Survivor: Fiji*, Season 14, episode 1, "Something Cruel Is About to Happen . . . Real Soon," aired February 8, 2007, on CBS. https://www.paramountplus.com/shows/survivor/.

17. *Survivor: Palau*, Season 10, episode 15, "Reunion," aired May 15, 2005, on CBS. https://www.paramountplus.com/shows/survivor.

18. *Survivor: Guatemala*, Season 11, episode 1, "Big Trek, Big Trouble, Big Surprise," aired September 15, 2005, on CBS. https://www.paramountplus.com/shows/survivor/.

19. *Survivor: Micronesia*, Season 16, episode 15, "Reunion," aired May 11, 2008, on CBS. https://www.paramountplus.com/shows/survivor/.

20. *Survivor: Micronesia*, Season 16, episode 15, "Reunion," aired May 11, 2008, on CBS. https://www.paramountplus.com/shows/survivor/.

21. Kathleen C. Riley "Surviving 'Survivor' in the Marquesas." *Anthropology News*, May 2002, 6.

22. Shawna Malcolm, "Survivor's New Look: Inside the New Tribal Council Set," *TV Guide*, September 29, 2007. https://www.tvguide.com/news/survivor-china-tribal -41810/.

23. CBS News, "'Survivor' Goes to China," *CBSNews*, September 20, 2007. https:// www.cbsnews.com/news/survivor-goes-to-china/.

24. Helen Gardner, "Explainer: The Myth of the Noble Savage," *The Conversation*, February 24, 2016. https://theconversation.com/explainer-the-myth-of-the-noble-savage -55316.

25. *Survivor: China*, Season 15, episode 1, "A Chicken's a Little Bit Smarter," aired September 20, 2007, on CBS. https://www.paramountplus.com/shows/survivor/.

26. Tzvetan Todorov, . *On Human Diversity: Nationalism, Racism and Exoticism in French Thought*, (Boston: Harvard University Press, 1998) 265.

27. *Survivor: 42*, Season 42, episode 9, "Game of Chicken," aired April 27, 2022, on CBS. https://www.paramountplus.com/shows/survivor.

28. Erin O'Mara Kunz, Jennifer L. Howell, and Nicole Beasley, "*Surviving* Racism and Sexism: What Votes in the Television Program *Survivor* Reveal About Discrimination," *Psychological Science* 34(6) (June 2023): 726–35.

29. Lynette Rice, "Altered Reality," *Entertainment Weekly*, February 2, 2022. https://ew.com/tv/cbs-diversity-survivor-big-brother/.

30. Joe Otterson, "CBS Sets Diversity Goal for Unscripted Shows," *Variety*, November 9, 2020. https://variety.com/2020/tv/news/cbs-unscripted-shows-diversity -1234826214/.

31. Eric Deggans, "'Do Right By Us': Black 'Survivor Alums Say the Reality Was Harmful Stereotypes,'" NPR, July 1, 2020. https://www.npr.org/2020/07/01/885750685/ do-right-by-us-black-survivor-alums-say-the-reality-was-harmful-stereotypes.

32. Rob Cesternino, Sean Rector, Julia Carter et al., Black Voices of SURVIVOR Roundtable LIVE, Rob Has a Podcast, June 24, 2020. https://www.youtube.com/watch?v =lqJM_05fFuk&t=5665s.

33. Julia Carter, "Push Me to the Edge: My Survivor Experience," thejuliacarter.co m. June 6, 2019.

34. Lynette Rice, "Altered Reality."

35. Nina Starner, "One Change Fixed the Series' Biggest Problem, According to Jeff Probst," *Looper*, April 24, 2024. https://www.looper.com/1569347/jeff-probst-survivor -mandate-changed-series/.

36. Dalton Ross, "Survivor Quarantine Questionnaire: Bret LaBelle Reflects on Coming Out as Gay on the Show," *Entertainment Weekly*, May 20, 2021. https://ew.com/tv/survivor-millennials-vs-gen-x-bret-labelle-quarantine-questionnaire-gay-coming-out/.

37. *Survivor: Millennials vs. Gen X*, season 33, episode 10, "Million Dollar Gamble," aired November 23, 2016, on CBS. https://www.paramountplus.com/shows/survivor/.

38. Mike Bloom "Survivor Contestant Bret LaBelle Recounts Coming Out on National Television," *Parade*, August 16, 2021. https://parade.com/1248679/mikebloom/survivor-bret-labelle-gay/.

39. *Survivor: Game Changers*. Season 34, episode 6, "What Happened on Exile, Stays on Exile," aired April 12, 2017, on CBS. https://www.paramountplus.com/shows/survivor/.

40. Patrick Gomez, "'Survivor''s Jeff Varner: How He Knew Zeke Smith Is Transgender and the 'Shame' He Feels for Outing Him," *People*, April 13, 2017. https://people.com/tv/survivor-jeff-varner-interview-outing-zeke-smith-transgender.

41. Sallie Tisdale, *The Lie About the Truck: Survivor, Reality TV, and the Endless Gaze* (New York: Gallery Books, 2021), 134.

42. *Game Changers*, Season 34, episode 6.

43. Jeff Varner, "Exclusive: 'Survivor' Contestant Jeff Varner in His Own Words: Outing Zeke Smith and the Shame That Followed," ETOnline, May 24, 2017. https://www.etonline.com/features/218256_survivor_contestant_jeff_varner_in_his_own_words.

44. Lesley Goldberg, "'Survivor': CBS Stands by Decision to Broadcast Transgender Outing," *The Hollywood Reporter*, April 13, 2017. https://www.hollywoodreporter.com/tv/tv-news/survivor-cbs-stands-by-decision-broadcast-zeke-smiths-outing-993757/.

45. Zeke Smith, "'Survivor' Contestant Opens Up About Being Outed as Transgender (Guest Column)," *The Hollywood Reporter*, April 12, 2017. https://www.hollywoodreporter.com/tv/tv-news/survivor-zeke-smith-outed-as-transgender-guest-column-991514/.

46. Tisdale, *The Lie About the Truck*, 134.

47. Dalton Ross, "Jackson Fox Reacts to Being Pulled from *Survivor 42*," *Entertainment Weekly*, March 10, 2022. https://ew.com/tv/survivor-42-jackson-fox-premiere-interview/.

48. *Survivor: Heroes vs. Healers vs. Hustlers*, Season 35, episode 14, "Reunion," aired December 20, 2017, on CBS. https://www.paramountplus.com/shows/survivor/.

49. Shannon Guss. Zoom interview with Joseph J. Darowski. April 2024.

50. Guss. Zoom interview.

51. *The Amazon*, season 6, episode 3, "Girl Power."

52. Rob Cesternino, Mary Kwiatkowski, and Maggie Morgan, Survivor All-Time Top 40 Rankings - #8 : The Amazon, Rob Has a Podcast, August 4, 2021. https://robhasawebsite.com/survivor-season-rankings-8-amazon/.

CONCLUSION

1. Suzanne Collins, *The Hunger Games* (New York: Scholastic Press), 2008.

2. Shirley Jackson, "The Lottery." In *Literature: Approaches to Fiction, Poetry, and Drama,* edited by Robert DiYanni (409–15).

3. Richard Connell, "The Most Dangerous Game." *Project Guttenberg*. https://gutenberg.ca/ebooks/connellr-mostdangerousgame/connellr-mostdangerousgame-00-h.html.

4. Richard J. Gerrig, "Introduction," in *The Psychology of Survivor: Overanalyze, Overemote, Overcompensate*, edited by Richard J. Gerrig (Dallas: Benbella Books, 2007), 1–2.

5. Mario Lanza, "The Funny 115: The 115 Funniest Things to Ever Happen on Survivor," *Funny 115*. http://www.funny115.com/hawaii/hawaii.htm.

6. Richard J. Gerrig, *The Psychology of Survivor: Overanalyze, Overemote, Overcompensate*. Dallas: Benbella Books, 2007.

7. Christopher J. Wright, *Tribal Warfare: Survivor and the Political Unconscious of Reality Television* (New York: Lexington Books, 2006).

8. Matthew J. Smith and Andrew F. Wood, *Survivor Lessons: Essays on Communication and Reality Television* (Jefferson, NC: McFarland, 2003).

9. Emily Longretta, "Jeff Probst on His Future on 'Survivor,' the Format Change He Was Told Would 'Kill the Franchise' and Already Planning for 51," *Variety*, June 18, 2024. https://variety.com/2024/awards/features/jeff-probst-survivor-format-changes-season-51-1236040161/.

APPENDIX

1. Jacob Rausch, "Survivor History: Determining the Six Eras of Gameplay," *Surviving Tribal*, January 29, 2018. https://survivingtribal.com/2018/01/29/survivor-history-six-eras-gameplay/.

2. Matthew Storrs, "The Different Eras of Survivor," Inside Survivor, February 1, 2020. https://insidesurvivor.com/the-different-eras-of-survivor-42297.

3. Jason P. Frank and Nic Juarez, "The Survivor Eras Tour," *Vulture*, June 4, 2024. https://www.vulture.com/article/survivor-guide-best-eras-seasons-players-moments.html.

4. Rob Cesternino and Josh Wigler, *The Evolution of Strategy: Volume 3*, "Chapter 22, Part 1: Rob vs. Russel; The Rematch," audiobook, *Rob Has a Website*, August 2015. https://robhasawebsite.com/evolution-of-strategy-chapters/.

5. Dalton Ross, "Jeff Probst Answers *Survivor 41* Season Premiere Burning Questions," *Entertainment Weekly*, September 22, 2021. https://ew.com/tv/survivor-41-jeff-probst-season-premiere-interview/.

BIBLIOGRAPHY

"5 Times Survivor Players Hacked Challenges." *Peridiam*. YouTube video. July 29, 2020. https://www.youtube.com/watch?v=cKsKUPlAMlk.

ABC News. "Did Network Reveal 'Survivor' Champ on Web?" *ABC News*. July 18, 2000.

———. "Original Survivor Claims Show Was Rigged." *ABC News*. February 6, 2001.

———. "Some 'Survivor' Scenes Were Reenactments." *ABC News*. May 10, 2001. https://abcnews.go.com/Entertainment/story?id=105494&page=1.

Apostol, Tyson and Riley McAtee with Cirie Fields. The Pod has Spoken: 'Survivor' Season 41 Finale. Podcast audio. December 16, 2021. https://www.theringer.com/2021/12/16/22839726/survivor-season-41-finale.

Apostol, Tyson and Riley McAtee with Todd Herzog. The Pod has Spoken: 'Survivor' Season 43, Episode 9. Podcast audio. November 17, 2022. https://podcasts.apple.com/us/podcast/the-ringer-reality-tv-podcast/id1580146037?i=1000586556150.

Apostol, Tyson and Riley McAtee with Xander Hastings. The Pod has Spoken: 'Survivor' Season 43, Episode 8. Podcast audio. November 10, 2022. https://www.theringer.com/2022/11/10/23451086/survivor-season-43-episode-8.

Associated Press. "Piercing Error Leads to More Prize Money for 2 'Survivor' Contestants." *Cleveland 19 News*. February 20, 2002. https://www.cleveland19.com/story/672757/piercing-error-leads-to-more-prize-money-for-2-survivor-contestants/.

Ault, Alicia. "Turning a Camera, Stress, and the Wild into a Sudden Hit." *The New York Times*. July 23, 2000.

Aviles, Gwen. "'Survivor' Alum Zeke Smith Reflects on Being Outed as Transgender on the Show," *NBC News*. July 17, 2020. https://www.nbcnews.com/feature/nbc-out/survivor-alum-zeke-smith-reflects-being-outed-transgender-show-n1234091.

Barker, Andrew. "Jeff Probst: Strong 'Survivor.'" *Variety*. June 20, 2013. https://variety.com/2013/tv/awards/jeff-probst-strong-survivor-1200498658/.

Bauder, David. "Television's 'Survivor' Dealing with #MeToo-Era Issues." *AP Top News Package*. December 18, 2019.

Bateson, Mary Catherine. "It's Just a Game, Really." *The New York Times*, vol. 149, no. 51493, August 27, 2000.

Asa Berger, Arthur. *Media and Society: A Critical Perspective*. New York: Rowman & Littlefield, 2012.

Berman, Judy. "Reality TV Has Reshaped Our World." *Time*. August 4, 2022. https://time.com/collection/reality-tv-most-influential-seasons/6199108/reality-tv-influence-on-world/.

Bianco, Robert. "Sold on Sex: Voyeuristic Views Can't Get Enough, So Reality . . ." *USA Today*. October 10, 2002.

Biressi, Anita and Heather Nunn. *Reality TV: Realism and Revelation*. London: Wallflower Press, 2005.

Bitette, Nicole. "Jeff Probst on 'Survivor's Ability to Outlast." *Paramount*. February 26, 2024. https://www.paramount.com/news/jeff-probst-on-survivors-ability-to-outlast.

Bloom, Mike. Zoom interview with Joseph J. Darowski. December 2021.

———. "Outwit, Outplay, Out-cut: How the Editing Team Has Kept the 'Survivor' Tribe Together Through 40 Seasons." Cinemontage.org. February 11, 2020. https://cinemontage.org/cbs-survivor-editors-editing/.

———. "Survivor Contestant Bret LaBelle Recounts Coming Out on National Television," *Parade*, August 16, 2021. https://parade.com/1248679/mikebloom/survivor-bret-labelle-gay/.

Bloomberg, David. "What Survivor Players Should Have Learned," Rob has a Website, September 14, 2021. https://robhasawebsite.com/blog/survivorrules/.

Boyle, Kellie. "'Survivor' Winner Kenzie Addresses Heated Q Exchange & Why Liz Could've Won." *TV Insider*. May 23, 2024. https://www.tvinsider.com/1137331/survivor-finale-season-46-winner-kenzie/.

Bradley, Laura. "Will Reality Television Ever learn How to Handle Misconduct Allegations?" *Vanity Fair*. November 15, 2019. https://www.vanityfair.com/hollywood/2019/11/survivor-dan-spilo-kellee-kim.

Brenton, Sean and Reuben Cohen. *Shooting People: Adventures in Reality TV*. New York: Verso, 2003.

Harbin, M. Brielle. "'Don't Make My Entertainment Political!' Social Media Responses to Narratives of Racial Duty on Competitive Reality Television Series." *Political Communication,* 40(4), March 30, 2023.

Bukszpan, Daniel. "And the Oscar for Not Paying Taxes Goes to . . ." *NBC News*, March 22, 2012. https://www.nbcnews.com/id/wbna46800653.

Burnett, Mark. "Mark Burnett on Casting Jeff Probst - EMMYTVLEGENDS.ORG." *FoundationINTERVIEWS*. YouTube video. June 8, 2011. https://www.youtube.com/watch?v=aOUvpJeSsP4.

———. "Mark Burnett on Casting Survivor- EMMYTVLEGENDS.ORG." *FoundationINTERVIEWS*. YouTube video. June 8, 2011. https://www.youtube.com/watch?v=9Q2ncu_iHwo.

———. "Mark Burnett on Creating Survivor - EMMYTVLEGENDS.ORG." *FoundationINTERVIEWS*. YouTube video. June 8, 2011. https://www.youtube.com/watch?v=jle_s0wZYOA.

Canfield, David. "Jeff Probst on a Survivor Season of Triumphs, Breakthroughs, and Quits: "I Was Shocked." *Vanity Fair*. December 13, 2023. https://www.vanityfair.com/hollywood/jeff-probst-survivor-45-successes-quits-emmys-interview-awards-insider.

Carley, Brennan. "Jeff Probst Is the Ultimate Survivor." *The New York Times*. September 19, 2021. https://www.nytimes.com/2021/09/18/style/jeff-probst-survivor.html.

Carter, Bill. "Britons Revamp American TV." *The New York Times*. July 18, 2000.

———. "CBS's 'Survivor' Is Winner for Network; Real-Life Show Pulls in Younger Viewers." *The New York Times*. June 2, 2000.

———. "CBS Is Surprise Winner in Ratings Contest." *The New York Times*. August 24, 2000.

————. "Survivor of the Pushiest." *New York Times Magazine*. January 28, 2001.

————. "TV Notes; Vicarious Thrills." *The New York Times*. May 24, 2000.

Carter, Julia. "Push Me to the Edge: My Survivor Experience," thejuliacarter.com. June 6, 2019.

CBS News. "Bush Appears with Regis." *CBS News*. September 21, 2000. https://www.cbsnews.com/news/bush-appears-with-regis/.

————. "'Survivor' Goes to China," CBSNews, September 20, 2007. https://www.cbsnews.com/news/survivor-goes-to-china/.

Cesternino, Rob. "Survivor 40 Premiere Red Carpet Interviews." *Rob Has a Podcast*. February 11, 2020. YouTube video. https://www.youtube.com/watch?v=f2rMdTJ-BUI&t=1s.

Cesternino, Rob, Chappell, and Chantele Francis. "Survivor All Time Top 40 Rankings: #40 Island of the Idols, Rob Has a Podcast. Podcast audio. January 7, 2021. https://robhasawebsite.com/survivor-all-time-top-40-rankings-number-40-survivor-island-of-the-idols/.

Cesternino, Rob with Christian Hubicki. Survivor 40 Episode 8 Recap with Christian Hubicki, Rob Has a Podcast. Podcast audio. April 2, 2020. https://robhasawebsite.com/survivor-40-episode-8-recap-with-christian-hubicki/.

————. Survivor All-Time Top 40 Rankings | #9: Cambodia with Christian Hubicki, Rob Has a Podcast. Podcast audio. July 28, 2021. https://robhasawebsite.com/survivor-season-rankings-9-cambodia/.

Cesternino, Rob with Ghandia Johnson and Teresa Cooper, Talking with T-Bird: Ghandia Johnson, Rob has a Podcast. Podcast audio. February 1, 2021. https://robhasawebsite.com/survivor-ghandia-johnson-interview-thailand-tbird/=.

Cesternino, Rob and Josh Wigler, *The Evolution of Strategy: Volume 3*, "Chapter 22, Part 1: Rob vs. Russel; The Rematch," audiobook, Rob Has a Website, August 2015. https://robhasawebsite.com/evolution-of-strategy-chapters/.

Cesternino, Rob with Mary Kwiatkowski, and Maggie Morgan. Survivor All-Time Top 40 Rankings - #8 : The Amazon, Rob Has a Podcast. August 4, 2021. https://robhasawebsite.com/survivor-season-rankings-8-amazon/.

Cesternino, Rob with Sean Rector, Julia Carter et al. Black Voices of SURVIVOR Roundtable LIVE, Rob Has a Podcast. June 24, 2020. https://www.youtube.com/watch?v=lqJM_05fFuk&t=5665s.

Chicago Tribune, "'Survivor' Finale Posts Ratings Even Larger than Show's Hype," *Chicago Tribune*, August 25, 2000, https://www.chicagotribune.com/2000/08/25/survivor-finale-posts-ratings-even-larger-than-shows-hype/.

Clarke, Steve. "How 'Survivor' Has Outplayed Its Competition for 25 Years." *Variety*. October 14, 2022. https://variety.com/2022/tv/global/survivor-25-years-anniversary-charlie-parsons-1235402539/.

Collins, Suzanne. *The Hunger Games*. New York: Scholastic Press, 2008.

Connell, Richard. "The Most Dangerous Game." Project Guttenberg. https://gutenberg.ca/ebooks/connellr-mostdangerousgame/connellr-mostdangerousgame-00-h.html.

Cook, Meghan. "'Survivor' Players Reveal What It's Really Like to Compete on the Show." *Business Insider*. March 11, 2022. https://www.insider.com/what-its-like-being-on-survivor-contestants-reveal-2021-6.

Conn, Peter. *Great American Bestsellers: The Books that Shaped America*. The Teaching Company. 2009. (audiobook).

Conrad, Roger. "T-Mobile US: The Sprint Merger So Far." *Forbes*. June 28, 2021. https://www.forbes.com/sites/greatspeculations/2020/06/23/t-mobile-us-the-sprint-merger-so-far/.

Darowski, Joseph J. and Kate Darowski, *Cheers: A Cultural History*. New York: Rowman & Littlefield, 2019.

DaSilva, Dan "Wardog" (@IAmTheWardog). "Analyzing the Best Reality Show on TV through the Lens of Gender Is Tiresome," Twitter, February 20, 2020. https://twitter.com/IAmTheWardog/status/1230874836664123393.

De Morales, Lisa. "ABC Aims at 'Survivor.'" *The Capital Times*. June 6, 2000.

Deggans, Eric. "'Do Right By Us': Black 'Survivor Alums Say the Reality Was Harmful Stereotypes." *NPR*. July 1, 2020. https://www.npr.org/2020/07/01/885750685/do-right-by-us-black-survivor-alums-say-the-reality-was-harmful-stereotypes.

Dehnart, Andy. "Answers to Survivor 46's Burning Questions." Reality Blurred. May 24, 2024. https://www.realityblurred.com/realitytv/2024/05/survivor-46-questions-answers/.

———. "Best Survivor contestants 'have really strong opinions, they know who they are.'" Reality Blurred. December 24, 2008.https://www.realityblurred.com/realitytv/2008/12/survivor-samoa-spillman_casting/.

———. "Bob Crowley: "I'm not playing the game, I'm here to have a good time.'" Reality Blurred. September 3, 2008. https://www.realityblurred.com/realitytv/2008/09/survivor-gabon-bob_crowley/.

———. "Did Survivor's Flirting, Furtive Foraging, or Puzzle Prep Pay Off?" Reality Blurred. March 8, 2023. https://www.realityblurred.com/realitytv/2023/03/survivor-44-episode-2-two-dorky-magnets-recap/.

———. "How Jeff Probst Made Me Fear for Survivor's Future." Reality Blurred. May 23, 2023. https://www.realityblurred.com/realitytv/2023/05/survivor-jeff-probst-podcast-fear/.

———. "Survivor: An Honest, Vulnerable Discussion of Race and Privilege Was Just One Part of an All-Time-Great Episode," Reality Blurred, October 30, 2019. https://www.realityblurred.com/realitytv/2019/10/survivor-island-of-the-idols-episode-6-suck-it-up-buttercup-recap/.

———. "Survivor rules: The Contract that Details Pay, Tie-Breakers, Prohibited Behavior, and More." Reality Blurred. May 31, 2010. Updated October 12, 2021. https://www.realityblurred.com/realitytv/2010/05/survivor-cast-contract/.

———. "'Survivor: Samoa' Rises to New Season of Challenges." NPR. September 16, 2009. https://www.npr.org/2009/09/16/112850247/survivor-samoa-rises-to-new-season-of-challenges.

———. "Why Sandra Sitting Out Back-to-Back Challenges Is Allowed." Reality Blurred. March 5, 2020. https://www.realityblurred.com/realitytv/2020/03/sandra-sitting-out-survivor-challenges/.

———. "Why Survivor Stopped Recruiting Players, and How Casting Has Changed Recently." Reality Blurred. October 27, 2020. https://realityblurred.com/realitytv/2020/10/survivor-casting-changes-recruits/.

Devens, Rick (@Rick_Devens). "Production Constantly Adding New Elements and Twists to the Show Is the Only Reason It's Been a Success for Going on 42 Seasons," Twitter, May 24, 2021, 9:38 a.m., https://twitter.com/Rick_Devens/status/1396868205252128768.

Dixon, Marcus James. "'Survivor' Nudity No Longer Allowed, Confirms Jeff Probst: 'Today It Wouldn't Get Past Our Producers for Half a Second,'" *Gold Derby*, February 12, 2020. https://www.goldderby.com/article/2020/survivor-nudity-jeff-probst-richard-hatch/.

Donaldson, Colby. "Commentary." Disc 1, *Survivor: The Australian Outback*, Season 2, episode 1, DVD.

Donaton, Scott, "Real Bad: The Backlash Begins Against Exploitative Tube Trend," *Advertising Age*, 71(41) (October 2, 2000).

Douglas, Susan J. *The Rise of Enlightened Sexism*. St. Marin's Press, 2010.

Dovey, Jon. "Studying Reality TV." In *The Television Genre Book*. London: Palgrave, 2015.

Drysdale, Jennifer. "'Survivor': How the Dan Spilo Controversy Was Addressed on 'Island of the Idols' Finale," *Entertainment Tonight*, December 18, 2019. https://www.etonline.com/survivor-how-the-dan-spilo-controversy-was-addressed-on-island-of-the-idols-finale-138260.

Ebenkamp, Becky. "Return to Peyton Placement." *Brandweek*, June 6, 2001.

ENews, "A History of Survivor's Most Controversial Twists," Eonline.com, September 22, 2021, https://www.eonline.com/photos/33298/a-history-of-survivors-most-controversial-twists.

Farberov, Snejana. "Fearless 'Survivor' Winner's Heartbreak after Her Son, 25, Is Killed in Car Accident 'Because He Wasn't Wearing a Seat Belt,'" *The Daily Mail*. December 11, 2013. https://www.dailymail.co.uk/news/article-2522095/Survivor-winner-Tina-Wessons-heartbreak-son-killed-car-accident.html.

Farrow, Ronan. "Les Moonves and CBS Face Allegations of Sexual Misconduct." *The New Yorker*. July 27, 2018. https://www.newyorker.com/magazine/2018/08/06/les-moonves-and-cbs-face-allegations-of-sexual-misconduct.

Flint, Joe. "CBS's Hit Show 'Survivor' Ends Summer Run with Huge Ratings." *The Wall Street Journal*, August 25, 2000.

Fishbach, Stephen. *People*. https://people.com/author/stephen-fishbach/.

Fonseca, Nicholas. "Details on the 'Bachelor'-Style Gay Reality Show," *Entertainment Weekly*, June 6, 2003. https://ew.com/article/2003/06/06/details-bachelor-style-gay-reality-show/.

FoundationINTERVIEWS, "Leslie Moonves Interview part 4 of 5 - EMMYTVLEGENDS.ORG, YouTube video, September 9, 2009. https://www.youtube.com/watch?v=uALSVBYHKP4&t=1191s.

Fournier, Holly. "Ex-'Survivor' Star Gets Up to 4 Years for Child Porn." *The Detroit News*. December 27, 2016. https://www.detroitnews.com/story/news/local/oakland-county/2016/12/27/ex-survivor-sentenced-child-porn-possession/95867296/.

Frank, Jason P. and Nic Juarez. "The Survivor Eras Tour," *Vulture*, June 4, 2024. https://www.vulture.com/article/survivor-guide-best-eras-seasons-players-moments.html.

Framke, Caroline. "'Survivor' Mishandling of Sexual Harassment Is Irresponsible and Infuriating," *Variety*, November 21, 2019. https://variety.com/2019/tv/news/survivor-island-idols-sexual-harassment-1203411590/.

Freberg, Malcolm. "'Survivor' Was Anyone's Game When I Played It, But Twists and Advantages Are Ruining What Makes the Show Special," *Business Insider*, December 1, 2021, https://www.businessinsider.com/former-survivor-player-whats-wrong-with-the-show-new-season-41-2021.

Friedman, James. *Reality Squared: Televisual Discourse on the Real*. New Brunswick: Rutgers University Press, 2002.

Gardner, Helen. "Explainer: The Myth of the Noble Savage." *The Conversation*. February 24, 2016. https://theconversation.com/explainer-the-myth-of-the-noble-savage-55316.

Garner, Todd with Jeff Probst, The Producer's Guide, podcast audio, September 13, 2018. https://podcastone.com/episode/Jeff-Probst.

George, Daniel. "Survivor's Jeff Probst: 'I Hear You. We're Not Gonna Do Edge (of Extinction) for a While.'" *Surviving Tribal.* February 11, 2020. https://survivingtribal .com/2020/02/11/survivor-jeff-probst-no-edge-extinction/.

Gerrig, Richard J. "Introduction," in *The Psychology of Survivor: Overanalyze, Overemote, Overcompensate*, edited by Richard J. Gerrig. Dallas: Benbella Books, 2007.

Gilbert, Sophie. "The Retrograde Shame of *The Biggest Loser*," *The Atlantic*, January 29, 2020. https://www.theatlantic.com/culture/archive/2020/01/the-retrograde-shame-of -the-biggest-loser/605713/.

Goldberg, Leslie. "'Survivor': CBS Stands by Decision to Broadcast Transgender Outing," *The Hollywood Reporter*, April 13, 2017. https://www.hollywoodreporter.com /tv/tv-news/survivor-cbs-stands-by-decision-broadcast-zeke-smiths-outing-993757/.

Gomez, Patrick. "'Survivor''s Jeff Varner: How He Knew Zeke Smith Is Transgender and the 'Shame' He Feels for Outing Him," *People*, Aprile 13 2017. https://people.com/tv /survivor-jeff-varner-interview-outing-zeke-smith-transgender.

Grant, Tamara. "'Survivor' Winner Richard Hatch Claims CBS Is Responsible for Controversial Incident," *Showbiz Cheatsheet*, February 8, 2020. https://www.cheatsheet .com/entertainment/survivor-richard-hatch-claims-cbs-is-responsible-for-incident -with-sue-hawk.html/.

Guss, Shannon. Zoom interview with Joseph J. Darowski. April 2024.

Harbin, M. Brielle. "Don't Make My Entertainment Political! Social Media Responses to Narratives of Racial Duty on Competitive Reality Television Series," *Political Communication*, March 30, 2023.

Hartman, Tilo and Charlotte Goldhoorn. "Horton and Wohl: Revisited: Exploring Viewers' Experience of Parasocial Interaction," *Journal of Communication*, 61(6) (December 2011).

Helling, Steve. "'Survivor' Contestant B.B. Anderson Dead at 77." *People*, November 1, 2013. https://people.com/tv/survivor-contestant-b-b-andersen-dead-at-77/.

———. "'Survivor' Contestant Dan Spilo Was Uninvited from Live Finale After His Removal from Show." *People*. December 12, 2019. https://people.com/tv/survivor -contestant-dan-spilo-was-uninvited-from-live-finale-after-his-removal-from-show/.

———. "'Survivor''s Dan Spilo Breaks Silence on His Behavior on the Show: 'I Am Deeply Sorry.'" *People*. December 17, 2019. https://people.com/tv/survivors -dan-spilo-breaks-silence-on-his-behavior-on-the-show-i-am-deeply-sorry/#:~ :text=%22I%20am%20deeply%20sorry%20for,again%2C%20clearly%20and %20unambiguously.%22.

Herman, Allison. "'Survivor' Is the Quintessential TV Show." *The Ringer*, May 12, 2020. https://www.theringer.com/tv/2020/5/12/21255075/survivor-legacy-40th-anniversary -reality-tv.

Hernandez, Brian Anthony. "*Survivor* Season 46 Winner Kenzie Talks Season 50 Cast Wish

List, Jury Votes, Q-Skirt and 'Mermaid Dragon' (Exclusive)." People.com. May 23, 2024. https://people.com/survivor-46-winner-kenzie-talks-season-50-cast-jury-votes-husband-baby-exclusive-8653352.

Hill, Annette, *Reality TV: Audiences and Popular Factual Television*. New York: Routledge, 2005.

Hill, Annette and Gareth Palmer. "Big Brother." *Television & New Media*, 3(3) (August 2002): 251–254. https://doi.org/10.1177/152747640200300301.

Holmes, Martin. "Birth of a Phenomenon—An Oral History of Survivor Borneo." Inside Survivor. May 29, 2020. https://insidesurvivor.com/birth-of-a-phenomenon-an-oral -history-of-survivor-borneo-43932.

———. "Casting Director Lynne Spiegel Spillman 'Let Go' from Survivor." Inside Survivor. July 1, 2018. https://insidesurvivor.com/casting-director-lynne-spiegel-spillman -fired-from-survivor-34504.

———. "Jeff Probst Says There Will Be No More Villains on Survivor." Inside Survivor. February 26, 2024. https://insidesurvivor.com/jeff-probst-says-there-will-be-no-more -villains-on-survivor-56582.

———. "Mike White Responsible for Survivor Ditching Fire Tokens Twist." Inside Survivor. September 9, 2021. https://insidesurvivor.com/mike-white-responsible-for -survivor-ditching-fire-tokens-twist-50592.

———. "Survivor Edgic—An Introduction." Inside Survivor. September 13, 2015. https:// insidesurvivor.com/survivor-edgic-an-introduction-3094.

Huff, Richard M. *Reality Television*. London: Praeger, 2006.

Hutcheon, Linda. *A Theory of Adaptation, second* edition. New York: Routledge, 120–28.

The Internet Movie Database. *The Weakest Link*. Episode aired on January 6, 2002. https:// www.imdb.com/title/tt0744761/.

Jackson, Shirley. "The Lottery," in *Literature: Approaches to Fiction, Poetry, and Drama,* edited

by Robert DiYanni. New York: McGraw Hill, (409–15).

Jenkins, Henry. *Convergence Culture: Where Old and New Media Collide*. New York: New York University Press, 2006.

Jensen, Jeff. "Bawdy and Sole: What's Up with that Reebok Ad?" *Entertainment Weekly*. August 11, 2000. https://ew.com/article/2000/08/11/bawdy-and-sole-whats-reebok -ad/.

Kaplan, Don. "'Survivor' 'Screw-Up' Costs CBS $200G." *New York Post*. February 20, 2002. https://nypost.com/2002/02/20/survivor-screw-up-costs-cbs-200g/.

Katz, Elihu, Hadassah Haas, and Michael Gurevitch. "On the Use of the Mass Media for Important Things." *American Sociological Review* 38(2) (1973): 164–81.

Kavka, Misha and Amy West. "Temporalities of the Real: Conceptualizing time in Reality TV." In *Understanding Reality Television*. New York: Routledge, 2004.

Kavka, Misha. *Reality TV*. Edinburgh: Edinburgh University Press, 2012.

Kellogg, Alex P. "A Game Theory for 'Survivor.'" *Chronicle of Higher Education*, 46(32) (April 20, 2001): A8.

Kelly, Emma. "Remembering The Swan—the Noughties' Most Controversial and Offensive Reality TV Series." *Metro*. October 22, 2019. https://metro.co.uk/2019/10/22 /remembering-swan-noughties-controversial-offensive-reality-tv-series-10962780/.

Koblin, John. "Fully Clothed and Barely Afraid," *The New York Times*, April 11, 2016.

———. "'Survivor' Defies Gravity to Hang on as CBS Ratings Stalwart." *The New York Times*. September 30, 2015. https://www.nytimes.com/2015/10/01/business/media/ survivor-defies-gravity-to-hang-on-as-cbs-ratings-stalwart.html.

Kuhagen, Christopher. "Survivor 40: Wisconsinites Who Have Played in the Hit Reality TV Show." *Milwaukee Journal Sentinel*. February 12, 2020. https://www.jsonline .com/picture-gallery/communities/2020/02/11/survivor-sue-hawk-andrea-boehlke -among-wisconsin-players-tv-show/4668113002/.

Kuppens, An and Jelle Mast. "*Ticket to the Tribes*: Culture Shock and the 'Exotic' in Intercultural Reality Television," *Media, Culture & Society*, 34(7) (October 2012): 799–814.

Lanza, Mario. "All-Star Survivor: Hawaii, A Fictional Serial Novel." *Funny 115*. http://www.funny115.com/hawaii/hawaii.htm.

———. *When It Was Worth Playing For: My Experience Writing about the TV Show "Survivor."* United States: CreateSpace Independent Publishing, 2015.

Lee, Felicia R. "'Home Edition' Shows the Softer Side of Reality TV," *New York Times*, November 4, 2004.

Liguori, Matt (@mattliguori), "We're Currently on a Streak of 9 Consecutive Women Getting Their Torch Snuffed," Twitter, February 20, 2020, https://twitter.com/mattliguori/status/1230692951614988288.

Longeretta, Emily. "Jeff Probst on His Future on 'Survivor,' the Format Change He Was Told Would 'Kill the Franchise' and Already Planning for 51." *Variety*, June 18, 2024. https://variety.com/2024/awards/features/jeff-probst-survivor-format-changes-season-51-1236040161/.

Lowe, Elaine. "'Survivor': CBS Adds New Guidelines Following Misconduct Allegations," *Variety*, December 17, 2019. https://variety.com/2019/tv/news/survivor-cbs-policy-change-dan-spilo-alleged-misconduct-1203446825/.

Lowry, Brian. "Decade's Big 'Survivor.'" *Variety*. December 18, 2009. https://variety.com/2009/tv/columns/decade-s-big-survivor-1118012985/.

Maas, Jennifer. "Reality TV Exec Who Launched 'Survivor' Sues CBS for Wrongful Termination, Discrimination." *The Wrap*. November 25, 2019. https://www.thewrap.com/survivor-exec-ghen-maynard-sues-cbs-wrongful-termination-discrimination/.

Malcolm, Shawna. "Survivor's New Look: Inside the New Tribal Council Set." *TV Guide*. September 29, 2007. https://www.tvguide.com/news/survivor-china-tribal-41810/.

———. "Three Tribes, 18 Seasoned Players, and Rich Is Still Naked," *TV Guide*, January 17–23, 2004.

McAtee, Riley. "'Survivor' Ejected Dan Spilo—but the Show's Harassment Crisis is Far from Over," *The Ringer*, December 12, 2019. https://www.theringer.com/tv/2019/12/12/21012988/survivor-dan-spilo-removed-harassment-season-39-episode-9.

McNett, Gavin. "The Wacky World of Television," Salon, March 13, 2000. https://www.salon.com/2000/03/13/wackytv/.

McQuillen, Kass (@KassMcQ). "This Had to Be Redone Because Trish's Mic Wasn't Working" Twitter, April 24, 2024. https://x.com/KassMcQ/status/1783124800522641682.

Millman, Joyce. "I Survived 'Survivor: The Australian Outback,'" Salon, May 3, 2001. https://www.salon.com/2001/05/03/last_survivor2/.

Mittell, Jason. *Television and American Culture*. Oxford: Oxford University Press, 2009.

Moynihan, Rob, "30 Seasons of Survivor: An Oral History of the Reality Competition That Changed the Game." *TV Insider*. September 18, 2015. https://www.tvinsider.com/1458/30-seasons-of-survivor-epic-blindsides-machiavellian-maneuvering-icky-bug-bites/.

Moonves, Leslie. "Leslie Moonves Discusses "Survivor" - EMMYTVLEGENDS.ORG." FoundationINTERVIEWS. YouTube video, January 23, 2013. https://www.youtube.com/watch?v=fQhrILJW6yU.

Murray, Susan. "'I Think We Need a New Name for It': The Meeting of Documentary and Reality TV," in *Reality TV: Remaking Television Culture*, 65–81. New York: New York University Press, 2009.

Nathani, Neha. "The Real Reason Survivor Doesn't Travel To New Locations Anymore." *Screen Rant*. March 24, 2024. https://screenrant.com/why-survivor-doesnt-travel -new-locations-anymore/.

Neal, Rome. "Hawk and Hatch: Getting Past It." *CBS News*, March 4, 2004. https://www .cbsnews.com/news/hawk-and-hatch-getting-past-it/.

Nordyke, Kimberly. "Caleb Bankston, 'Survivor' Competitor, Dies at 26 in Railway Accident." *The Hollywood Reporter*. June 25, 2014. https://www.hollywoodreporter.com/ news/general-news/caleb-bankston-dead-survivor-competitor-714851/.

Norwin, Alyssa. "'Survivor' Finale Reunion: Why Is Alec Merlino Missing from the Live Show?" *Hollywood Life*. December 19, 2018. https://hollywoodlife.com/2018/12/19/ where-is-alec-survivor-david-vs-goliath-reunion-finale/.

O'Mara, Erin, Kunz, Jennifer L. Howell, and Nicole Beasley, "Surviving Racism and Sexism: What Votes in the Television Program Survivor Reveal About Discrimination," *Psychological Science* 34(6) (June 2023).

Oleszczak, Leigh. "Survivor: Production Steps in for First Time Despite Past Issues," Surviving Tribal, November 17, 2019. https://survivingtribal.com/2019/11/17/survivor -island-idols-production-steps-in/.

Olson, Alexandra. "CBS Denies Former CEO Les Moonves $120 Million Severance," *Associated Press*, December 18, 2018. https://apnews.com/television-arts-and -entertainment-general-news-7858ff2dc8044b139c99a20aed18c502.

Otterson, Joe. "CBS Sets Diversity Goal for Unscripted Shows." *Variety*. November 9, 2020. https://variety.com/2020/tv/news/cbs-unscripted-shows-diversity-1234826214/

Oullette, Laurie and James Hay. *Better Living Through Reality TV*. Malden, MA: Blackwell Publishing, 2008.

Parker, James. "Race to the Bottom: Why There Are So Many Naked People on TV These Days," *The Atlantic Monthly*, October 2015.

Peridiam. "The 'Intentional Matsing' Strategy in Survivor." YouTube. January 24, 2018. https://www.youtube.com/watch?v=jXtOj32Tx4U.

Peyser, Marc, et al. "'Survivor' Tsunami," *Newsweek*, 136(9) (August 8, 2000): 52.

Pierce, Scott D. "Despite #MeToo, 'Survivor' and CBS Failed Women and Heads Should Roll," *The Salt Lake Tribune*, December 15, 2019. https://www.sltrib.com/artsliving /2019/12/15/scott-d-pierce-despite/.

———. "'Survivor' Changed TV as We Know it," *Deseret News*, December 22, 2009. https://www.deseret.com/2009/12/22/20360166/scott-d-pierce-survivor-changed-tv -as-we-know-it/.

Pittman, Jeff. "Doing Their Dest, despite . . ." True Dork Times. November 29, 2020. https://www.truedorktimes.com/s17/recaps/e3.htm.

Poniewozik, James. "Aaargh! CBS Is Playing 'Survivor' Mind Games," *Time*. August 3, 2000.

———. "Survivor's Rulebook Leaks Out." *Time*. June 1, 2010. https://entertainment.time .com/2010/06/01/survivors-rulebook-leaks-out/.

Probst, Jeff (@jeffprobst). BREAKING NEWS Get ready to see returning players on #Survivor: 50! April 27, 2024. https://www.instagram.com/reel/C6SheDqLLVy/?utm _source=ig_web_copy_link&igsh=MzRlODBiNWFlZA==.

———. "Jeff Probst | A Peek Behind the Scenes of Survivor's 20-Year Success," Talks at Google, February 20, 2020, YouTube video, https://www.youtube.com/watch?v =azzJur0cukc&t=2905s.

———. "Jeff Probst on fighting to become host of "Survivor." FoundationINTER-VIEWS. September 17, 2013. YouTube video. https://www.youtube.com/watch?v=3_ojDBrkx8k.

———. "Jeff Probst REVEALS His Favorite Moments From 20 Years of 'Survivor' | Full Interview." *Entertainment Tonight.* February 15, 2020. YouTube video. https://www.youtube.com/watch?v=biN72tLAN6E.

———. "Jeff Probst Won't Snuff Out the Torch for Survivor Quitters." LiveKellyand-Mark. November 15, 2023. YouTube video. https://www.youtube.com/watch?v=MQh5O9mQOlc&t=51s.

Probst, Jeff, Brittany Crapper and Jay Wolfe, Designing Challenges: On Fire with Jeff Probst: The Official *Survivor* Podcast, podcast audio, March 22, 2023. https://podcasts.apple.com/us/podcast/designing-challenges/id1673596832?i=1000605479451.

———. Shooting *Survivor*: On Fire with Jeff Probst: The Official *Survivor* Podcast, podcast audio, May 3, 2023. https://podcasts.apple.com/us/podcast/shooting-survivor/id1673596832?i=1000611662379.

———. Your Burning *Survivor* Questions: On Fire with Jeff Probst: The Official *Survivor* Podcast, podcast audio, May 10, 2023. https://podcasts.apple.com/ca/podcast/your-burning-survivor-questions/id1673596832?i=1000612566616.

Probst, Jeff, Jay Wolff, and Dee Valladares. Play or Get Played: On Fire with Jeff Probst: The Official *Survivor* Podcast. Podcast audio. May 16, 2024. https://podcasts.apple.com/us/podcast/play-or-get-played/id1673596832?i=1000655737413.

———. What's Up, Jeff? On Fire with Jeff Probst: The Official *Survivor* Podcast. Podcast audio. April 10, 2024. https://podcasts.apple.com/us/podcast/whats-up-jeff/id1673596832?i=1000652089872.

Rausch, Jacob. "Survivor History: Determining the Six Eras of Gameplay," Surviving Tribal, January 29, 2018. https://survivingtribal.com/2018/01/29/survivor-history-six-eras-gameplay/.

Reality TV World Staff, "Fox Releases Details of 'Playing It Straight''s Unaired Conclusion," Reality TV World, July 28, 2004. https://www.realitytvworld.com/news/fox-releases-details-of-playing-it-straight-unaired-conclusion-2782.php.

Rees, Alex. "*Survivor*'s New Season Brings Back Many of the Show's Most Influential Winners. Where Is Original Champion Richard Hatch?" *Time*, February 12, 2020. https://time.com/5781331/survivor-winners-season-richard-hatch-harassment/.

Reinstein, Mara. "Jeff Probst Reveals Why Richard Hatch Is Not Part of 'Survivor' Season 40," *US Weekly*, January 15, 2020. https://www.usmagazine.com/entertainment/news/jeff-probst-why-richard-hatch-is-not-on-survivor-winners-at-war/.

———. "Through Two Decades and 40 Seasons, the Tribal Council Remains the Heart of 'Survivor.'" The Ringer. May 12, 2020. https://www.theringer.com/tv/2020/5/12/21254206/survivor-tribal-council-evolution-behind-the-scenes.

Rice, Lynett. "Altered Reality," *Entertainment Weekly*, February 2, 2022. https://ew.com/tv/cbs-diversity-survivor-big-brother/.

———. "'Survivor' Issues Rare Statement to Viewers." *Deadline.* May 30, 2024. https://deadline.com/2024/05/survivor-issues-statement-to-viewers-consider-embracing-kindness-1235945399/.

Rickenbacker, Davie (@WheresDavie). "lol since we talking about reshoots . . ." Twitter. April 24, 2024. https://x.com/WheresDavie/status/1783177491546316857.

Riley, Kathleen C. "Surviving 'Survivor' in the Marquesas." *Anthropology News*, May 2002.

Rivera, Christopher. "Cast of 'Survivor' Season 1: Where Are They in 2024!" After Buzz TV, May 22, 2024. https://www.afterbuzztv.com/cast-of-survivor-season-1-where -are-they-in-2024/.

Rose, Veronica, "'Roar': A Throwback to Heath Ledger's Irish Prince Stint." *The Series Regulars*, July 13, 2020.

Ross, Dalton (@DaltonRoss). "The 1 Big Bummer Is that Panama Was the Last Season with a Final 2 (with rare injury exceptions). Producers Then Changed to Final 3 after Watching Terry Not Make It . . ." *Twitter*, June 15, 2021. https://twitter.com /DaltonRoss/status/1404826841660243969?s=20.

———. "All Hands on Deck: Behind the Scenes of a Survivor Marooning." *Entertainment Weekly*. February 20, 2019. https://ew.com/tv/2019/02/20/survivor-edge-of -extinction-marooning/.

———. "How to Get on Survivor: Behind the Scenes of Casting Season 45." *Entertainment Weekly*. September 18, 2023.https://ew.com/tv/survivor-45-behind-the-scenes -casting-cover-story/.

———. "Jackson Fox Reacts to Being Pulled from *Survivor 42*," *Entertainment Weekly*, March 10, 2022. https://ew.com/tv/survivor-42-jackson-fox-premiere-interview/.

———. "Jeff Probst Answers *Survivor 41* Season Premiere Burning Questions." *Entertainment Weekly*. September 22, 2021.https://ew.com/tv/survivor-41-jeff-probst -season-premiere-interview/.

———. "Jeff Probst Addresses His Future as Survivor Host." *Entertainment Weekly*. December 7, 2022. https://ew.com/tv/jeff-probst-future-survivor-host/.

———. "Jeff Probst Explains Why *Survivor* Just Made a Huge Rules Change." *Entertainment Weekly*. October 4, 2023. https://ew.com/tv/survivor-45-jeff-probst-explains -huge-rules-change/.

———. "Jeff Probst Explains Why They Brought Edge of Extinction Back on Survivor: Winners at War." *Entertainment Weekly*. January 24, 2020. https://ew.com/tv/2020 /01/24/survivor-winners-at-war-jeff-probst-edge-of-extinction/.

———. "Jeff Probst Explains Why They Are Sticking with 26-Day Survivor Seasons." *Entertainment Weekly*. May 15, 2024. https://ew.com/survivor-jeff-probst-explains -not-going-back-to-39-day-seasons-8649115.

———. "Jeff Probst on Tony's Three Days of Survivor Dominance." *Entertainment Weekly*. April 23, 2020, https://ew.com/tv/survivor-jeff-probst-winners-at-war-tony -vlachos-episode-11-interview/.

———. "Jeff Probst Reveals the Survivor Concept Season We Never Saw." *Entertainment Weekly*. April 13, 2023. https://ew.com/tv/survivor-jeff-probst-concept-season -we-never-saw/.

———. "Jeff Probst Says Survivor May Never Go Back to 39 Days." *Entertainment Weekly*. September 7, 2021. https://ew.com/tv/survivor-41-jeff-probst-26-day-game -instead-of-39/.

———. "Jeff Probst Says Survivor Quitters Will No Longer Get Torch Snuffed." *Entertainment Weekly*. November 15, 2023. https://ew.com/survivor-jeff-probst-quitters -no-longer-get-torch-snuffed-8402222.

———. "Jeff Probst Wants Survivor to Stay in Fiji Permanently." *Entertainment Weekly*. September 12, 2017. https://ew.com/tv/2017/09/12/survivor-jeff-probst-fiji/.

———. "Meet the Cast of Survivor 41." *Entertainment Weekly*. August 30, 2021. https:// ew.com/tv/survivor-41-cast-photos-bios/.

———. "Omar Zaheer Reveals Unseen Idol Nullifier that Led to His Survivor Demise." *Entertainment Weekly*. May 19, 2022. https://ew.com/tv/survivor-42-omar-zaheer-interview/.

———. "Survivor's 35 Best Challenges Ever." *Entertainment Weekly*. August 22, 2022. https://ew.com/tv/survivor-the-35-best-challenges-ever/.

———. "'Survivor: Cagayan': Jeff Probst Weighs in on the Latest Blindside." *Entertainment Weekly*. April 17, 2014. https://ew.com/article/2014/04/17/survivor-cagayan-jeff-probst-blindside/.

———. "Survivor Considered Filming in Georgia and Hawaii Due to COVID." *Entertainment Weekly*. September 1, 2021. https://ew.com/tv/survivor-41-georgia-hawaii-covid-jeff-probst/.

———. "Survivor Host Jeff Probst Explains the Show's New Intro," *Entertainment Weekly*. October 3, 2019. https://ew.com/tv/2019/10/03/survivor-jeff-probst-island-of-the-idols-episode-2/.

———. "'Survivor' Host Jeff Probst on the Pair that Dropped Out and a Possible Final Two." *Entertainment Weekly*. September 8, 2014. https://ew.com/article/2014/09/08/survivor-jeff-probst-san-juan-del-sur-final-2/.

———. "Survivor Host Jeff Probst Says Mike White Helped Get Rid of Redemption Island." *Entertainment Weekly*. November 13, 2014. https://ew.com/article/2014/11/13/survivor-jeff-probst-mike-white/.

———. "*Survivor* Host Jeff Probst Talks about First Player Ever Ejected from the Game," *Entertainment Weekly*. December 11, 2019. https://ew.com/tv/2019/12/11/survivor-host-jeff-probst-dan-spilo-removed-episode-13/.

———. "*Survivor* Host Jeff Probst Weighs in on Jamal and Jack's Racial Incident." *Entertainment Weekly*. October 31, 2019. https://ew.com/tv/2019/10/31/survivor-jeff-probst-island-of-the-idols-episode-6/.

———. "Survivor Finale: Jeff Probst Explains Reason behind Controversial Twist." *Entertainment Weekly*. December 21, 2017. https://ew.com/tv/2017/12/21/survivor-finale-jeff-probst-twist/.

———. "'Survivor': Jeff Probst on 'the Most Frightened I've Been in All My Time' on the Show." *Entertainment Weekly*, March 10, 2016, https://ew.com/article/2016/03/10/survivor-jeff-probst-kaoh-rong-caleb-alecia-debbie-episode-4/.

———. "Survivor Recap: Dumbest. Tribe. Ever." *Entertainment Weekly*. February 27, 2015. https://ew.com/recap/survivor-one-world-episode-4/.

———. "Survivor Quarantine Questionnaire: Andrew Savage Was 'Deeply Haunted' by the Outcast Twist." *Entertainment Weekly*. February 8, 2021. https://ew.com/tv/survivor-pearl-islands-cambodia-andrew-savage-quarantine-questionnaire/.

———. "Survivor Quarantine Questionnaire: Bret LaBelle Reflects on Coming Out as Gay on the Show." *Entertainment Weekly*. May 20, 2021. https://ew.com/tv/survivor-millennials-vs-gen-x-bret-labelle-quarantine-questionnaire-gay-coming-out/.

———. "Survivor Quarantine Questionnaire: Crystal Cox on Why Survivor Needs More Minority Editors." *Entertainment Weekly*. October 22, 2020. https://ew.com/tv/survivor-gabon-crystal-cox-quarantine-questionnaire/.

———. "*Survivor* Quarantine Questionnaire: David Wright Buried a Fake Idol . . . before the Season Even Began!" *Entertainment Weekly*, June 1, 2021. https://ew.com/tv/survivor-david-wright-millennials-vs-gen-x-edge-of-extinction-quarantine-questionnaire/.

———. "Survivor Quarantine Questionnaire: Kelly Shinn Talks about Her Infamous 'Purple Edit' in Nicaragua." *Entertainment Weekly*. September 8, 2020. https://ew.com/tv/survivor-nicaragua-kelly-shinn-purple-quarantine-questionnaire/.

———. "Survivor Quarantine Questionnaire: Jolanda Jones on Being Portrayed as the 'Bitch' in Palau." *Entertainment Weekly*. October 2, 2020. https://ew.com/tv/survivor-palau-jolanda-jones-quarantine-questionnaire/.

———. "Survivor's 35 Best Challenges Ever." *Entertainment Weekly*. August 22, 2022. https://ew.com/tv/survivor-the-35-best-challenges-ever/.

———. "The Best and Worst Survivor Twists Ever." *Entertainment Weekly*. June 18, 2019.https://ew.com/tv/2019/06/18/survivor-best-and-worst-twists/.

———. "Why Ghandia Should Change Her Name to Gone-dia." *Entertainment Weekly*. October 11, 2002. https://ew.com/article/2002/10/11/why-ghandia-should-change-her-name-gone-dia/.

Santos, Thiago Oliveira, Abel Correia, Rui Biscaia, and Ann Pegoraro. "Examining Fan Engagement through Social Networking Sites," *International Journal of Sports Marketing and Sponsorship* (October 2018).

Scalzi, John. *Red Shirts*. New York: Tor Publishing Group, 2012.

Schneider, Michael. "100 Most-Watched TV Series of 2023-24: This Season's Winners and Losers." *Variety*, May 28, 2024. https://variety.com/2024/tv/news/most-popular-tv-shows-highest-rated-2023-2024-season-tracker-survivor-1236015844/.

Shales, Tom. "Reality Faked Out." *Electronic Media*. June 4, 2001.

———. "Summer of Silliness." *Electronic Media*. July 3, 2000.

Schapiro, Barbara Ann. "Who's Afraid of Being Kicked Off the Island?" in *The Psychology of Survivor: Overanalyze, Overemote, Overcompensate*, edited by Richard J. Gerrig (3–15). Dallas: Benbella Books, 2007.

Shiels, Maggie. "Women's Group Attacks Reality Show." *BBC*, January 17, 2003. http://news.bbc.co.uk/2/hi/entertainment/2668029.stm.

Shin, Dong-Hee. "Do Users Experience Real Sociability Through Social TV? Analyzing Parasocial Behavior in Relation to Social TV," *Journal of Broadcasting & Electronic Media*, 60 (2016).

Sigesmund, B. J. "The Tribe Has Spoken." *Newsweek*, September 5, 2001. https://www.newsweek.com/tribe-has-spoken-152053.

SirNiceGuy. "Follow/FavPokémon Survivor: South Hoenn." FanFiction. August 1, 2020. https://www.fanfiction.net/s/13660255/1/Pokémon-Survivor-South-Hoenn.

Skeggs, Beverley and Helen Wood. "Introduction." In *Reacting to Reality Television: Performance, Audience and Value*. New York: Routledge, 2012.

Smith, Matthew J. and Andrew F. Wood, *Survivor Lessons: Essays on Communication and Reality Television*. Jefferson, NC: McFarland, 2003.

Smith, Zeke. "'Survivor' Contestant Opens Up About Being Outed as Transgender (Guest Column)." *The Hollywood Reporter*. April 12, 2017. https://www.hollywoodreporter.com/tv/tv-news/survivor-zeke-smith-outed-as-transgender-guest-column-991514/.

Stanley, Alessandra. "So Rowdy, They Discomfit the Royal Hell-Raiser." *New York Times*. May 19, 2014. https://www.nytimes.com/2014/05/20/arts/television/i-wanna-marry-harry-a-reality-series-on-fox.html.

Starner, Nina. "One Change Fixed the Series' Biggest Problem, According to Jeff Probst." *Looper*. April 24, 2024. https://www.looper.com/1569347/jeff-probst-survivor-mandate-changed-series/.

Starr, Michael. "He Was Robbed! - Wrong Team Won 'Survivor' Challenge." *New York Post.* March 4, 2004. https://nypost.com/2004/03/04/he-was-robbed-wrong-team -won-survivor-challenge/.

Storrs, Matthew. "The Different Eras of Survivor," Inside Survivor, February 1, 2020. https://insidesurvivor.com/the-different-eras-of-survivor-42297

"Survivor: Inside the Phenomenon." *Survivor - The Complete First Season.* DVD. 2004.

SurvivorQuotesX (@SurvivorQuotesX),."'I'm saying to you, heart to heart, friend to friend, human being to human being." *Twitter.* April 23, 2024. https://x.com/ SurvivorQuotesX/status/1782776979214704805.

Survivor Stories. FanFiction. https://www.fanfiction.net/community/Survivor-Stories /76449/.

"Survivor (US)." Survivor Wiki. Accessed July 30, 2024. https://survivor.fandom.com/ wiki/Survivor_(U.S.).

"Survivors Falling Over for 17 Minutes." Eager Tortoise. YouTube video. February 12, 2021. https://www.youtube.com/watch?v=bBMK9sV_YLA.

Thomas, Lauren. "Sears, Mattress Firm and More: Here Are the Retailers That Went Bankrupt in 2018." *CNBC.* December 31, 2018.https://www.cnbc.com/2018/12/31/ here-are-the-retailers-including-sears-that-went-bankrupt-in-2018.html.

Time Cover. *Time.* June 26, 2000. https://content.time.com/time/covers/0,16641,20000626 ,00.html.

Tisdale, Sallie. *The Lie about the Truck: Survivor, Reality TV, and the Endless Gaze.* New York: Gallery Books, 2021.

TMZ. "'Survivor' Contestants Violate NDA $5 Million Fine on the Line." TMZ. May 15, 2018. https://www.tmz.com/2018/05/15/survivor-season-37-contestants-out -themselves-5-million-dollar-nda/.

Todorov, Tzvetan. *On Human Diversity: Nationalism, Racism and Exoticism in French Thought.* Boston: Harvard University Press. 1998.

Travis, Emlyn. "Keith Nale, Two-Time Survivor Contestant, Dies at 62." *Entertainment Weekly.* April 19, 2023. https://ew.com/tv/keith-nale-dead-survivor-contestant/.

Tucker, Jessica. "After More than 40 Seasons on Air, How Much Does Survivor Rake in for CBS?" TheThings.com. March 29, 2023. https://www.thethings.com/how-much -money-does-survivor-make-for-cbs/.

Varner, Jeff. "Exclusive: 'Survivor' Contestant Jeff Varner in His Own Words: Outing Zeke Smith and the Shame That Followed," *ETOnline,* May 24, 2017. https://www .etonline.com/features/218256_survivor_contestant_jeff_varner_in_his_own_words.

Walker, Christine S. "'I'm So Sick of This Race Talk. Boo Hoo": Perceptions of Race on 2021-22 CBS *Survivor,*" *Howard Journal of Communication,* April 5, 2023. https:// www.tandfonline.com/doi/pdf/10.1080/10646175.2023.2195058.

Walsh, Charlotte. "Survivor's Jeff Probst Explains Why the Hourglass Twist Has Been Voted Off the Island." Yahoo Entertainment. September 14, 2022. https://www .yahoo.com/entertainment/survivor-jeff-probst-explains-why-191900876.html.

The Week Staff. "'Bridalplasty': A New Low for Reality TV?" *The Week.* January 8, 2015. https://theweek.com/articles/490971/bridalplasty-new-low-reality-tv.

West, Ed. "The Reality Show that Supersizes Cruelty." *Spiked,* March 6, 2009. https:// www.spiked-online.com/2009/03/06/the-reality-show-that-supersizes-on-cruelty/.

White, Peter. "CBS Sets Diversity Targets for Reality Casts; 50% of Talent Must Be BIPOC & Commits 25% Of Unscripted Development Budget To BIPOC Creatives."

Deadline. November 9, 2020. https://deadline.com/2020/11/cbs-diversity-targets
-reality-casts-bipoc-commits-unscripted-development-budget-1234611548/.

———. "'Survivor': CBS Planning 'Year-Long' Celebration for Season 50." *Deadline*,
June 11, 2024. https://deadline.com/2024/06/survivor-cbs-season-50-1235970491/.

Whitten, Lee. "Survivor 42: Why the Hourglass Twist Is a Creative Failure." Screenrant.
April 17, 2022. https://screenrant.com/survivor-42-hourglass-twist-creative-failure
-jeff-probst/.

Wright, Christopher J. *Tribal Warfare:* Survivor *and the Political Unconscious of Reality
Television.* New York: Lexington Books, 2006.

Yahr, Emily. "'Survivor' Changed Television Forever and It Still Endures. What's the
Secret?" *The Washington Post*, May 29, 2015, https://www.washingtonpost.com/
news/arts-and-entertainment/wp/2015/05/29/survivor-changed-television-forever
-and-it-still-endures-whats-the-secret/.

Yahr, Emily, Caitlin Moore, and Emily Chow. "How We Went from 'Survivor' to More
Than 300 Reality Shows: A Complete Guide." *The Washington Post*, May 29, 2015.
https://www.washingtonpost.com/graphics/entertainment/reality-tv-shows/.

Yu, Kaila. "I Worked on 'Survivor.' We Tested Challenges before Contestants, Stayed in
Island Resorts, and Got Front-Row Seats for Filming." *Business Insider*. September
29, 2022.
https://www.businessinsider.com/survivor-dream-team-job-test-challenges-before-cast
-contestants-2022-9.

EPISODES

Survivor at 40: Greatest Moments and Players. Aired February 5, 2020, on CBS.
https://www.paramountplus.com/shows/survivor/.

Survivor 41. Season 41, episode 1, "A New Era." Aired September 22, 2021, on CBS.
https://www.paramountplus.com/shows/survivor/.

Survivor: 41. Season 41, episode 8, "Betraydar," Aired November 10, 2021, on CBS.
https://www.paramountplus.com/shows/survivor.

Survivor: 42. Season 42, episode 1, "Feels Like a Rollercoaster," Aired March 9, 2022, on
CBS. https://www.paramountplus.com/shows/survivor.

Survivor: 42. Season 42, episode 9, "Game of Chicken," Aired April 27, 2022, on CBS.
https://www.paramountplus.com/shows/survivor.

Survivor: 44. Season 44, episode 1, "I Can't Wait to See Jeff." Aired March 1, 2023, on
CBS.https://www.paramountplus.com/shows/survivor/.

Survivor: 44. Season 44, episode 13, "Absolute Banger Season." Aired May 24, 2023, on
CBS. https://www.paramountplus.com/shows/survivor/.

Survivor: 46. Season 46, episode 1, "This is Where the Legends Are Made," Aired February 29, 2024. https://www.paramountplus.com/shows/survivor/.

Survivor: 46. Season 46, episode 7, "Episode Several." Aired April 11, 2024. https://www
.paramountplus.com/shows/survivor/.

Survivor: 46. Season 46 episode 13, "Friends Going to War." Aired May 22, 2024, on
CBS. https://www.paramountplus.com/shows/survivor/.

Survivor: Africa. Season 3, episode 1, "Question of Trust." Aired October 11, 2001, on
CBS. https://www.paramountplus.com/shows/survivor/.

Survivor: Africa. Season 3, episode 14, "The Final Four: No Regrets." Aired January 10, 2002, on CBS. https://www.paramountplus.com/shows/survivor/.

Survivor: Africa. Season 3, episode 15, "Reunion." Aired January 10, 2002, on CBS. https://www.paramountplus.com/shows/survivor/.

Survivor: All-Stars. Season 8, episode 3, "Shark Attack." Aired February 12, 2004, on CBS. https://www.paramountplus.com/shows/survivor/.

Survivor: All-Stars. Season 8 episode 5, "I've Been Bamboozled!" Aired February 26, 2004, on CBS. https://www.paramountplus.com/shows/survivor/.

Survivor: All-Stars. Season 8 episode 6, "Outraged." Aired March 4, 2004, on CBS. https://www.paramountplus.com/shows/survivor/.

Survivor: All-Stars. Season 8 episode 18, "America's Tribal Council." Aired May 13, 2004, on CBS. https://www.paramountplus.com/shows/survivor/.

Survivor: The Amazon. Season 6, episode 3, "Girl Power." Aired February 27, 2003, on CBS. https://www.paramountplus.com/shows/survivor/.

Survivor: The Amazon. Season 6, episode 7, "Girls Gone Wilder." Aired March 26, 2003, on CBS. https://www.paramountplus.com/shows/survivor/.

Survivor: The Amazon. Season 6, episode 15, "Reunion." Aired May 11, 2003, on CBS. https://www.paramountplus.com/shows/survivor/.

Survivor: The Australian Outback. Season 2, episode 1, "Stranded." Aired January 28, 2001, on CBS. https://www.paramountplus.com/shows/survivor/.

Survivor: The Australian Outback. Season 2, episode 6, "Trial by Fire." Aired March 2, 2001, on CBS. https://www.paramountplus.com/shows/survivor/.

Survivor: The Australian Outback. Season 2, episode 7, "The Merge." Aired March 8, 2001, on CBS. https://www.paramountplus.com/shows/survivor/.

Survivor: The Australian Outback. Season 2 episode 12, "No Longer Just a Game." Aired April 12, 2001, on CBS. https://www.paramountplus.com/shows/survivor/.

Survivor: The Australian Outback. Season 2, Episode 13, "Enough is Enough." Aired April 19, 2001. https://www.paramountplus.com/shows/survivor/.

Survivor: The Australian Outback. Season 2, episode 15, "The Most Deserving." Aired December 15, 2001, on CBS. https://www.paramountplus.com/shows/survivor/.

Survivor: The Australian Outback. Season 2, episode 16, "Reunion." Aired December 15, 2001, on CBS. https://www.paramountplus.com/shows/survivor/.

Survivor: Blood vs. Water. Season 27, episode 1, "Blood is Thicker Than Everything." Aired September 18, 2013, on CBS. https://www.paramountplus.com/shows/survivor/.

Survivor: Blood vs. Water. Season 37, episode 7, "Swoop in for the Kill." Aired October 30, 2013. https://www.paramountplus.com/shows/survivor/.

Survivor: Borneo. Season 1, episode 1, "The Marooning." Aired May 31, 2000, on CBS. https://www.paramountplus.com/shows/survivor/.

Survivor: Borneo. Season 1, episode 2, "The Generation Gap." Aired June 7, 2000, on CBS. https://www.paramountplus.com/shows/survivor/.

Survivor: Borneo. Season 1, episode 3, "Quest for Food." Aired June 14, 2000, on CBS. https://www.paramountplus.com/shows/survivor/.

Survivor: Borneo. Season 1, episode 5, "Pulling Your Own Weight." Aired June 29, 2000, on CBS. https://www.paramountplus.com/shows/survivor/.

Survivor: Borneo. Season 1, episode 6, "Udder Revenge." Aired July 5, 2000, on CBS. https://www.paramountplus.com/shows/survivor/.

Survivor: Borneo. Season 1, episode 7, "The Merger." Aired July 12, 2000, on CBS. https://www.paramountplus.com/shows/survivor/.

Survivor: Borneo. Season 1, episode 8, "Thy Name Is Duplicity." Aired July 19, 2000, on CBS. https://www.paramountplus.com/shows/survivor/.

Survivor: Borneo. Season 1, episode 9, "Old and New Bonds." Aired July 26, 2000, on CBS. https://www.paramountplus.com/shows/survivor/.

Survivor: Borneo. Season 1 episode 11, "Long Hard Days." Originally aired August 9, 2000. https://www.paramountplus.com/shows/survivor/.

Survivor: Borneo. Season 1 episode 12, "Death of an Alliance." Aired August 16, 2000. https://www.paramountplus.com/shows/survivor/.

Survivor: Borneo. Season 1, episode 13, "The Final Four." Aired August 23, 2000. on CBS. https://www.paramountplus.com/shows/survivor/.

Survivor: Borneo. Season 1, episode 14, "The Reunion." Aired August 23, 2000, on CBS. https://www.paramountplus.com/shows/survivor/.

Survivor: Cagayan. Season 28, episode 3, "Our Time to Shine." Aired March 12, 2014, on CBS. https://www.paramountplus.com/shows/survivor/.

Survivor: Cagayan. Season 28, episode 13, "It's Do or Die." Aired May 22, 2014, on CBS. https://www.paramountplus.com/shows/survivor/.

Survivor: Cagayan. Season 28, episode 14, "Live Reunion Show." Aired May 22, 2014, on CBS. https://www.paramountplus.com/shows/survivor/.

Survivor: Cambodia. Season 31, episode 1, "A Second Chance." Aired September 23, 2015, on CBS. https://www.paramountplus.com/shows/survivor/.

Survivor: Cambodia. Season 31 episode 6, "Bunking with the Devil." Aired October 28, 2015, on CBS. https://www.paramountplus.com/shows/survivor/.

Survivor: Caramoan. Season 26, episode 5, "Persona Non Grata." Aired March 13, 2013, on CBS. https://www.paramountplus.com/shows/survivor/.

Survivor: Caramoan. Season 26, episode 14, "Last Push." Aired May 12, 2013, on CBS. https://www.paramountplus.com/shows/survivor/.

Survivor: China. Season 15, episode 1, "A Chicken's a Little Bit Smarter." Aired September 20, 2007, on CBS. https://www.paramountplus.com/shows/survivor/.

Survivor: China. Season 15, episode 5, "Love is in the Air." Aired October 18, 2007, on CBS. https://www.paramountplus.com/shows/survivor/.

Survivor: Cook Islands. Season 13, episode 2, "Dire Strengths and Dead Weight." Aired September 21, 2006, on CBS. https://www.paramountplus.com/shows/survivor/.

Survivor: Cook Islands. Season 13, episode 15, "This Tribe Will Self-Destruct in 5, 4, 3 . . ." Aired December 17, 2006, on CBS. https://www.paramountplus.com/shows/survivor/.

Survivor: David vs. Goliath. Season 37, episode 9, "Breadth-First Search." Aired November 2022, 2018, on CBS. https://www.paramountplus.com/shows/survivor/.

Survivor: David vs. Goliath. Season 37, episode 10, "Tribal Lines are Blurred." Aired November 28, 2018, on CBS. https://www.paramountplus.com/shows/survivor.

Survivor: Edge of Extinction. Season 38, episode 13, "I See the Million Dollars." Aired May 15, 2019, on CBS. https://www.paramountplus.com/shows/survivor/.

Survivor: Fiji. Season 14, episode 1, "Something Cruel Is About to Happen . . . Real Soon." Aired February 8, 2007, on CBS. https://www.paramountplus.com/shows/survivor/.

Survivor: Gabon. Season 7, episode 13, "Say Goodbye to Gabon." Aired December 14, 2008, on CBS. https://www.paramountplus.com/shows/survivor/.

Survivor: Game Changers. Season 34, episode 4, "Dirty Deed." Aired March 30, 2017, on CBS. https://www.paramountplus.com/shows/survivor/.

Survivor: Game Changers. Season 34, episode 6, "What Happened on Exile, Stays on Exile." Aired April 12, 2017, on CBS. https://www.paramountplus.com/shows/survivor/.

Survivor: Game Changers: Season 34, episode 12, "No Good Deed Goes Unpunished." Aired May 25, 2017, on CBS. https://www.paramountplus.com/shows/survivor/.

Survivor: Ghost Island. Season 36, episode 12, "Always Be Moving." Aired May 16, 2018, on CBS. https://www.paramountplus.com/shows/survivor/.

Survivor: Ghost Island. Season 36, episode 1, "Can You Reverse the Curse." Aired February 28, 2018, on CBS. https://www.paramountplus.com/shows/survivor/.

Survivor: Guatemala. Season 11, episode 1, "Big Trek, Big Trouble, Big Surprise." Aired September 15, 2005, on CBS. https://www.paramountplus.com/shows/survivor/.

Survivor: Guatemala. Season 11, Episode 9, "Secrets and Lies and an Idol Surprise." Aired November 11, 2005, on CBS. https://www.paramountplus.com/shows/survivor/.

Survivor: Heroes vs. Healers vs. Hustlers. Season 35, episode 11, "Not Going to Roll Over and Die." Aired December 6, 2017, on CBS. https://www.paramountplus.com/shows/survivor/.

Survivor: Heroes vs. Healers vs. Hustlers. Season 35, episode 12, "The Survivor Devil." Aired December 13, 2017, on CBS. https://www.paramountplus.com/shows/survivor/.

Survivor: Heroes vs. Healers vs. Hustlers. Season 35, episode 13, "Million Dollar Night." Aired December 20, 2017, on CBS. https://www.paramountplus.com/shows/survivor/.

Survivor: Heroes vs. Healers vs. Hustlers. Season 35, episode 14, "Reunion." Aired December 20, 2017, on CBS. https://www.paramountplus.com/shows/survivor/.

Survivor: Heroes vs. Villains. Season 20, episode 9, "Survivor History." Aired April 16, 2010, on CBS. https://www.paramountplus.com/shows/survivor/.

Survivor: Heroes vs. Villains. Season 20 episode 15, "Reunion." Aired May 16, 2010, on CBS. https://www.paramountplus.com/shows/survivor/.

Survivor: Island of the Idols. Season 39, episode 1, "I Vote You Out and That's It." Aired September 25, 2019, on CBS. https://www.paramountplus.com/shows/survivor/.

Survivor: Island of the Idols. Season 39, episode 6, "Suck It Up Buttercup." Aired November 6, 2019, on CBS. https://www.paramountplus.com/shows/survivor/.

Survivor: Island of the Idols. Season 39, episode 8, "We Made it to the Merge." Aired November 13, 2019, on CBS. https://www.paramountplus.com/shows/survivor/.

Survivor: Island of the Idols. Season 39, episode 12, "Just Go for It." Aired December 11, 2019 on CBS. https://www.paramountplus.com/shows/survivor/.

Survivor: Kaôh Rōng. Season 32, episode 4, "Signed, Sealed and Delivered." Aired March 9, 2016, on CBS. https://www.paramountplus.com/shows/survivor/.

Survivor: Marquesas. Season 4, episode 8, "Jury's Out." Aired March 20, 2002, on CBS. https://www.paramountplus.com/shows/survivor.

Survivor: Marquesas. Season 4, episode 13, "A Tale of Two Cities." Aired May 16, 2002, on CBS. https://www.paramountplus.com/shows/survivor/.

Survivor: Marquesas. Season 4, episode 14, "The Sole Survivor." Aired May 19, 2002, on CBS. https://www.paramountplus.com/shows/survivor/.

Survivor: Marquesas. Season 4, episode 15, "Reunion." Aired May 19, 2002, on CBS. https://www.paramountplus.com/shows/survivor/.

Survivor: Micronesia. Season 16, episode 6, "It Hit Everyone Pretty Hard." Aired March 13, 2008, on CBS. https://www.paramountplus.com/shows/survivor/.

Survivor: Micronesia. Season 16, episode 13, "If It Smells Like a Rat, Give It Cheese." Aired May 8, 2008, on CBS. https://www.paramountplus.com/shows/survivor/.

Survivor: Micronesia. Season 16, episode 15, "Reunion." Aired May 11, 2008, on CBS. https://www.paramountplus.com/shows/survivor/.

Survivor: Millennials vs. Gen X. Season 33, episode 10, "Million Dollar Gamble." Aired November 23, 2016, on CBS. https://www.paramountplus.com/shows/survivor/.

Survivor: Nicaragua. Season 21, episode 1, "Young at Heart." Aired September 15, 2010, on CBS. https://www.paramountplus.com/shows/survivor/.

Survivor: Nicaragua. Season 21, episode 2, "Fatigue Makes Cowards of Us All." Aired September 22, 2010, on CBS. https://www.paramountplus.com/shows/survivor/.

Survivor Nicaragua. Season 21, episode 12, "You Started, You're Finishing." Aired December 2, 2010. https://www.paramountplus.com/shows/survivor/.

Survivor: One World. Season 24, episode 4, "Bum-Puzzled." Aired March 7, 2012, on CBS. https://www.paramountplus.com/shows/survivor/.

Survivor: One World. Season 24, episode 9, "Go Out with A Bang." Aired April 11, 2012, on CBS. https://www.paramountplus.com/shows/survivor.

Survivor: One World. Season 24, episode 14, "Perception Is Not Always Reality." Aired May 13, 2012, on CBS. https://www.paramountplus.com/shows/survivor/.

Survivor: Palau. Season 10, episode 1, "This Has Never Happened Before!" Aired February 17, 2005, on CBS. https://www.paramountplus.com/shows/survivor/.

Survivor: Palau. Season 10, episode 5, "The Best and Worst Reward Ever." Aired March 16, 2005, on CBS. https://www.paramountplus.com/shows/survivor/.

Survivor: Palau. Season 10, episode 9, "I Will Not Give Up." Aired April 15, 2005, on CBS. https://www.paramountplus.com/shows/survivor/.

Survivor: Palau. Season 10, episode 14, "The Ultimate Shock." Aired May 15, 2005, on CBS. https://www.paramountplus.com/shows/survivor.

Survivor: Palau. Season 10, episode 15, "Reunion." Aired May 15, 2005, on CBS. https://www.paramountplus.com/shows/survivor.

Survivor: Panama. Season 12, Episode 4, "Starvation and Lunacy." Aired February 24, 2006, on CBS. https://www.paramountplus.com/shows/survivor/.

Survivor: Pearl Islands. Season 7, episode 7, "What the . . . Part 1?" Aired October 31, 2003, on CBS. https://www.paramountplus.com/shows/survivor/.

Survivor: Pearl Islands. Season 7, episode 8, "What the . . . Part 2?" Aired November 7, 2003, on CBS. https://www.paramountplus.com/shows/survivor/.

Survivor: Redemption Island. Season 22, episode 8, "This Game Respects Big Moves." Aired April 6, 2011, on CBS. https://www.paramountplus.com/shows/survivor/.

Survivor: San Juan del Sur. Season 29, episode 4, "We're a Hot Mess." Aired October 15, 2014, on CBS. https://www.paramountplus.com/shows/survivor/.

Survivor: San Juan del Sur. Season 29, episode 13, "This is My Time." Aired December 18, 2014, on CBS. https://www.paramountplus.com/shows/survivor/.

Survivor: South Pacific. Season 23, episode 7, "Trojan Horse." Aired October 27, 2011. https://www.paramountplus.com/shows/survivor/.

Survivor: South Pacific. Season 23, episode 15, "Loyalties Will Be Broken." Aired December 18, 2011, on CBS. https://www.paramountplus.com/shows/survivor/.

Survivor: Thailand. Season 5 episode 1, "The Importance of Being Eldest." Aired September 19, 2002, on CBS. https://www.paramountplus.com/shows/survivor/.

Survivor: Thailand. Season 5 episode 3, "Family Values." Aired October 3, 2002, on CBS. https://www.paramountplus.com/shows/survivor/.

Survivor: Thailand. Season 5, episode 14, "Slip Through Your Fingers." Aired December 19, 2002, on CBS. https://www.paramountplus.com/shows/survivor/.

Survivor: Thailand. Season 5 episode 15, "Reunion." Aired December 19, 2002, on CBS. https://www.paramountplus.com/shows/survivor/.

Survivor: Tocantins. Season 18 episode 13, "The Martyr Approach." Aired May 14, 2009, on CBS. https://www.paramountplus.com/shows/survivor/.

Survivor: Vanuatu. Season 9, episode 14, "Spirits and the Final Four." Aired December 12, 2004. https://www.paramountplus.com/shows/survivor/.

Survivor: Worlds Apart. Season 30, episode 9, "Bring the Popcorn." Aired April 23, 2015, on CBS. https://www.paramountplus.com/shows/survivor.

Survivor: Worlds Apart. Season 30, episode 13, "It's A Fickle, Fickle Game." Aired May 21, 2015, on CBS. https://www.paramountplus.com/shows/survivor/.

Survivor: Winners at War. Season 40, episode 1, "Greatest of the Greats." Aired February 12, 2020, on CBS. https://www.paramountplus.com/shows/survivor/.

Survivor: Winners at War. Season 40, episode 14, "It All Boils Down to This." Aired May 13, 2020, on CBS. https://www.paramountplus.com/shows/survivor/.

INDEX

ABOUT THE AUTHORS

Joseph J. Darowski holds a PhD in American studies from Michigan State University and is assistant professor of English at Brigham Young University. He is the editor of The Ages of Superheroes essay series. He is the author of *X-Men and the Mutant Metaphor: Race and Gender in the Comics* (Rowman & Littlefield, 2014) and coauthor of *Frasier: A Cultural History* (Rowman & Littlefield, 2017) and *Cheers: A Cultural History* (Rowman & Littlefield, 2019).

Kate Darowski has a master's degree from Parsons School of Design, where she studied the history of decorative arts and design, with an emphasis on twentieth-century modern design and pop culture in design. With her brother, Joseph, Kate is the coauthor of *Frasier: A Cultural History* (Rowman & Littlefield, 2017) and *Cheers: A Cultural History* (Rowman & Littlefield, 2019).